The Spare and The Heir

James D. Wood

Copyright © 2023 by James D. Wood.

All rights reserved.

No part of this publication may be reproduced, distributed, or transmitted in any form or by any means, including photocopying, recording, or other electronic or mechanical methods, without the prior written permission of the publisher, except as permitted by copyright law. For permission requests, contact the author or the publisher, Kensington Square, 201 Goldhawk Road, London W12 8EP, UK.

The story, all names, characters, and incidents portrayed in this production are fictitious. No identification with actual persons (living or deceased), places, buildings, and products is intended or should be inferred.

Published by Kensington Square.

ISBN 979-8-3993733-6-2

For Melissa

Cast of Characters
In Order of Appearance

Tilly Hentzau
13 year old daughter of Ruritanian government minister Rupert Hentzau.

Christopher Wainwright
27 year old telesales executive from Stoke Newington, London.

Johann Blicker
Artist president of the newly independent Republic of Ruritania.

Rudolph Rassendyll
The long dead hero of Anthony Hope's 1894 novel, *'The Prisoner of Zenda'*.

Queen Flavia
Former Queen of Ruritania from *'The Prisoner of Zenda'*, rumoured to be Rassendyll's lover.

Cast of Characters

Donald
Owner and MD of TravelCo, a coach tour company based in Covent Garden, London.

Horst Bangermann
Art director of the Ruritanian government, formerly Prada VP of International Sales (South East Europe).

Sophie Bernenstein
23 year old PR assistant and official 'influencer' of the Ruritania Government, best friend of Rose Elphberg (see below).

Boris Kurtz
Minister of Economics.

Rupert Hentzau
Minister of Trade, former Oligarch, owner of Zenda Castle, descendent of Count Rupert of Hentzau, the antagonist of *'The Prisoner of Zenda'*.

Rose Elphberg
Distant cousin of the former Royal Family of Ruritania, the Elphbergs, and heir to the throne of Ruritania.

Andrew Hentzau
Rupert Hentzau's playboy son, engaged to Rose Elphberg.

Yuri Lougouev
Russian CEO of Globalny Foods Inc, importer of fast food and soap operas.

Cynthia
Donald's assistant at TravelCo.

John H. Bigelow
A Hollywood movie producer.

Roger
A TravelCo tour manager.

Coach Jackson
Coach of a visiting team of American football players, the Arkansas Angels, passengers on 'The Land That Time Forgot', TravelCo's inaugural coach tour to Ruritania.

Hank, Joe, Leroy
Three members of the Arkansas Angels.

Martha Fierstein
Young female passenger of the tour group.

Henry and Mary Finkelburger
Elderly passengers of the tour group.

Joseph Spinelli
A VIP passenger of the tour group, and representative of Universal Foods Inc.

Michael
Tour group coach driver.

Roderick Fraser
A dead person.

Prologue

She knew that it was unlikely to change anything. She'd already made up her mind. You only had to look around you. The place was going to the dogs. Still, she wanted to give him one last chance. To see for herself.

As the speck became a dot, and the dot an aeroplane, the dignitaries shuffled around her. Musicians stood rigidly to attention, instruments idling, the odd discordant tuning note the only sound on the breeze. Tilly fingered two long chestnut tresses, each intertwined with the traditional red, white and yellow of her country, and adjusted the spray of roses one final time. It wasn't nerves. She'd done it countless times since her father had been in government, presenting posies to a succession of VIPs – even a US Secretary of State on one occasion.

The plane touched down, and an excited buzz rose from the crowd. The engines whined to a halt, a hydraulic door swung out slowly against the gleaming white fuselage, the band struck up the national anthem, and the man they had all been waiting for stepped gingerly into the sunlight.

It didn't look good. He was even shorter and scruffier up

close. His startled eyes darted uncertainly from the reception committee to the band and back again. Finally he waved a pudgy hand, and lumbered down the steps.

Tilly shifted one final time, posy at the ready. He approached across the tarmac, guided by a functionary, and automatically she stepped forward, as she'd been trained. For the first time he seemed to notice her, and it began to dawn on her with mounting horror that he was going to pat her on the head. He was beginning to look at her with those kiddy eyes that adults sometimes affected when faced with young children – generally adults who had none of their own and no clue. Tilly suddenly wanted to puke. She gritted her teeth, and as his outstretched hand bore down on her she deftly curtsied and shoved the roses at him. He started. She took a step back.

The first president of the newly democratic Republic of Ruritania smelt the flowers, sneezed all over her, and moved away, past the crowd of press hounds.

"Mr President! Mr President!" they clamoured. "Welcome home! Can you tell us about your trip? Did the IMF say yes, Mr President!"

As the pack moved away, engulfing their prey like a tourist in a Marrakech medina, she pulled out her iPhone and fired up Twitter.

"Blicker just landed," tweeted @MatildaMay99. "Hashtag FAIL."

Chapter 1

As in the Bishopric

Christopher Wainwright was having a bad day. One of a string, a whole series, an uninterrupted caravan of dog days stretching back as far as he cared to remember.

It was extremely hot. Inside the offices of the Direct Publishing Company – who had not seen fit to install air-conditioning - the air was stale, the result of fifty plus human beings sitting in cubicles in a confined space for eight hour stretches. Beads of sweat glistened on his forehead, dark patches discoloured his underarms, and the cold, clammy feel of damp cotton on skin made him shudder as he embarked on his fiftieth call of the morning. The headset at a jaunty angle, he clumsily tugged at his tie with his left hand while his right tapped out a number on his keyboard from a spreadsheet on his screen.

The number rang. Someone answered and he took a deep breath.

"Hi. Morning," he began confidently enough. "May I speak to James Thompson?" Beginning was easy. "Please. That's right, your managing director. The name's Edmund Salisbury."

He coughed, anticipating the next four words of the script – four words that, annoyingly, he could never quite get out of his head.

"As in the bishopric. No, I called a few days ago and spoke to his assistant. Thank you *so* much."

While Christopher waited he doodled idly on a pad: *'As - in - the - bishopric'*. Edmund Salisbury was his *nom de plume*. They all had them. It made them sound – well, more respectable than their own names in most cases. Their one and only task in this job was to sell advertising in a 'yearbook' published 'annually' by Direct Publishing called the Global Trade Monitor – though they all knew no one actually read this yearbook, that the bulk of the copies were delivered to the paying advertisers themselves, and the remainder to a hand picked selection of CEOs and Managing Directors who had never actually asked for them, but could nevertheless be promoted as the 'readership'. 'Annual', too, could be a fairly elastic concept.

"Hello? Mr Thompson? I'm sorry to bother you, Edmund Salisbury here, from the Special Projects Office of the World Trade Organisation in Geneva."

From where he wasn't, clearly. For when he stood up in his cubby hole ("talk down to your prospects" was a maxim the more timid salesmen were encouraged to take literally) he had a clear view of a number 22 bus stopping to pick up a gaggle of North London schoolgirls. Someone had once told him Lenin used to take that bus route. From Putney to the British Library Reading Room. It was hard to imagine.

"Now the reason I'm calling, Mr Thompson, is that we are currently putting together a new year book for the WTO, which will also be widely distributed and read by ambassadors..."

He consulted a grubby crib-sheet tacked to the wall in front of him.

"...diplomats, chief executive officers of major corporations and...er...and so forth. Now the reason I've come through to you, Mr Thompson, is that your company has been identified by our research department as one of the top half dozen outfits in waste retreatment in the UK, and one that is doing an increasing amount of business with... I'm sorry, Mr Thompson?…Brexit? Well I'm just coming to that. You see this year the emphasis is going to be on recycling issues with a foreword by HRH William, Prince of Wales and a profile of David Attenborough, whose environmental credentials as I am sure you are aware are very well recognised both here and abroad. Now Mr Thompson you're probably also aware of the tremendous growth in this field over recent years and we at the WTO...sorry, Mr Thompson?... Tariffs?"

He paused for a moment to reflect. What tariffs did the guy mean? Tariffs on shit? He gathered himself for one more push.

"No, Mr Thompson, sewage retreatment won't go anywhere...what?...no, the European Commission.... quite, well we've naturally been flooded with requests from business leaders and trade delegations across Europe asking for information and, more importantly, reputable companies such as yourselves who might be able to continue servicing their needs post-Brexit. Now as I say, since your company has been specifically identified as being at the cutting edge of...er...um..."

He became aware of a dull ache in his head. Concentrate, Christopher. A young woman stooped over his desk with a tray of machine-made coffee, her hair brushing his arm. There was a waft of something warm, musty, cheap. He had a sudden urge to do something inappropriate, something so outrageous that for a moment he thought he was going to faint and topple off the desk. He ground his teeth and the urge passed, but he'd lost his thread. Glancing absentmindedly at the multiple sheets taped to the wall he continued:

"...of...urn...soft toy manufacture, bears, tanks, plastic

models, that sort of thing, I'm very pleased to be able to offer you, for a strictly limited period, the opportunity to..."

Fuck. He was reading from the wrong script. The line went dead.

He sighed, wearily dragging off his headphones, and surveyed the room. It was pandemonium. Cubicles and desks were crammed side by side down the length of the long narrow office, thirty salesmen and women jabbering into headsets all at once. Some were hunkered down in front of their screens; others roamed their square metre of carpet on bluetooth like pet monkeys. One or two were actually sitting on the floor. At the far end of the room a man lay full stretch on the carpet, waving at the ceiling. Perhaps it was to get a better view of the fifty quid note that was pinned there each day as an incentive. The 'Reach for the Sky' award they called it. Christopher had yet to reach anywhere near it. He turned around and started. One of the team leaders was standing directly behind him.

"What d'you think you're doing, Wainwright?"

Wainwright? That sort of thing really pissed him off.

"What's the watchword?"

"Pitch, re-pitch, objection," recited Christopher without enthusiasm. It was emblazoned on a huge banner at the far end of the room, rather like in a Nissan factory.

"Exactly. I want ten sales out of you this week, is that clear?"

He watched the man stalk away and scrolled through the prospect list for the fifty-first time that morning. He was a university graduate, for heaven's sake. BA Hons in Philosophy, Psychology and Scientific Thought. How the hell had it come to this?

. . .

An hour later he was picking at a sandwich on a park bench. He knew full well why it had come to this.

"I hate this bloody job."

"Why do it then?" replied Ali, a workmate.

"Money, mate. I need 2k, and fast."

"What the fuck for?"

Christopher raised an eyebrow. "It's a long story, Ali…"

"Try me."

Christopher sighed. "If I don't cough up in -" he glanced at his phone "- a few weeks time… well, something tragic will happen."

Ali looked alarmed. "You mean for you?"

But Christopher had already taken a chunk out of his sandwich – mature cheddar with strong pickle, the same he had most days - and let the question hang. As for Ali, he wasn't eating today - it was Ramadan. They lapsed into silence. A girl they'd both noticed working in the CEO's office on the next floor down sauntered past, and they followed her with their eyes as she settled two benches along, wiping the seat carefully with a tissue. Spring was here, change was in the air. Christopher felt a vague longing, something that he couldn't quite put his finger on. He needed a girlfriend, a proper one, he realised. He was sick and tired of Tinder.

"If only I could get away. Wave some magic wand, go travelling for a while, screw all this. It's torture sitting up there spouting that bullshit while out here the sun's shining and real life is passing me by."

"I hate to tell you, but this is it, mate. This *is* real life."

"Mmm," Christopher replied. "Not convinced." He knew he didn't believe it. He was a fish swimming in an alien pond. An outsider. Ali was the only one he spent time with at work, and then only during their lunch break or occasionally for a beer in the evening. The others he worked with just thought he was a bit weird. Perhaps they all had degrees too, he had no idea. Everyone had degrees nowadays, didn't they? Still, this was not what he had expected to graduate to. Counting every penny. There had to be something better than this, surely?

He flicked idly at a stray crisp packet.

"You believe in luck, right?" said Ali.

"Sure," laughed Christopher. "Bad luck."

"What kind of attitude is that! How can lady luck help you if you don't let her help you?"

"She's a woman then, is she? Can't rely on them. Besides, I scratch my card each week, don't I? What more do I have to do?"

Which was a lie. He had bought a lottery card with Ali, the previous week, just on the off chance he could win the money he needed, despite the fact that the National Lottery was just a scam to fleece poor people. In his opinion.

"That's fantasy, man. Just a bit of fun. You don't get nothing for nothing." Ali paused. "Look, Chris, put it this way. Sitting up there, feeling frustrated, doing something you don't enjoy. That's your situation. Nothing can change unless you give it a chance. If you believe in luck, then it will come to you. But you gotta believe, man. And you've got to give it the opportunity. Get out there, mess about a bit, make things dodgy like. If you keep the faith, she'll help you, man, things'll happen. All she can do up there," he jerked his thumb in the direction of the office block they worked in, "is give you a good sale. But that's not the kind of luck you need." He sniffed the air. "I don't think."

Christopher grunted.

"Here." Ali grabbed the copy of the London Evening Standard from the bench beside him, and flicked through the pages. "You got enough for a flight?"

"I very much doubt it."

"Pay day's tomorrow. How many sales you made?"

Christopher shrugged. "Two. Three maybe." He knew Ali

was right. He wasn't cut out for sales. It wasn't that he couldn't lie. It was just the people you had to deal with. They were such arseholes. He wasn't as thick-skinned as Ali - fifty abortive calls made him depressed. It was a shabby, soul-destroying business.

"Hey, listen to this!" Ali exclaimed. "Presentable, well-spoken Tour Manager wanted. Exciting new tours to Eastern Europe. Contact a Ms Cynthia Fraser. £3k+ a week OTE. How about that, eh?"

Christopher glanced at it sceptically. OTE was like a big red flashing beacon. The OTE figure that had lured him into the sales job was a joke.

"I don't have the first clue about the tourism industry."

"So? You don't know fuck all about the shit industry, either, but that doesn't stop you jerking off about sewage retreatment like an expert."

Christopher laughed. "I think you'll find sewage is an unfortunate metaphor, Ali. Talking shit is the one thing we are experts in." Christopher jabbed a finger at the newspaper. "Plus I think you missed a bit. It says *experience essential*."

Ali rolled his eyes. "Hasn't this job taught you anything?"

They lifted their arms and smacked their palms together. Two benches along the girl from downstairs jumped, startled.

"Bullshit!" they chimed in unison.

Chapter 2

Roses are White

"*Where the hell are we going? The cabinet meets in fifteen minutes.*"

They were already twenty minutes out of the airport and still nowhere near anywhere Johann Blicker could recognise. He sucked hungrily on his cigarette and peered anxiously out of the window of his armoured Mercedes as it sped rapidly through the bleak, abandoned streets. Police outriders weaved an erratic path ahead of them.

The reason for the diversion soon became apparent. As they rejoined the main highway, weaving to avoid two gaping potholes, a massive statue of Lenin hove into view to their right. It was being dismantled by a crane, and lurched alarmingly against a backdrop of gesticulating workmen. A street of traffic was blocked off and shoppers waited patiently on the other side of the road as the godfather of communism swung above them.

Which reminded him, Blicker thought to himself, he'd have to find a replacement. He'd be sad to lose the Merc, with its cocktail bar and ice machine. He chuckled as he remembered the first time he ridden in it, a few months previously, on first being elected president; how he'd picked up the old school phone - red, naturally - and pressed a button to listen to a recording in Russian: *"I'm sorry caller, this line is no longer in use. We are unable to put you through to the Kremlin switchboard at this time. Please check your number..."* The Russians had evidently got fed up with jittery dictators phoning up to beg for assistance at all hours of the day and night.

After several minutes the huge bulk of Strelsau Palace, his official residence, came into view. A small crowd of onlookers – noticeably absent from the airport, Blicker thought to himself anxiously – stood outside the gates to greet his return. A ragged cheer went up. As they swung through the entrance, a line of security guards held back a group of boys waving red and white flags. Blicker frowned. The black Armani suits would have to go. With their holstered Colt 45s bulging out from under their fitted jackets, and their mirrored dark glasses, they looked like extras from "The West Wing". It was not at all the look they should have in these times of austerity. Besides, he wanted an open, traditional administration, not this ship of fools he suddenly found himself at the helm of. He made a mental note to raise the matter in Cabinet.

THE PALACE AT STRELSAU, CAPITAL OF RURITANIA, FORMERLY the Royal Palace of the Elphbergs, had changed little since the days of *'The Prisoner of Zenda'*, that famous historical account of Ruritania written by Anthony Hope in 1894. It was situated in the main square of what was now commonly called The Capital, as if the exhaustion of three name changes in the space of a century – from Strelsau to Molotovgrad to 21st September Grad and now back to Strelsau again – had stripped the townspeople of any last vestige of civic pride. But the palace gardens were still exquisitely manicured, and the exterior stucco work gleaming and white. Only the interior was in need of refurbishment. For some reason none of the billions of dollars that had been poured into Ruritania in recent years under the benevolent auspices of the EU had found its way into this old palace – the EU and their local standard bearers preferred the flashing glass pyramids of the new business district, now standing eerily empty. Or the fifty-one story Hyatt Hotel, whose menu these days was rarely available, and whose guests were almost entirely accountants and bankers – circling like vultures to see how much of what they poured in they could now claw back.

None of this, however, was visible to the casual bystander. The only tell-tale sign of the momentous changes that had been, and continued to be, wrought in a century of Ruritanian history was the large patch of discoloured stucco above the main portal, where once the imposing golden eagle of the Royal House of Elphberg had stood. But unless it was pointed out, a casual bystander would never have guessed, for the empty space was large and rectangular, not at all eagle-shaped. Just long enough, in fact, for a more recent incumbent – the words, in Cyrillic script, *'Autonomous Federation of Khomsova.'*

For history buffs, a brief resume of modern Ruritania goes as follows. It all started in 1870, with the coronation of King Rudolf, as chronicled in *'The Prisoner of Zenda.'* The King's brother, Prince Michael, so the legend goes, had him drugged and imprisoned in the Castle of Zenda just before the coronation was due to take place. However, in a desperate attempt not to give Prince Michael the excuse to claim the throne for himself, two of the King's ministers persuaded his doppelgänger distant cousin, and namesake, the half Scots, half English Rudolf Rassendyll, to impersonate the King at the Coronation. Said doppelgänger was so-called because he was the descendent of a woman who had had an affair with an earlier Ruritanian King, and he had inherited the famous

Ruritanian red hair and sharp, straight nose. The likeness with the King was said to be astonishing, and they could not be told apart.

So this doppelgänger, a 19th century forerunner of James Bond, was duly crowned King. And, in true Bond fashion, he fell in love with the King's fiancé, Princess Flavia, who noticed a marked change in the romantic attentions of her paramour - for the better. But imagine the agony: he can't tell her who he really is, and when the real King is finally rescued and restored to his throne, he is forced to leave, his love for Flavia unconsummated. Or was it?

The events had a tragic ending some years later. Rassendyll returned to Ruritania to see his former love, to tell her the truth, but became involved in a bitter dispute, and he and the King were killed.

Queen Flavia, tragic and alone, lived on until 1927, apparently without an heir.

On her death, the country was taken over in a bloody coup by the Bolsheviks, and it became a satellite of the Soviet Union. Nestled in a mountainous region between the Balkans and Central Europe, half in one and half in the other, it was a significant stepping stone in the Red's march to the west.

In the years that followed, the Soviets erased all traces of the old Ruritania, renaming it Khomsova. And so it remained for sixty years, until 1989, when, along with the neighbouring revolutions in Bratislava, Prague and Bucharest, Khomsova fell. But it proved to be a false dawn. One set of dictators was replaced with another. The rule of the Oligarchs had begun.

Two decades later came the worldwide financial crash, and it all changed again. Up until then, the Oligarchs had run the place almost as their private fiefdom. Billions had been poured in, initially through bonds issued in their own currency, the ruro, pegged to the ruble, and then, when Russia's economy started to falter, in loans from the EU. Factories had been set up, state industries privatised, infrastructure built. Various dodgy internet companies had sprung up, and the .fk domain - for 'Federation Khomsova' - had been extremely lucrative for a while. But it was the EU-backed rag trade that had been the true engine of growth, manufacturing garments in huge quantities for Italian labels like Gucci, Prada and Armani. It was good for Khomsova and it was fantastic for the EU - their very own backyard sweatshop. But here's the thing – they all said *'Made in the Autonomous Republic of Khomsova (ARK)'*. No one was any the wiser. Even the bankers doing the lending didn't have a clue where they were lending to – all they saw were balance sheets, profit and loss, and PE ratios. Speculators in Panama, the Cayman Islands and the Isle of Man would study their portfolios and come to the line – *'Credit default swaps, ARK'*. They understood junk bonds and subprime mortgages, but ARK? None of them wanted to admit they did not understand this mysterious acronym. They imagined it was some kind of funky new derivative and besides, it had a kind of environmental ring to it. It was only when it started to plummet, the day after the financial crash kicked off, that they got on the phone.

To save the country from ruin, Khomsova needed a massive loan. They turned to the EU, and there was even talk of applying for membership. But Brussels had one major condition: Khomsova must hold free and fair elections.

It had taken a few years to agree - the Oligarchs did not cede power without a struggle - but when elections finally came, something extraordinary happened. The candidate who won was a complete outsider. Although he was known abroad on the international art circuit, few in Ruritania knew much about him. But his one overwhelming advantage was that he was the only person of any stature to have remained untainted by a half century of communism and the capitalist excess that followed. He was duly elected with a massive majority to form a National Government of Reconstruction. The new state was to revert to its former name, Ruritania.

So this benighted semi-Balkan country, for so long in the dark shadow of foreign powers and oligarchs, was now, blinking and hesitant and through no fault of its own, suddenly naked. It was as if the people had toiled, sweating and stumbling, through the steep dark forests of a very tall mountain, forced to shed the habits of centuries as they went, building fabulous highways and bridges, conference centres and garment factories, underpaid and exploited. Only to emerge from obscurity at 25,000 feet hopelessly unequipped to deal with sudden glare of this new dawn. They were still panting, hot and expectant. Sure, the view was fantastic. But as they were beginning to realise, it was cold up here.

There was one man above all others who knew what that meant. Though he was certainly not responsible for having dragged them up to this magnificent but inhospitable peak, there was no doubt about his responsibility for their future. For their hopes, fears, expectations. It was one aspect of the job that terrified him.

That man was Johann Borovski Blicker. Abstract painter.

Chapter 3

Rafting down the Zambezi

The offices of TravelCo were at the top of four flights of stairs in Covent Garden, so by the time Christopher arrived he was badly out of breath. The leather jacket had gone, as had the frayed tie, to be replaced by a blazer with gold buttons and a red polka dot tie. He smelt vaguely of moth repellent. As he entered, the receptionist followed his progress with an unusual amount of attention. He introduced himself and her face broke into a wide grin.

"Glad to see you. You've just made me ten quid."

"I beg your pardon?"

She giggled.

"The lift was out of order," he explained.

She lowered her voice and leant towards him conspiratorially. "We don't have lifts here, we have elevators. Remember that."

"I see." Though he really didn't. He consulted the torn out ad from the Evening Standard which he'd stuffed in his wallet. "I'm here to see someone called Ms Cynthia…"

"Donald's who you're seeing." She gestured to a chair.

Christopher sat down heavily and surveyed his

surroundings. The entire operation seemed to consist of two small rooms. Into the first, along with the receptionist, were jammed four other desks at which two people sat, wall to wall with filing cabinets. Both had an unhealthy, subterranean pallor about them, made faintly luminous by the bank of LED lights above. Beyond was a glass partition that gave onto the second office. Ensconced inside, Christopher could see a large man in shirtsleeves gesticulating into an old fashioned desk phone. The receptionist caught his eye, in response to which he flapped a hand in Christopher's direction.

"Donald says to go right in."

"Mike, we don't give refunds, you know that as well as I do!" the man was bellowing into the receiver as Christopher entered. He waved him to a chair with a tight smile.

"I realise it's in the brochure, but we have to have the boat back a day early to pick up the next group so you're going to have to give them Luxor in the dark. Isn't there a *Son-et-Lumiere* or something? No? You mean it's pitch black? You better pray for a full moon then, Mike."

He roared with laughter, a deep throaty boom which startled Christopher. He watched a small bead of sweat break out on the man's forehead and trickle slowly down the bridge of his nose, and then a grubby handkerchief was fished out of a pocket to wipe it away.

"Of course you don't tell them that. Tell them...tell them the tides are wrong. Beyond our control, that sort of stuff. Oh, not tidal at Luxor?" The man paused, scratching his head. "Isn't that extraordinary," he continued, "d'you know, I never knew that? Well make up something, for Pete's sake, because if I have letters of complaint that hold us liable then you'll be on the Moscow run for the rest of the season. Exactly. Thank you,

Mike. Goodbye. Oh and Mike? Try and have a sense of humour."

He put the receiver down with a clatter and swung round.

Donald was a large man with a round, puffy face and a paunch just cresting the lip of his desk. His breath came in short, sharp wheezes, and his hand shook slightly as he held it out for Christopher to shake. It felt clammy.

"Find us alright?"

"No problem."

"We didn't know quite what to expect. We were running a book in the office on whether you'd be vertically challenged."

"Vertically challenged?" said Christopher, startled. "I'm the person who's come about the job."

"Yeah, and the guy who took those wheelchair tours rafting down the Amazon, right?"

Christopher was seized by a sudden blind panic. What the fuck was the man talking about?

"The Amazon?" he blinked, fingering his collar.

"Or was it the Yangtze?" Donald rummaged around on his desk, a chaotic swirl of loose papers, spreadsheets, brochures and a pile of passports bundled together with a rubber band. Out of it emerged a stapled two-sheeter that looked to Christopher very much like the CV Ali had typed up for him a week earlier.

"Christopher Aidan Wainwright, age 29, single, driving licence, London-Dakar rally experience, French and Italian speaking," read Donald. "That you?"

The bastard, thought Christopher.

"Conversational French. And the Italian's...er...a bit rusty."

"After university, led a specialist French wine tour in the Bordeaux region."

Christopher gulped. He didn't like the specialist bit. He kicked himself for not having read through the final draft before Ali had emailed it off. He had a horrible feeling he'd been stitched up.

"Yes," he countered warily. "That's right."

"Following year, conducted a trip to Rome for the Pope's Easter Blessing with St Mary's Convent, Chicago, Illinois."

They had come up with Rome because it was a city he knew well. But a convent? That was a late addition, and a pure fiction of Ali's. "That a school or a bunch of nuns?"

"A school," he improvised hastily.

"How old?"

"Oh…" Christopher waved a hand nonchalantly. "15... 16. Nightmare trip. Never partied so much in my entire life."

He tried to laugh but all that emerged was a snigger. Donald shot him a sidelong glance and went on.

"Here we are. Oh, my mistake. The Zambezi. Took fifteen paraplegic guests in wheelchairs rafting down the Zambezi. Zambian medal for bravery for the rescue of two clients from a raging torrent." Donald raised an eyebrow. "Bit colourful, isn't it?"

Tie and face merged into one, if you ignored the polka dots. "My sister wrote that bit."

"Did she now?" They eyed each other. "So how did you secure these...wheelchairs? Onto the rafts I mean?"

Christopher cleared his throat noisily, desperate for the extra seconds to help him frame a reply. He wondered for a moment whether to come clean, but decided he had to tough it out.

"Oh, we had a special one built...excuse me," he spluttered, gobbing noisily into his fist.

"You alright?" said Donald, concerned. "Can I get you a glass of water?" Christopher shook his head, suddenly seized by a coughing spasm.

"Here, use my handkerchief," he added, getting the rag

out, but Christopher's head shake only became more vigorous, his face puce.

"I'll be OK," he gasped, "honestly, thanks, I just need a few seconds."

He took a deep breath and pointed to his throat, forcing a smile, "Something must have gone down the wrong way," all the time trying to compose a plausible reply.

"You were saying…" said Donald eventually. "About the special raft."

"Oh yes, the raft, yes, the thing is, it had these…er…steel rails, onto which the wheelchairs were fixed."

"So what happened?"

"How do you mean?"

"With these two gentlemen who went overboard into a raging torrent?"

"Oh… them. They…er…most unfortunate, they… er…they forgot to lock their brakes and when the raft had to do a sudden turn to avoid some rocks the back dipped and they shot off the end."

Donald stared at him in silence, mesmerised. Eventually he let out a low whistle. "Amazing. You mean like they sort of…*pirouetted* into the rapids? Spun out of control?"

"Exactly."

"So what in hell's name did you do?"

"I leapt in after them, didn't I?"

"Wow." Donald laid down the CV. "Well. You're either a foolhardy maniac or a more than capable liar. Either way you sound eminently suited for this kind of work." He grinned. "OK, now there's just a few questions I'd like to ask you."

Christopher sat back heavily, barely disguising a sigh of relief. He could feel the sweat trickling down from under his armpits.

"Fire away."

"Ninety-nine per cent of our clients are Americans. When

you arrive in a hotel, what's the first thing you point your passengers to?"

Christopher thought for a moment.

"The toilet?"

"You mean the restroom. No, that's not it. Try again."

"Er...the restaurant?"

"Warmer. The elevators. Lifts are what they do to their breasts." He reached across his desk and took a swig out of a can of Pepsi.

"Two," he continued. "When a passenger asks you a question you don't know the answer to, what do you say?"

He was on more familiar ground here. Direct Publishing had a number of recommended strategies for this one. "Get a sudden attack of cramp?"

"That'll do. Just never say 'I don't know'. Remember, that's not in your lexicon. Three. All the hotels we stay in are air-conditioned. It's right there in the brochure. If by any chance you find no evidence of any air actually being conditioned, it means the hotel management have switched it off. Why?"

"Presumably because they're trying to save money."

"Precisely. In order to give the difference to an African orphan appeal. You'll find it's a very popular appeal. Any questions?"

Christopher rubbed his chin. "Where exactly do your tours go to?"

Donald swung round in his swivel chair. "Where don't they go? France, Germany, Italy, Spain, North Africa. Plus some in Eastern Europe. Hungary, Russia, all those weird little republics. So. When can you start?"

Christopher shifted uneasily in his seat.

"You mean...I've got the job?"

"Don't see why not. Let me see now." He leant back. On a wall-chart behind his desk was a large printed year planner with a series of names, numbers and lines in a variety of colours. "How about next week? Comprehensive European, eighteen days. If you can handle the Zambezi, you should be able to handle that lot."

"Which...er...which country's that then?"

"Most of them." He flipped through the brochure until he found it. "Here we are. Paris, Bordeaux, Lourdes, Avignon, Nice, Florence, Sorrento, Rome, Venice, Vienna, Lucerne, Brussels, Amsterdam. London."

"Jesus."

"Yeah, it's a rapid one, but you'll make good money. Our clients are the best, Wainwright. These guys have serious wallets. We call it the pyjama tour."

"Pyjama tour?"

"No time to unpack."

"Sounds...er...complicated. So when...what about training? When does that take place?"

"Training?" The man appeared genuinely shocked. "You train on the job, dear boy! Our guides generally come in and pick up their documents just before they leave - sometimes even from the airport - meal vouchers, hotel lists, visa details if applicable, that sort of stuff. Then you're off." He snorted. "Good Lord, there's no time for luxuries like training."

"No?" Christopher was rapidly feeling out of his depth. "And...er...how big are these groups, generally speaking?"

"Forty, fifty. If you're lucky."

Christopher blanched. "50?" Christ. "And if I'm unlucky?"

"Maybe twenty five, thirty."

"I see." But he didn't see at all.

There was a short silence. Donald seemed to be waiting for Christopher to say something.

"So," he said finally. "Any further questions?"

"Well, yes actually," said Christopher. "Your ad mentioned £3k OTE a week. What's the salary?"

Donald stared at him. "I beg your pardon?"

"I mean, d'you pay me by the tour, a fixed salary or what? Weekly, monthly?" He trailed off.

"We don't pay you anything."

Christopher appeared baffled.

"Forgive me, perhaps I'm being slow here, but I don't understand. What d'you mean, you don't pay anything?"

"You pay us, my friend. Fifty dollars a head."

Christopher fingered the nape of his neck.

"I...pay...you," he repeated slowly.

"Exactly."

"So...er...what's in it for me?"

"What's in it for you? Christ, Wainwright, who've you been working for all these years? Here I am offering you fifty loaded Americans on a two and a half week tour, and you're asking ME how YOU make money?"

Suddenly he burst out laughing.

Chapter 4

Potatoes or Rice?

"Left a bit, right a bit, hold it!" An explosion of white light lit up the studio, followed by the urgent whine and whirr of a camera.

"Encore une fois. Turn the epaulette a touch towards me. Ach … too much! That's it!" Two more flashes came in quick succession. Horst, balding 42 year old art director to the new National Government of Reconstruction and formerly, before the factory closed, Prada VP of International Sales (South East Europe), straightened up.

"Voila! Next!"

A door opened and a head appeared,

"Oh..Mr President...Johann...good morning."

The President of the new Republic of Ruritania surveyed the room with bewilderment. He was on his way to see his minister of finance, and had stopped briefly to check in on the art department. There was so much going on here that he didn't understand.

"Listen, Horst – what exactly is the position on those police uniforms?"

"You mean the palace guard? Let me see now... the jackets

are on approval from...*Georgi darling, who are those jackets on loan from? You know, the police jackets?*" Someone mumbled an answer through a mouthful of pins in an adjoining room.

"That's the one. It's from the unsold Armani stock. The denims are from Dolce and Gabbana, the belts..."

"Denims?"

"Uh-huh, you like them? Special order that was undelivered, black with silver rivets. Been sitting in the warehouse for years."

"They're certainly...distinctive," Blicker said doubtfully. He wondered about all this unsold stock. When orders from the multinational fashion houses had begun to dry up after the crash and the banks had finally pulled the plug in the face of Chinese competition, half the garment factories across the country had had to close. Suddenly they were in possession of vast quantities of undelivered black pants, silk shirts and designer swimming shorts. He was amazed they'd not been burnt. There had been talk about flogging the lot to Net-a-Porter, especially now the fashion for autumn colours had come full circle. But buried somewhere in the small print had been a clause forbidding their re-sale. Presumably the brands themselves did not want to flood the market.

"We'll discuss them later. I can't stop, I'm late for a meeting..."

Blicker made to leave but Horst held up a hand.

"*Une moment,*" he said, flinging open a drawer. "Before you go, I need a decision. We're in a quandary." He pulled out two little round buttons and fingered them nervously. "What do you think about these? Black or silver? Georgi reckons silver but I'm not so sure."

"What are they?" Blicker glanced at his watch, impatient to get on.

"Buttons, chief, buttons. For the dress coat." He beckoned to a rather uncomfortable youth who was standing idly in one corner. He was dressed in a peacock blue tunic. Horst beckoned him over.

"I like the black because it goes quite well with the yellow epaulettes. See? But the silver is somehow more...*militaire*." Horst squinted, gently twirling his ginger moustache.

But Blicker had already left the room.

OUTSIDE IN THE CORRIDOR A PROCESSION STARTED UP, BLICKER at its head. To his left was his social secretary, a large battle-axe of a woman with a fat file cradled in her arm, who kept up a low but insistent monotone in his left ear. To his right was a white bundle of gesticulation in a chef's hat, brandishing a piece of paper. A small army of grey suited functionaries, the civil servants, fanned out behind like a school of pilot fish.

They marched through galleries, along corridors, past ante-rooms. Everywhere was evidence of feverish renovation – scaffolding, workmen, half drunk cups of tea. Along one corridor a series of old portraits were coming down, and some new modern works were going up in a cloud of dust. Elsewhere metres of shimmering material was being measured out for curtains, while tall young men staggered past with huge works in steel and glass.

Blicker worried whether he had made the right decision with Horst. His idea to recycle all this design-wear had been right in principle, and the jobs they had found for the bloated bureaucracy in the palace renovations were welcome – but Blicker was concerned that they would end up as a laughing stock. It was no good pointing out to people that the suede flare pants didn't actually have labels and were otherwise destined for the scrap heap. They were meant to be in austerity mode.

They reached a large hallway. A line of stopped clocks high up on the wall read Moscow, Beijing, Havana, Tripoli.

Evidently no one had bothered to change them since 1989. Below them, stacked neatly against a reception desk, were three freshly painted legends waiting to replace them: Beijing, New Delhi, Berlin, New York, London. The order was significant. A clue to where the new Ruritania felt its economic salvation might come from.

A man and a woman emerged from a doorway. Blicker greeted them as he swept past.

"Morning Ivan."

"Good morning Johann."

Blicker wondered whether he should stamp out all this informality.

"As I was saying, Mr President," continued the man in the stained chef's hat. "Leeks with cranberries is what I thought we'd do next, with rice or potatoes..."

And that was another thing, thought Blicker. It was all very well welcoming back the odd cordon-bleu Ruritanian chef, but the banquets that Horst was putting on, mostly for representatives of the BRIC nations, were not sending the right signal. They were looking for loans, and here were the waiters resembling something out of an avant-garde production of Hamlet, all pastels and polar necks. It was distracting. Occasionally they'd been heard to act that way too: *"Something is rotten in the state of Ruritania..."* and so on, whispered in hushed tones to the Brazilian ambassador between coffee and liqueurs.

"And here's the letter to the Chinese basketball player..." intoned the battle-axe, and without breaking stride Blicker signed the bottom of it, "and here's the one to that F1 fellow." He scribbled again. "Last, the footballer."

"The footballer?"

"Yes sir. Our honorary cultural attaché in Buenos Aires."

He grunted. Several stars in the world of sport and the arts, in particular from the developing world, were being invited to be honorary cultural attaches to the new republic. None had as yet accepted. Without breaking step he signed the letter inscribed "Dear Lionel", walked on a few paces, and came to a door. He stopped, and gripped the handle.

The procession came to a sudden, noisy halt. Blicker turned in bewilderment.

"God, who are all these people?" he hissed to his secretary, eyeing the pack of civil servants and some new additions now jostling for position behind them. What had started out as five had now grown to nearer fifteen. Two men hurried by with mumbled apologies. A young, anxious looking girl found herself exposed before him. He eyed her with suspicion.

"You, for instance. Who are you, young lady?"

The girl had long fair hair and looked acutely embarrassed.

"Sophie Bernenstein," she stammered. "From the PR department. One of your influencers, sir."

Influencers? What new madness was this? Blicker groaned inwardly. This crazy bureaucracy was out of control. Half the country seemed to be in public service. He'd been in office for six months now and still people kept appearing out of the woodwork. How on earth was he supposed to pay all these salaries?

He turned, opened the door, and disappeared inside, slamming it shut behind him.

Boris Kurtz, it said. Minister for Economic Affairs.

Chapter 5

A Rumour

"Well?" said Blicker, without pleasantries or pre-amble, slumping heavily into an armchair. "What do you suggest we do?" He was squat and heavily built, just short of sixty, with greying hair around the temples and an untidy mop of what was left on top. "How they think we're supposed to boost our GDP by slashing jobs I do not understand."

"Fuck the IMF," said his Finance Minister from behind his desk. "We simply cannot accept a loan under those conditions."

Blicker lit up a Camel cigarette.

"The point is, Boris, if we don't get a loan from the IMF, where do we get one from?" He waved a hand. "Back to the EU?"

"We already owe them from the last loan. They have their own problems, now Britain's gone. It cost them billions. Besides, you heard what the Germans said. They cannot promise us membership for at least ten years."

"The Chinese?"

"Well, yes, there's always the Chinese. Perhaps we can get in on their Belt and Braces initiative."

"You mean their Belt and Road initiative. Unwise. We'd be giving away our infrastructure."

"Whatever".

"So who else? The Americans?"

"You know very well, Johann, what I think about that," muttered Boris.

Blicker threw up his hands. "Well, we need to get revenue from somewhere, and quickly. We must sort out the economy. The people are expecting it, we have a window of opportunity, but if we fail, who then will be the beneficiary?"

He looked at his finance minister meaningfully, and was met with a grimace.

"Exactly, the Russians. They will be all over us. You saw how they tried to prevent my election. All those social media bots. It's not like they have gone away." He clenched a fist involuntarily.

Boris smirked. "Well, boss, I did have one off the wall idea…"

AT JUST 26, BORIS KURTZ WAS THE BABY OF THE CABINET. Tall and lanky, with blond hair gathered back into a ponytail, a wispy goatee and a boyish grin, Boris had been plucked from the examination halls of the London School of Economics to head up Blicker's financial team. It was a significant choice. It was clear that Blicker needed some fresh thinking.

Boris was one of only a few Ruritanians who had been able to study abroad, paid for by generous grants from the previous administration. When Blicker's scouts had come to find him in his Bayswater bedsit, he was just finishing a condensed degree in Economics at the LSE, following a spell at the University of Southern California. Blicker was pleased at the report that came back. Here was a young man passionately attached to a Green economic agenda: decentralised, community based industry; mandatory recycling of waste; and freshwater seaweed farming. All of which, he pointed out, could be introduced into Ruritania at a fraction of the cost that would be necessary in a more developed country.

Blicker's man had told Boris that he could consider himself a candidate for a post in a new Think Tank. But to everybody's surprise, Boris had said that what he really wanted was the Economics portfolio. After a hasty trip home to Strelsau, and to the amazement of everyone, he had got it.

Not surprisingly, given his green convictions, Boris had very soon established himself in the new administration as the leader of a group of ministers who believed that Ruritania needed to wipe the slate clean and start again, this time with a sustainable growth agenda. This was the very opposite of the unrestrained capitalism and free-market economics pursued for the past thirty years, with, he maintained, such disastrous consequences.

It had been clear, even when he was at the LSE, what had been going on under the Oligarchs. The country had been flooded with all sorts of cheap credit, loan guarantees and business development grants. Running through all this interest was a poison ivy, it seemed to him: the West's overwhelming desire to open up the old Russian territories as a new market for their overpriced, over-resourced and over-rated goods, while at the same time getting access to a cheap labour force that was a fraction of the distance away when compared to China or India. It wasn't hard for Boris to twig. It was what they had taught at the LSE.

Opposing Boris in Cabinet was Rupert Hentzau. Where Boris's supporters were known as the hard whites, Hentzau's were labelled the off-whites. 58, tall, good looking and of aristocratic bearing, Hentzau was a former oligarch, and junior minister in the previous regime. He was also from an old Ruritanian family, a forebear and namesake having featured prominently in *'The Prisoner of Zenda'*, and the grandson of the last Count of Zenda – though the title had been defunct since 1929.

However, as the only oligarch not to have fled abroad, Blicker had included him in the new Government because, as a former banker, he provided a useful bridge and reassurance to the international financial community. In his former role as Minister for Home Affairs he had been one of the most enthusiastic sponsors of foreign investment, and he had become rich on the proceeds. In making him Minister of Trade, Blicker relished the rather neat symmetry of having the man part responsible for the mess they were in, deal with the fallout.

"WELL?" SNAPPED BLICKER WHEN BORIS DID NOT FOLLOW through. "Let's hear it then."

Boris's smirk morphed to a grin. "What would you say if someone told you that the Red Army had left a large stockpile of military hardware up in a bunker near Felixtown?"

Blicker raised an eyebrow. "What kind of hardware?"

"Let's say…" Boris began stroking his goatee. "A stash of warheads. Nukes."

"I'd say they were nuts."

"The Russians?"

"No, no, the person…" Blicker stopped. "Look, Boris, where did you hear this ridiculous rumour?"

"No rumour, Johann. Reliable sources. Deep down in a bunker, apparently, close to the border, somehow got overlooked. Pretty old, probably decayed, and almost certainly without means of delivery. But lethal nevertheless, if they get into the wrong hands."

"Overlooked? Are you sure they did not leave them there as an excuse to come back in again? You know the way it goes, false flags, prevent them getting into the wrong hands etcetera etcetera…"

"Possible, but unlikely, because they would need maintenance. In which case it would have to be done secretly, and the risk of them getting found out is rather high, don't you think?"

Blicker began to pace up and down the room, thinking furiously.

"We must destroy them. At once," he said decisively. "Under the auspices of the UN. They're set up for this kind of thing."

"You mean give them up for free?" Boris glanced at his boss meaningfully. "I mean, look what happened to Ukraine."

"Well, I hope that you're not suggesting…"

"I'm not proposing anything *specific*," returned Boris hastily. "And we'd have to run it past the cabinet. But think about it. The Arab states still have a shedload of oil. Our oil import bill is crippling, it'll take another five years for our wind farms to take up the slack. Now if…"

"No! No! No!" cried Blicker. He shook his head in disbelief. "I cannot believe you can even think that!"

"Hear me out! I'm not proposing we sell them the uranium..."

"The tech?" Blicker whispered, aghast.

"Boss, I'm not proposing we sell anything to anybody. We just threaten to sell them. And we let the Arabs woo us with easy loans. Nothing is guaranteed to make the IMF – the Brits, the Germans, the Americans - come running back faster than that. We've just got to make them realise that there's competition for our business."

Blicker regarded Boris with amazement.

"And there I was all the time thinking you were …. heard of Machiavelli by any chance? We'd be pariahs."

"It's an idea, anyway," continued Boris. "It would have to

be conducted in total secrecy. If it ever became public there'd be hell to pay, and the Russians would be forced to demand them back."

"What about Ukraine? There's another Dutch auction for you!" Blicker chuckled. "Maybe we could make out that we developed them ourselves. You can imagine the headline: *Returning Ruritanian boffins* etc."

"Are there any?" chuckled Boris.

"I'm sure we could invent a few." They laughed. "Sorry Boris, but that's a lousy idea. We must contact the Kremlin and ask them to take them away, before they can use them as an excuse to march in."

Boris sighed. "Well, have you got a better one? It's a lot less crazy than that scheme Hentzau came up with the other day."

Blicker raised an eyebrow at the mention of Hentzau.

"Don't you remember? Ah, no, that's right, it was when you were in Brussels. He said we should - get this - resurrect the fucking monarchy!" With that he got up from his desk and walked over to a side table. "Can I get you a drink boss? I think we deserve one, don't you?"

Blicker didn't reply immediately. There was the clink of ice as Boris filled the heavy Ruritanian crystal from a silver bucket.

"Say that again?" said the President.

"Whisky, brandy, roochi and tonic?"

"No, no, before that. You said something about resurrecting the monarchy."

"Yes, preposterous, isn't it?" Boris turned round, and noticed a peculiar look on Blicker's face. "Calm down boss, I didn't mean it."

He turned back to the side-table and poured himself a whisky. "So, what'll it be?"

"But it's a brilliant idea, Boris."

Boris put the glass down heavily. "Oh for God's sake, Johann, please, I've had a hard morning."

The Spare and The Heir 39

Blicker's expression resembled that of the first accountant to be told about the pocket calculator.

"My God, you are serious," continued Boris. "Here, drink this."

He poured a small glass of the national drink – a type of local grappa called roochi - and handed it to a distracted looking Blicker. But the President ignored it.

"Put it this way," he said, jumping up excitedly and beginning to pace the room. "Consider our new tourism strategy, to attract visitors into the country. To show them we exist. A restored monarchy would be the perfect family attraction."

It was true - the new Ruritania faced a major problem, which Blicker's new tourism initiative was intended to correct. Soon after he'd been elected President they'd commissioned some market research, held some focus groups, and the results had stunned them. If high-school kids in Hicksville, Ohio, thought Bulgaria was a disease – or even a type of yoghurt – Ruritania conjured up a cross between Dracula, Tintin and a cheap brand of foreign wine. Their brand recognition was non-existent. Even their recent triumph of winning the World Marbles Championship had gone largely unnoticed. No one had heard of them, except a few cinemascope bores old enough to have seen Stewart Granger play the King in Metro Goldwyn Mayer's 1952 production of *'The Prisoner of Zenda'*. And even then, they discovered, people didn't actually believe they existed. After a lot of time-consuming research they'd traced it back to a shocking misclassification of Anthony Hope's original book by the British Library as fiction. *Fiction?* Their new ambassador to the court of St James had nearly had a heart attack in the British Library Reading Room.

"Well, it's one plank, Johann, just one plank in our revenue plan. Monarchy isn't something you can switch on and off you know. It's a serious commitment. By the time our wind turbine farms are complete and…"

"Yes, yes, yes…" Blicker waved the air impatiently. "And the hormone-free beef exports, and the renewable timber…blah blah blah… but I'm talking about real revenue, now. Otherwise there will be no new industries, of any kind whatsoever. And it's no good waiting for the garment industry to pick up again. Now…" He turned to Boris, "…how do you suppose UK plc survives?"

"UK plc?" Boris wished he'd lay off the acronyms.

"Think." He sucked his teeth. "Tourism, of course. They've got castles, dukes, they've got heritage. Above all, they've got a monarchy."

"Sure, but aren't you forgetting one thing?" Boris peered at Blicker over the rim of his glass like a schoolmaster correcting a wayward pupil. "Two things actually. First there was North Sea oil, and now…"

Blicker started to interrupt.

"Wait. Let me finish. I did go to the London School of Economics, you know, so I do understand a thing or two about the British economy." He paused. "Financial services. The City. It's still the best there is, even out of the EU. Besides, a lot of people want to get rid of their monarchy. If they really believed it made money, they wouldn't be that stupid."

"Don't you believe it. Look at what that Thatcher woman did to their industrial base. I'm not so sure you're right about their monarchy, either. I mean look at it the other way round." Blicker was well into his stride now, a man possessed.

"Why do you think that the King - when he was Prince of Wales, the one with the ears - married someone so unsuitable in the first place? She never liked architecture, of any description, she couldn't talk to plants, she had none of his eco interests. She was more than ten years younger, for God's sake, she liked disco dancing and shopping. And who can blame her? He would never have chosen her himself, not in a million years. No, she was chosen for him, by the powers that be."

"What," interjected Boris, "you mean because she was a virgin?"

"No, no, no, you idiot, because she was a cover girl." Boris started to protest. "Yes, I know, ended in disaster blah blah, and then the poor girl had that awful accident. But why else was Diana on more covers than anyone else in the history of the world? She was a fairy-tale princess to match their fairy-tale grandmother. They knew which way their biscuits were coated."

"Or they thought they did."

"They weren't to know how it would turn out. It started as one enormous public relations stunt. And so it goes on. You have to give them credit for trying again with this new one. I mean how can we ever forget that wedding…"

"I was screwing a girl in the Adriatic…"

"Precisely. You remember exactly what you were doing. It was a world event."

"Hardly," muttered Boris, flicking his pony-tail.

"I'll grant you, it backfired in the end. And sure, tourism's not everything. But it's a huge slice. Because what else we got?" He paused. "Besides, there's another reason why this could be a genius idea."

"Which is?" said Boris.

"The Russians. We all know how skilled they are at manipulating elections, meddling in a country's politics for their own ends, but it's much harder to overthrow a homegrown monarchy. This anchors us to our heritage. You can't manipulate birthright. The only issue I can see is that it will need popular support, but I am sure we can manage that, considering how much nostalgia there is in this country for our historical roots."

Boris fell silent for a few moments.

"Mmm, I see what you mean," he replied eventually. "From that angle it does look attractive." He paused to stroke his goatee. "However, I don't mean to be a downer or anything, but there's another problem. Just suppose we decide to do it, to resurrect the monarchy. OK, so we proclaim the heir. And guess who that turns out to be? Some garage mechanic in Zenda. Certainly no Leonardo DiCaprio."

Blicker marched over to Boris's desk and pressed a buzzer.

"Let's find out, shall we?" He waited for the receptionist to answer, then issued a string of instructions. Boris got up.

"Seriously, Johann. The Elphberg line died out with Queen Flavia, remember?"

"Well OK, the Elphberg line might have, but weren't there some third cousins or something claiming the throne in 1927? Don't you remember? They must have descendants."

"Shouldn't think so. Weren't they all butchered in '45?"

"So we'll invite someone to take the throne. Someone already famous and popular."

Boris gazed at him in wonder. Perhaps the Boss had finally flipped. The idea seemed to have gone to his head. He only hoped the heir turned out to be a supermarket shelf-filler or something equally unmarketable. Better still, a figurative painter. Blicker would soon drop the idea. He snorted out loud.

Blicker scowled at him. "What's so funny?"

"I've got it." He paused for dramatic effect. "*Tom Cruise!*"

There was a split second of silence before Boris dissolved into howls of laughter, clutching at his sides in agony.

"Oh my God...oh my God...can you imagine..." He rocked from side to side, tears beginning to roll slowly down his cheeks. So engrossed was he in his own joke that he failed to notice Blicker storm out. All that registered was the slamming of the door.

. . .

The Spare and The Heir

HALF AN HOUR LATER THE PRESIDENT RETURNED.

"What's so urgent?" he said, striding back into the room.

"Which d'you want first?" said a beaming Boris, who'd just put the phone down to his private secretary. "The good news, or the bad news?"

Boris handed him a piece of paper. It was the black and white scan of a young woman with long dark hair. Despite the blurred image, it was clear she was very pretty. Large, round, liquid eyes stared out from a fresh looking face, with an ambiguous mix of innocence and mischievousness which made her look positively angelic. Blicker stared at it.

"Who's this? The new Mrs Boris?" he ventured.

"It's the good news. She's called Rose Elphberg."

He waited for a reaction, but none came. Blicker just kept staring at the grainy image. God, he was slow sometimes, thought Boris.

"The heir to the throne," he added.

By the time Blicker spoke again it was in a whisper. "My God..." He beamed. "What did I tell you? So the Elphberg line didn't die out after all..."

"I wouldn't be so sure. She's actually descended from the cousins, so why she calls herself Elphberg, I've no idea. It's not strictly correct. We'll need to investigate, of course. And she's only the unofficial heir - that is she's..."

"Official, unofficial, Elphberg, Smithski, what does it matter?" cried the President.

"...the nearest relation still living here. I was right when I said the majority of the ex-royals fled in 1945. But whether they got away is another matter. We all know how RUSK and the other security services operated. The whole thing's been under wraps for years. Mind you, there was a rumour..."

"Sod the rumour. That's academic now."

"Perhaps. Perhaps not," said Boris cryptically.

"There's no perhaps about it! Just look at her. Besides,

there's a vacancy right now for a fairy tale queen, what with the Queen of England gone." Blicker waved the image in the air.

"And there's more." Boris smiled. "I think we might be onto something here."

"Ah, 'we' now is it?"

Boris handed over another document. This one was torn and yellowing.

"A letter from the Bank of England dated 8th January 1945. It appears that the Russians attempted to withdraw a large quantity of Gold bullion - here described as the 'Royal Gold', but were refused on the grounds that due title was not proved. Note the last sentence."

Blicker read: 'According to the instructions of our late client Her Majesty Queen Flavia the fore-mentioned shall only be restored, with interest at a rate to be determined from time to time by the Bank in accordance with the Bank's base lending rate, to the National Bank of Strelsau at such time that the heirs to the Elphberg dynasty are restored to the throne, or, after an agreed period of years to the rightful heir regardless of status, whichever is the sooner. In the latter case a notification will be sent to the National Bank of Strelsau in accordance with international law.'

Blicker looked up, wide-eyed. "How much is it? Do we know?"

Boris turned to another slip of paper. "We certainly do. I have a note of it here. In 1945 it was worth 45,467,888 pounds, six shillings, and nine pence."

Blicker let out a low whistle. "My God. And what about notification? Have we had one?"

"We have no record of any notification. The agreed period was up a few months ago. But I'll tell you something else. I checked up on this Rose Elphberg, and for the past two years she's been drawing welfare payments. So what does that tell us?"

Blicker frowned. "Mmm…"

"There's only one snag. The bad news."

"What are you trying to tell me? That she's a…a.." Blicker squinted at the picture, trying to imagine what drawback there could possibly be. Dark images flashed before him of a man in heels with unpronounceable pronouns.

"Worse."

He blinked. "*Worse?*"

"She's engaged to Hentzau's son." He paused. "So unless we move fast, it leaves him with the gold."

It took a while to sink in.

"And us?" whispered the President.

"What it leaves us with," replied Boris, "is the rumour I was telling you about."

Chapter 6

Tilly

"You've got to do something about it, Papa."

Tilly was pacing up and down in front of Rupert Hentzau's desk, looking cross. Her father, Trade and Business Minister in Blicker's cabinet, was engrossed in a pile of documents spilling out from a red government box.

"Mmm, sweetheart?"

"It's rubbish," she spat out in her husky, 13 year old voice. "Hashtag fail." She stopped pacing and faced him squarely.

Hentzau sighed. He didn't need his daughter to remind him. He was still smarting from the rebuff he had received in the cabinet just a few days previously over his plan to import a new type of fast food product from Russia. It was a sure way of making savings to the schools budget, which he'd been told to slash by 20%. He'd negotiated with Globalny Foods the sale, at a knock-down price, of 5000 *'TV-Eezy Cook'* meals each week to support the new school dinners programme, along with a deal to stream fifty episodes of the TV reality show *'Nevsky Prospekt' (sponsor: Globalny Foods in association with Netflix)* - the Russian equivalent of *'Made in Chelsea'* following the rich kids of St. Petersburg. As a quid quo pro, Globalny had agreed to sponsor the refurbishment of Zenda Castle, his country seat, in time for the wedding of his son to Rose Elphberg and the tourist season - though he had been careful not to highlight that part of the bargain.

But all that that pony-tailed creature of an 'economics minister' could see was the threat to his pet organic agriculture programme, whilst the culture minister queried the wisdom of importing Russian programming. Eventually President Blicker had cut the discussion short and suggested they remit the decision to the TV Regulatory Committee. Instead they went on to talk about his pet Artsfare scheme. This was a programme to offer extra welfare payments to practising artists in return for providing regular works of art to the State. Hentzau had asked, acidly, what was to stop every out-of-work scrounger deciding he was an artist? It didn't take much wit to exhibit an unmade bed these days, he'd pointed out. Soon they'd have warehouses of the stuff. But would Blicker listen? It was a shambles.

"Guess what we had for school lunch today? Just guess?"

"What's that, my darling?" Hentzau went back to his papers and scanned a page absent-mindedly.

Tilly screwed up her face in disgust. "Vegan mush. Organic vegan mush. Yuk!" She shuddered.

"Really?"

"Yuk!!" she repeated, stamping her foot violently. Hentzau looked up, alarmed.

"Hey, little lady, why aren't you in school, anyway?"

She made a face, trying to suppress a look of triumph. "I got suspended, that's why. You're not listening to a word I say!" She snatched the paper out of her father's hands and stormed out of the room.

He found her upstairs in her bedroom under the eaves. Every available surface was covered in posters, flags and memorabilia – except for one corner, which was piled up with china dolls and cuddly toys. On one wall was a huge poster of Che Guevara, on another a picture of Lenin next to one of some heroic industrial workers in Minsk. A framed certificate from her school stood on her bedside table, beside a signed photograph of an unidentifiable man coming down a flight of airline steps. And, rather surprisingly, a press cutting of Margaret Thatcher. Behind the door a crudely made darts board hung limply from a hook, a much torn picture of Mikhail Gorbachev barely intact in the middle. His bald cranium was almost completely obliterated.

Hentzau came in and closed the door gently. Tilly was reading on her bed, head propped up on her elbows, legs waving lazily in the air. On her bedside table were two unopened TV-Eezy Cooks. *'Frigo Wonder Chicken'* flavour.

"Go away."

"What was all that about?" he said softly.

"GO. A. WAY! I'm not talking to you." She said it without looking up from her book. He lowered himself into a battered old armchair, moving a large furry bear to make room.

"Careful!" she said angrily, glancing at him sideways. "He doesn't like being shoved around. Least of all by a member of this stupid government!"

He couldn't help smiling to himself. She really was something. Top student at the special school for the children of Government functionaries, a junior leader of the Zenda Youth Brigade, one of only ten pupils to go on an exchange visit to Caracas. He was tremendously proud of her. So would her mother have been. She was going to turn into one hell of a young woman.

But now, he knew, all that was finished. First of all the school had opened its portals to all sorts of riff-raff. Anyone who would pay in fact. Tilly still studied there, still got to do the honours when dignitaries arrived at the airport, but somehow of late she'd lost her enthusiasm for it. What was all this about being suspended, he wondered? It would have been unthinkable a year ago. The Youth Brigade had been disbanded, to be replaced with some ludicrously over-dressed 'Pioneer Scouts'. Everyone knew what it was really about: an excuse for that silly little man Horst, the government's so-called 'artistic director', to show off again, this time at the World Scout Jamboree in Seoul.

He shuddered to think. Ruritania was rapidly becoming a laughing stock, with its designer scout jackets and its nut roast banquets. Still, Tilly's political awakenings alarmed him. She had just turned thirteen, she should be doing things other girls of her age did – drinking cider (or rather vodka, if her older brother was to be believed) and flirting with boys. Instead of which, she had this crazy notion that the solution to Ruritania's economic malaise was to take it back to pre-revolutionary days – to a Communist nirvana that had never actually existed.

Hentzau idly picked up a commemorative plate that was mounted on a kind of wooden frame on the table beside him. A portrait of Mao Tse Tung was displayed in the middle, above the legend 1893-1993.

"You're a great fan of Mao, aren't you?"

"Well aren't you?" Tilly retorted.

She was referring to her father's early political career, when he had been a leading light in the youth wing of the Communist Party before the oligarchs moved in. It had been a romantic time of high ideals.

"Of course, darling, of course. But we're living in changed times now. We've got to adapt to circumstances. As we find them."

"Rubbish!" It seemed to be her favourite word of late. Tilly sat up suddenly and swung her star spangled legs over the side of the bed. Hentzau had a momentary flash of anxiety: she's too young for stockings. But it passed.

"Tilly! That's no way to speak to your father… you're a Hentzau, remember!"

"Well you're obviously not! All I ever hear from you is *'cir-cum-stanc-es'*, *'out of my hands'*. That's so lame! You're supposed to be a do-er, Papa. Look what's happening to our country now. It's falling to bits. It's been taken over by a bunch of losers."

"My sweet, I know it's difficult for you, what with school and everything, but…"

"Oh…it's not me! It's our country. I can't think why you're not really worried. I've even heard some people calling you a traitor! It's horrible! I can't stand it!" She was on the verge of tears.

Hentzau reached out for her but she held out an arm to fend him off, eyes averted.

"Look, sweetheart, we've been through all this before, you know we have. I don't like it any more than you do. Honestly. I only agreed to be a part of it so I could change it."

"And a fat lot of good you're doing. It's going from bad to terrible."

"It takes time. You must trust your father. And anyway, don't listen to what other people say. Now. What's all this about you being suspended?"

"That's another stupid thing. First of all they make us all eat disgusting organic yuck - whatever organic means. Poisoned probably - then they try and change all the history books and tell us that the Liberation in 1945 was really an invasion. Well it wasn't. Just think of the poor working class peasants who had to slave away for all those nasty Lords and everybody who…"

"Like us, you mean?"

"Well we're not the Zendas anymore are we, Papa? Besides, we were pretty good ones, weren't we?"

"Depends on which book you read, my sweet. So tell me -

you got suspended for raising the red flag?" Her father couldn't help laughing. Tilly flushed.

"I'm just doing what's right, like you taught me! Someone has to, around here!" She flounced up angrily and went over to her bookshelf.

"You're a clever girl, Tills. I'm sure you'll make an excellent politician one day. But trying to bring back communism is going to do no good at all. People don't want that anymore, they…"

"It's nothing to do with what they want, it's what's good for them!" Tilly said with feeling, mustering all the conviction her thirteen years would allow her. A conviction that helped explain the pin-up of the Iron Lady. "Nobody thinks of that anymore, do they? It's all just about themselves now, *Papa*." The last word was spat out with heavy sarcasm.

Hentzau sighed. He knew it was impossible arguing with a thirteen year old girl. He imagined what Greta Thunberg's parents must have gone through.

"So what are we going to do about it?" Tilly challenged him with her pale blue eyes and her turned up nose. He was grateful for the 'we' : she still had faith in him.

He paused, wondering whether to tell her. He'd trusted her with secrets before, and, surprisingly for a child, she had not yet let him down.

"Well, actually, there is a plan. But you have to promise me to keep it to yourself for now. Everyone will know soon enough."

"Of course papa."

"Well, step one, we're going to get Andrew married off to Rose…"

Tilly snorted, " 'bout time, they've been engaged for three years."

"…and then we're going to reinstate the monarchy."

It took a while for the words to sink in.

"The monarchy?" Her eyes widened. "You mean the King?"

"Well, actually the Queen."

Tilly looked at her father, puzzled.

"But that's...*reactionary*, papa!"

Hentzau laughed. "She'll be a figurehead only of course. Opium for the people and all that. But…" He tapped his nose knowingly, and could have sworn he felt something fall out of it. "It's the power behind the throne that counts."

"So you mean, we'll still be in charge?"

"Of course, my darling, who else?"

"And she'll just be for the tourists?"

He shrugged. "Something like that."

Her face, which had hitherto taken on a rather pinched expression as she tried to digest all the ramifications of this startling news, suddenly cleared.

"Why, that's brilliant!" she exclaimed, clapping her hands excitedly. She fell upon him, her arms reached up to his shoulders, her head on his breast, so that he had to steady himself to prevent falling over.

"And then we can get rid of all those idiots who are running the country…" he beamed, brushing his lapel just to make sure, "…with their carbon credits, their nut roast banquets, their seaweed toilet paper…"

∽

BUT SHE BARELY HEARD HIM. SHE WAS ALREADY FANTASISING about herself as sister-in-law to the Queen. About carriages, ball-gowns, curtsies - no, wait, she reflected, on second thoughts they'd do away with those: about dashing suitors and handsome footmen. She'd always wondered about footmen. What they actually did. Attend to her feet she supposed.

For Andrew was Tilly's brother. And she well knew that

The Spare and The Heir

Rose Elphberg was descended from the old royals. It had always counted against her in Tilly's book. Now, though, she began to see the whole thing in a completely different light. Suddenly a disturbing thought dawned on her. She drew away from her father, her eyes narrowing.

"But does that mean that Andrew will be the *King*?"

"Not exactly, sweetheart. Consort, I think you call them. But I'm sure we can make you a Princess. Now if you'll excuse me, I really must get on."

～

As Hentzau came down the stairs, clutching a slightly crumpled document of state in his hand, he mulled over what Tilly had said. He was glad she'd taken it so well. He'd not meant to reveal his hand so soon, but she was right, things were going from bad to worse. It was time to stop this rot. Open government? Millions of ruros lavished on art and culture? It was practical anarchy. Before long the whole country would be addicted to tofu and meat would have become indigestible.

And then there was Andrew. She had a point there. Her bewilderment at the dawning realisation of Andrew's responsibility in the affair sprang not from some natural sibling rivalry, but rather from the painful truth that Andrew was something of a waster. At that very moment, in fact, at ten o'clock in the morning, his father would not be at all surprised if his son was still in bed, and with one of any number of young women. Singly or together. As the natural heir to the Countdom of Zenda and the son of a cabinet minister, Andrew had plenty to choose from.

Few knew he was engaged to Rose Elphberg, and Andrew was happy to keep it that way. It was an attitude that pained his father, who had gone to great lengths to arrange the match.

His son's philandering he could forgive, but it was Andrew's indiscretion that he couldn't understand. Did he want to alienate the girl? Then there was his penchant for cocaine, embarrassingly revealed to Hentzau by the internal security service RUSK a year previously. He didn't think his son really realised what was at stake here. Was he an idiot, or just plain stupid? Hentzau hadn't actually spelt it out to him at the time. He hadn't thought it necessary. He realised now he might have made a mistake.

But if he didn't act soon it might all be too late. The question was: when? It was a fine judgement: whether to leave Blicker and Boris to make such a mess of things that the country was clamouring for another change, or whether to prevent their reforms from taking too deep a root. What was the expression he'd read about soldiers facing the enemy in battle? Hold your fire until…

His landline began to ring. He bounded down the last few steps.

"Hentzau!" he barked.

A female voice came over a crackly line.

"Hold the connection please. I have the President of Globalny wishing to speak with you."

It was an introduction that always maddened him. Why couldn't the man come on himself, if he insisted on calling him at his home number? There was always at least a minute's delay. Who did these CEOs think they were? God?

Then, at once, he remembered. His heart missed a beat. What on earth was he going to tell the man?

"Good morning Hentzau. Lougouev here!"

"Mr. Lougouev, how are you? So nice to hear from you!" Hentzau found himself having to practically shout down the phone.

"I'm fine, I'm fine."

"Mr. Lougouev...Yuri...this is a terrible line, you'll have to speak up!"

"Yes, I am very sorry about this, my people hev tried your mobile phone, they could not get through. I'm on Kira." Typical, thought Hentzau, recognising the name of his yacht. "But listen, vat I vant to know is, when do I send over my associate to sign?"

"To sign?" Hentzau hesitated for a second while he rapidly collected his thoughts. "Oh, to sign! Yes, of course...um...well... er... there's going to be a little bit of a delay I'm afraid.."

"*De-lay*?" Lougouev sounded menacing. "What is the meaning of *de-lay*?"

Hentzau ran his hand through his hair nervously. "It's been referred to our TV regulatory committee, Mr. Lougouev. Probably a formality, but just in case that's an issue, would you…"

"You know the deal." The line suddenly seemed to become crystal clear. Hentzau winced. "Nevsky's non-negotiable. You understand the meaning in your part of world? *Non-neg-ohshe-abull.*"

"Understood, Yuri, non-negotiable," Hentzau said hurriedly, "and I'd like to personally thank you for your support on our Zenda renovations, things are really beginning to take shape down there."

"Fan*tas*tic." The Russian put a particular emphasis on the word. "Let's get this signed. You hev two weeks Hentzau. Otherwise vee will need the advance back."

"The advance? But they're practically all eaten. We got a few Frigo Wonder Chicken left but…"

The President of Globalny Foods was gone. In a flash Hentzau remembered that expression: the whites of their eyes. They were getting that close. This couldn't go on.

Chapter 7

Blue Circles

Two hundred miles away in the Capital, the sun was beginning its long slow dip towards the horizon through wisps of cloud. President Blicker was doing something he did all too rarely these days: painting.

His green corduroy sports jacket was slung behind the door, and he'd donned a dirty blue painting smock. He was midway through one of his 'Blue circle' works, and in the background a reworked version of 'Candle in the Wind' provided soothing background music. He had primed the canvas, painting on a sketchy layer of raw sienna - in this case mixed with a touch of cadmium yellow. Next came the blue circle. For this particular work, a square canvas, he'd decided to place it just left of centre, and in a shade of blue just a touch brighter and more vibrant than usual. He wanted the circle to sing.

Now was the time for the household paint. He was proud of this technique. By using two different types of decorators paint - one matt, one vinyl silk - and mixing each with enough water or oil to make them translucent, he was able to drag a succession of textured veils over the circle in the middle, creating a 'veritable mystery within', as an art critic had so aptly put it in a recent review. The trick was in the randomness, marrying intention and chaos in such a way as to produce what the critic had labelled a 'resonant reflection of the magic that is Nature'.

Blicker gave the matt mix one final swirl with his stick, tipped the ash off his cigarette, and got up on a chair. The canvas was propped up against the wall in front of him, cradled in a huge expanse of transparent polythene to catch the dripping paint. Gently he poured it from the can in five bold stripes so it ran down horizontally in five broad rivers. Satisfied, he climbed down. The important thing here was not to interfere with gravity. The integrity of the work was everything. He took a step back and squinted. The lights dimmed, flickered, and went out. Bravo, he thought sarcastically, bang on time. Tuesday and Friday evenings, Saturday and Sunday afternoons for repeats. Regular like clockwork. The first commercial break in whatever episode was then playing of '*Nevsky Prospekt*', as millions of kettles around the country switched on simultaneously for their first cup of tea. He was damned if he was going to authorise fifty episodes of this Russian propaganda. It was obvious: there was no way Rurolectric's grid could cope.

He glanced at a wall clock and suddenly remembered that he had arranged to call an old friend in the US State Department an hour ago. The man was on the Balkans desk, and was always in meetings. Cursing silently, he fished his mobile out of a pocket with one hand, wiping a smear of paint off the other.

Luckily his friend was not in a meeting. Blicker got straight to the point. He had a favour to ask. A rather peculiar favour, his friend decided, when he mulled over the conversation with his wife later that night.

No, admitted the American, he hadn't heard the rumour.

Nor had he any idea whether any of the ex-Royal family had fled to the United States in 1945, or even 1927, come to that. His department had nothing to do with applications for asylum. Sure, he could find out. Urgently? Hell, why not. But hey, this was a kind of coincidence wasn't it? Because he'd literally just put the phone down to an editor who'd mentioned a feature he'd been offered by a PR agency in the Cayman Islands on some Elphberg princess, and the editor had wanted a quote, knowing that he was an authority on Balkan politics. Some girl living in a most unregal fashion somewhere in the north of Ruritania, apparently. That was the angle anyway. The editor had said they were planning a whole series of them, and had been offered unrivalled access.

Blicker swore. Who was this editor, he wanted to know? Was he from a local cable station? Nothing like that, replied his friend. No, the girl was guaranteed huge coverage, because he was the editor of the international 'Ciao' magazine, massive circulation, read by every…

Most peculiar, the State Department official thought afterwards. The President had kind of gone all weird on him at this point. Something to do with the article. Said he'd be sending some people over, and could his friend liaise with them.

Liaise about what, for Pete's sake?

Chapter 8

The Great Resignation

It had been two weeks now since Christopher's interview with TravelCo. Nothing had arrived by post or email and no one had been in touch. He was beginning to think they'd forgotten him. Which maybe was just as well. He had been in two minds about the job. They expected him to know instinctively what to do with a party of forty demanding Americans on a night out in Rome, or Paris, or Vienna. And he was still none the wiser as to how you were supposed to earn a living out of the job, despite Donald's assurance that the $50 a head 'tour levy' would be covered five times over. Like the money they had promised him he would be able to earn at Direct Marketing, he reminded himself ruefully - £200 per week plus expected commission of £300-400. Oh yes? It took an average of eight to twelve weeks to figure out you weren't going to get there, by which time Direct Marketing had had the use of your enthusiastic services for a fraction of that. He'd managed to save precisely one and a half grand. True, a single all-media deal could net him almost what he needed to close the gap, to pay the money he'd promised. But if he didn't land it in the next two and a half weeks... It didn't bear thinking about.

Ali nudged him and he looked up. The Team Leader was wandering in their direction, tapping a rolled-up newspaper menacingly against his thigh. Christopher punched a number into his keypad at random. Unexpectedly, it started to ring.

"Hello?" answered a quavery voice. Female, seventy plus.

Christopher cleared his throat. The team leader came to a halt directly behind him. He should have stopped it right there and hung up. But he panicked into pressing on.

"Hello, can I speak to John Thomas, please."

"Who did you say, dear?"

"Thank you so much. Edmund Salisbury from the World Trade Organisation in Geneva."

"I can't hear you. Did you want to speak to John?"

"That's right. As in the bishopric."

He could feel a warm breath on his neck. How long would the fucker stand there? Why couldn't he go and pester someone else? But he knew he'd been singled out - the technique of this particular bastard was to stand behind you until he'd heard one complete pitch, convincingly delivered.

Christopher had an idea. He would demonstrate his double bluff. Ali and he had practised it to perfection.

"Oh hello Mr Thomas, how nice to speak to you again."

"*Helloo?*" An elderly male voice had come onto the line.

"Edmund Salisbury, that's right, from the WTO in Geneva."

"Geneva?"

"Last time we spoke you expressed an interest in the new Year Book and website feature we are currently putting together for the members of the WTO, but that you had a small cash-flow problem."

"No I did not."

"Exactly." Christopher chuckled personably, casually, impressing the team leader no doubt with his easy charm and command of the conversation. "Widely distributed and read by ambassadors, diplomats, chief executive officers of major Corporations and so forth. You've got the gist, Mr Thomas."

He paused for breath. Don't get cocky. He felt the air stir behind him as the Team Leader shifted slightly, but he failed to move on. As Christopher had suspected, he was settling in for the long haul. Beside him, Ali had his head down into the receiver on a routine of his own, not daring to look up.

"Look excuse me, I haven't got the gist. Could you please explain what this is all about? Is this about my accident?"

"By all means." However hard he tried, Christopher couldn't completely cut out the party at the other end of the line. It was a strange sensation, as if the other person, whoever he was, was right there with him.

"Call for Christopher Wainwright line 6!" boomed a voice from the other end of the room. He glanced up at the corner of his screen, but there was no indication of any incoming call.

"The reason I'm calling again is that our design department are just about to go to press this afternoon, and they've just called me to say there are a limited number of spaces left which we are prepared to give away at a 10% discount, in order to fill the publication completely you understand. We also offer additional website coverage, for free." Here he glanced briefly at the Team Leader behind him. The man's face remained impassive. It was acceptable practice to offer up to 15% discounts to difficult prospects as a last resort, so long as they closed immediately.

"Of course I instantly thought of you, Mr Thomas, in the light of our previous conversation, and because I know you are keen to reach the wide readership of ambassadors, diplomats, chief executive officers of major multinationals and so forth that our publication is aimed at. Of course Mr Thomas these spaces will only be available for an hour or so, so if you've got a pen handy…"

Out of the corner of his eye he noticed Ali signalling to him.

"You're trying to sell something, aren't you?" growled the man angrily. "Well whatever it is I don't want any. Thank you and goodbye."

The line went dead.

"I tell you what I'll do Mr Thomas," continued Christopher blithely, now speaking into an empty line "I'll need authorisation, but I'll see if I can get a further 5% discount for you, making 15%. How's that? If you'll excuse me for one minute.." He gently removed his headset and picked up another that Ali was holding out to him. They'd helped each other out with this double bluff technique often enough that it was by now second nature. *Pitch, objection, counter, re-pitch.*

"Hello Mr Churchill?" he said, loudly enough for the supposed party on the other line to be able to overhear him. Sam Churchill was Ali's particular nom-de-plume. Quite an ambitious one, Christopher often thought, considering Ali's Essex accent. "Edmund Salisbury here. I have a client…"

It was at this point he noticed Ali madly waving at him, mouthing something. He frowned.

"…on the other line who I'd like to be able to offer a 15% discount, and I was wondering how many spaces we now have left in the WTO Handbook. Yes, sir, I know we're wrapping it up in a few hours, that's why…"

He paused for breath. There was an odd quality to the silence at the other end. Somewhere at the back of his mind something was telling him: shouldn't there be a dialling tone?

"…one left, well that's brilliant news…oh, it's been promised to another client? I see, well can't you see a way, I mean I'd really appreciate it if you could release this one to my client, sir, you see he's terribly keen although cash-flow problems…"

He paused again. Out of the corner of his other eye he saw that the team leader was now glaring at him.

"Is that Wainwright?" Horrifyingly, there was a voice at the other end, and it was somehow familiar.

"..I promise I won't ask another favour again sir, that's terribly generous of you sir…yes right away. I understand sir."

"Wainwright! For Christ's sake! It's Donald."

Christopher stopped dead.

"Get your bags packed, you're leaving tomorrow."

For a moment he could say nothing. He became aware of something else - a faint, monotonous tone emanating from his own headset, the one still lying idle at his elbow in order to overhear his masterful sales bluff.

The Team Leader stretched over him and gently tugged the headset cable out of his PC.

"Tomorrow Donald? What time?" he said into the other headset.

Beside him, Ali's eyes were developing stalks.

"Come in here at nine for your papers. It's a 16 day trip."

"Fantastic! Where to?"

"See you tomorrow."

Donald hung up. Christopher slumped back, exhausted.

"Wainwright…" hissed the Team Leader. "What the hell d'you think you're doing? Who was that prospect?"

"Which prospect?"

"The one you just called. All your calls are recorded, you know. I'll be reviewing that one this afternoon."

Christopher felt a coin flipping in his head, and landing with a thump at his feet. Sod it, what did he have to lose? What were the chances of closing a big one in the next two weeks? Close to zero, if he was being honest with himself. He swivelled his chair and pulled off his headphones.

"Go ahead," he said. "I quit."

There was something else he had been wanting to say too, for some time. He held it back just long enough to retrieve his jacket and head for the door.

"Arsehole."

Chapter 9

A Golden Opportunity

Boris had his feet up, shod in the very best calf-length cowhide and tooled by a man in Texas, when the President burst in. He was watching the surf report from La Jolla, California, on a 52 inch screen.

"Boris, we need to talk."

Boris muted the sound, startled. He'd had no wind of the president's visit. His secretary poked her head around the door apologetically and mouthed the word 'sorry'. But too late - Blicker caught her out of the side of his eye.

"Thanks, Brenda, milk no sugar," improvised Boris hastily. "Coffee, boss?"

The President shook his head and started to pace, hands behind his back, fingers clasping and unclasping distractedly. The door closed.

"Mind if I sit?"

Boris gestured to a new sofa that Horst had re-upholstered for him. The President took some time to settle down on it, brushing away a stray hair with the side of his hand.

"I've been thinking," he said eventually.

Boris was used to Blicker's mannerisms. It was best to say

nothing, like an interviewer, and wait for Blicker to get it off his chest. What he was looking for was a *'What's the matter, Johann? You look under stress. Is anything wrong?'* and so on. He cast a furtive glance back at the screen, where the credits showed two surfers slicing into a massive tube of rolling water.

"You were right. I've been making enquiries. We can find no record of any Elphberg Royals emigrating abroad after the dissolution of the monarchy on Queen Flavia's death."

The wave dissolved. So that was what he had come to talk about. He dragged himself away and said "Not even to London?"

"I tried Washington, I tried Paris, I tried London. OK, so maybe some of them slipped out to Argentina. But quite frankly, Boris, I think we should leave those well alone."

Boris got up, stretched, and went to the window.

"I agree," he said. "London would have been the obvious place."

"You think so?"

"Why yes. Their breeding requirements are legendary." Boris sniggered.

Blicker looked blank.

"They've had to resort to commoners, Johann. If there'd been any spares of ours floating around, you can be sure they'd at least have had first crack at them in London, eh?"

Blicker sighed. "I'm serious Boris, this is no laughing matter. The point is, Rose Elphberg is the only credible heir around. Officially that is. It would be unlike Hentzau not to have done his homework."

"You think Hentzau actually engineered this with a view to a Restoration?"

"That's exactly what I think. Besides, I've now got proof. It's what I wanted to talk to you about. You remember you said you thought it was strange the woman had the name Elphberg, when in fact she's really a cousin, a Tarlenheim? It seems her name was changed by deed-poll, and on Hentzau's authority, around the same time she became engaged to his son."

"Why would she need to do that? She's the heir regardless."

"Precisely. It can only be because she, or rather Hentzau, means to make use of her claim. The only way a Restoration will work with our people is if they want it. What romance is there in the name Tarlenheim? A distant cousin of the original line, more an aristocrat than a royal. But Elphberg, now that's a different matter entirely. It has romance, it has history, it has everything our people yearn for - past glories, a link with the Habsburgs, a time when the world had heard of us, paid us attention." He frowned. "It's obvious. It's a PR job."

They were silent for a moment as they both worked through the implications.

"Nevertheless," countered Boris, stroking his ponytail. "Don't you think you're being a touch cynical? I mean, OK, so Hentzau's a greedy son-of-a-bitch, wants power any way he can get it, but this is more to do with his social climbing ambitions than anything else. He can't surely expect a Restoration of the monarchy to work?"

"What d'you mean?" cried the President. "We do, don't we?"

"You mean you do."

"I seem to remember you getting rather excited about the prospect. What d'you imagine I've been doing all this time, why d'you think I'm looking for alternative heirs? Because we've decided it is feasible."

"I've never thought it was remotely feasible."

"Oh, great, thanks Boris, thank you for sharing that with me!"

"Johann, the bank letter, remember? The loot goes to the heir regardless of status. That's what it said. Whether they're on the throne or not. The letter was drawn up in 1945. The deadline has passed. We don't want a frigging monarchy. Not even for the tourists. What we want - or rather what we don't want - is for all that money to get into Hentzau's bloody pocket. That's why we need an alternative heir. In return to securing the restoration of his, or her, inheritance - financial, mind, not historical - the Republic - note the emphasis, my friend, will take a hefty commission. Follow me?"

Blicker sank down further on the sofa and tapped a cigarette from a crumpled packet.

"Well Boris, all I can say is that you'd better change your tune. Hentzau is about to agitate for a Restoration. The only way we're going to stop it is to find another heir. And put him, or her, on the throne."

Boris shook his head. He knew what Blicker's problem was. He wasn't coming at this with a straight bat. It wasn't really tourism at all, or Hentzau. He just wanted someone else to take the heat.

"It's all very well for you to shake your head, Boris, but I've got proof. In a day or two an American journalist is due to fly into Zenda. She's from Ciao Magazine. She's doing a big profile on Rose and her fiancée Andrew Hentzau, in advance of their wedding next month."

Boris sat up. "They're getting married next month? You never told me that."

"I just found out. The story came to them via a Public Relations agency based out of the Cayman Islands. Why the Cayman Islands? Presumably because the person or persons who have retained them don't want to be traced so easily."

"Hentzau!"

"Precisely. So here's what I propose. We follow up on the rumour. Illegitimacy was never a bar to succession in the past."

"You mean the child born to Princess Flavia in 1886? The one supposed to be fathered by that English spy?"

"Yes, he was said to have been smuggled to England. I've

done some preliminary research. The senior descendent of Rassendyll's family is a fellow called John MacHuff of MacHuff who lives on an estate in Angus. that's where Flavia's child would've gone. What I propose we do is persuade the baby's descendant to take the throne in return for the gold." He clucked his tongue. "If he exists."

Boris did a rapid calculation in his head. This was an angle he hadn't considered. If the gold in 1945 was worth forty-five million...

"Of course we'd keep some of the gold, commission and so forth."

Boris twitched. "Wait a minute, I thought you said in *return* for…"

"Well yes. It might not be that easy. It's a hell of a job. Not many would agree to take it on voluntarily. Look what happened to poor…"

Boris winced. If he heard that name one more time, swear to God he'd scream.

"...bulimia, forced to seek solace with that cavalry officer…"

"Yes, OK!" cried Boris, "but you actually mean to give the man the gold? Do you have any idea what that might be worth now, for God's sake? More than a billion! Imagine. Someone wakes up to find he's been offered a throne and a billion pounds sterling. He'd jump off a bridge!" His face lit up. "Come to think of it, that wouldn't be a bad scenario. Gold reverts to the State, throne lapses through gross disrepute."

"Don't be facetious Boris. I don't intend he should keep all of it. Take what you think appropriate. State taxes, et cetera."

"I've just put the et cetera up to 85%," muttered his Finance Minister.

Chapter 10
Ciao

"Ciao," she began.

"Ciao," answered Andrew.

"Ciao," echoed his father.

The journalist stretched out an elegant finger with a tinkle of wrist-wear and tapped the screen of her recording device.

"I'm sorry, excuse me," she turned to Hentzau senior. "I'm sorry, I should have explained: I just need one ciao. Just one ciao, OK?"

"Of course. I'm terribly sorry, just one ciao, right."

She tapped 'record' a second time. The bracelets shook.

They were sitting in the main reception room of Zenda Castle: Hentzau, his son Andrew, and a journalist from Ciao Magazine - West Hollywood, New York, Madrid, London. The ceiling had been recently regilded, and the huge hammer beams towering above them, with their bold colours and grinning gargoyles, looked like something out of a film set. New tapestries - copies of originals from eighteenth century engravings, specially woven in China - were draped on the walls, while up at one end a throne was being erected. It was not strictly correct - the Ducal court in the old days didn't include a throne - but Hentzau was sure the tourists would want to see one.

It was with some chagrin, therefore, that he had listened to the blasé first impressions of the journalist. Or rather not listened, because she'd walked into the magnificent room without a single comment, as if she conducted interviews in these sorts of environments every day. Or perhaps that's what hanging out with celebrities did for you, he mused: nothing was for real anymore.

"Ciao," she began for the second time.

"Ciao."

"Please tell us, Andrew, about your upbringing. Where did you grow up?"

Andrew Hentzau sniffed. "Here. At least not in this castle, it belonged to the state in those days, but in a lodge in the grounds."

"You must remember that the castle," interjected Hentzau senior, "is a national treasure, and as such it was for a long time, after liber...the revolution...I mean the first one...felt right that it should be the responsibility of the State."

"I see." The journalist from Ciao magazine seemed annoyed. She tapped her recording device once again. "Look..."

"Yes," pursued Hentzau "and now it has been privatised again, we Hentzaus are once more guardians of this great national treasure. Young Andrew here might have been brought up, by myself and my dear departed wife, in comparatively humble circumstances..." he timed a pause "...very humble in fact, but you should remember that our family has had a connection with Zenda for over six centuries now and we are very conscious that we have been given a unique legacy which we...which we have to uphold."

Silence.

"After all," he went on, "Zenda Castle will be the country residence of Andrew and Rose once they are married."

He sat back, his brogue shoes gently squeaking. The girl leant forward. "I'm sorry, Mr. Hentzau. There's been a slight misunderstanding. The interview is with your son, OK? It's very important that only his voice is on the podcast. We are of course happy for you to sit in provided..."

Hentzau glared at his son, who had begun to light a cigarette, staring out of the castle window with a bored expression. He followed Rupert's gaze. Far below, young Tilly, in jeans, sneakers and an outsize baseball cap sporting the logo of Globalny Foods Inc., was supervising her team of pioneer scouts. Hentzau felt a momentary glow of pride. They were getting the place ready for the expected influx of tourists, busy dredging out the moat that separated the old castle, where the interview was taking place, from the newer 'Chateau' beyond. This moat had been allowed to get into an appalling state, emptied of water and head high in weeds and rubble. Their adolescent frames groaning under the weight of large lumps of concrete, and a long fat overflow pipe that they were attempting to fix into the wall of the Castle.

"Ciao."

Hentzau snapped back to the task at hand.

"Come on, Andrew, wakey wakey!" he said angrily.

Andrew jerked out of his reverie. "Mmm..?"

"Ready?"

"Yeah."

The recording machine sprang into life for a fourth time.

"Ciao."

"Ciao," sniffed Andrew.

"Please tell us, Andrew, about your upbringing. Where were you brought up?"

"I was born and brought up very near here, in the lodge house in fact, before we moved back to the castle, which

The Spare and The Heir

is...er...both a national treasure and a family responsibility, for which we have...er...a great legacy."

Hentzau squirmed. His son was in dire need of a makeover. Publicity alone was obviously not going to be sufficient, and on current form it might even back-fire. He decided to get on to an image consultant that very afternoon.

The journalist from 'Ciao' ploughed on.

"You've talked lovingly about your parents..." she intoned.

Really? thought Hentzau and his son simultaneously. That was news to them.

THE INTERVIEW LASTED AN HOUR. WHEN SHE HAD FINISHED, Hentzau took her on a tour of the Castle, for it was essential to get in a few details of what was being done in the way of renovation, if only to placate his sponsor. They descended a steep stone stairwell into what used to be the dungeon.

"And down here," Hentzau was saying, "is where King Rudolf was imprisoned by Black Michael of Strelsau at the end of the last century. You've read the book, I presume?"

"The book?"

"The Prisoner of Zenda."

"No...I don't think I've read that one."

"Anthony Hope? Published at the end of the nineteenth century?"

Still she looked blank.

"Really? How extraordinary." The girl was not much older than his daughter and in Hentzau's opinion, completely incompetent. Didn't they do any background prep for God's sake? Any reading at all, come to that. Mr. Ciao must be raking it in, employing amateurs like her.

"Well let me tell you about it." He would obviously have to enlighten her. He dared not imagine what she might write otherwise.

"Absolutely true story. The Count, you see, Black Michael of Strelsau, was the King's brother, and very determined to get the throne. Rudolf, the King, was a very weak man, and it was felt, by a large proportion of the people I might add, that the Kingdom needed strong leadership at that particular juncture in its history. It was a very difficult time in Europe then, you understand, just prior to the First World War. Black Michael also, let me tell you, had rather a penchant for the King's bride-to-be, Princess Flavia."

Hentzau fixed the journalist with his steely blue eyes.

"So he kidnapped the King just prior to the Coronation, and locked him up in here." They turned a corner, and entered a small, stone walled cell high above the moat. "After you…"

The journalist shuddered, and entered reluctantly. She got claustrophobia in places like this, especially with men like him.

"Unfortunately he and his chief lieutenant, my namesake and great grandfather, the famous Rupert Hentzau, had a piece of extraordinarily bad luck. A man called Rudolf Rassendyll, a particularly odious Highlander who was here on a smash and grab raid for the British Museum as well as tasks for the British Secret Service, was recruited by the King's camp to step in…"

"I see."

She was nothing if not monosyllabic, he thought testily. Perhaps she was just programmed in Ciao-speak, to spew out all those facile questions: *how many years have you lived in this lovely part of the world? You have two wonderful children. How old are they? How long has your brother/father/grandma been battling against this terrible disease?* It was amazing what you had to do nowadays if you wanted a bit of publicity. It was just important he kept the end in sight, he told himself. But she surprised him.

"So what happened to the King?"

"The King? Well he…er… was rescued, but my great

grandpa managed to escape. Mind you, he himself was killed in the end, a few years later, as indeed was my great grandfather by that red-headed Scottish shit."

"Sounds like a blood bath," she giggled. Hentzau's expression turned thunderous. "What about the Princess?" she added hastily.

"She reigned on alone, as the Queen of course. She died in 1927, the last of the Elphbergs, and the People's Republic was declared. Except she wasn't quite the last," he continued, "because as you know Rose is her descendant, through a second cousin." She bloody well ought to know. Presumably she'd read the copy from Rose's interview.

The journalist relapsed into silence. He led her out of the cell and along a corridor.

"And if you were to ask me whether there is any call for the monarchy at the present time," he continued, with heavy irony (she hadn't been intending to, but it was amazing, she reflected, what you had to put up with to earn a buck these days), "I would have to answer in the affirmative. The people love their royal past. For instance take a look at this…" They turned a corner and passed into a large refectory.

The sudden change in noise level was startling, the thickness of the stone walls preventing even the most vigorous of hammer blows from penetrating more than a few yards. Workmen were everywhere, as partitions went up and crates were unloaded.

"Now this will interest you!" Hentzau raised his voice to be heard above the din. "It's going to be called *'The Zenda Experience'*. An audio-visual recreation in 3D of *'The Prisoner of Zenda'* in words, images and wax-work models. Sponsored by Globalny Foods Inc!"

He turned to her to gauge the effect. It appeared to be limited. And this was another thing that bugged him: there wasn't a notebook in sight. Nowadays it was all i-this and i-that, her own version of which she appeared to have left in the throne room. He said: "You should write that down."

She looked surprised. "Write what down?"

"Globalny Foods. I think it would be useful. And make sure you get the full title. They're most particular about that. *'Globalny Foods Inc. We are what you eat TM'* You got that?"

Her bracelets jangled.

"Erm…can I borrow a pen?"

Chapter 11

Cynthia

"*The People's Republic of what?*"

Christopher sat wide-eyed in Donald's office.

"Don't ask me," said Donald, wiping his forehead shakily. "Does it matter?" He pocketed the rag and tapped a wall-map with a stick. "It's between here and here. Apparently."

"Never heard of it. Are there guidebooks?"

"No, perhaps you can write one. Oh, there is one book. Let's see now, what on earth was it called?" He scratched himself. "The something of Zenda."

Great, thought Christopher sarcastically.

"Me, I had never heard of the place until this company called Universal Foods called me up asking did we do tours there. It's a corporate special, a cultural exchange type of thing. Looked it up in the atlas and couldn't find it, had to get onto the Foreign Office. Even they had no idea, until it suddenly appeared on this hand-drawn map emailed from the Russian Embassy."

He pointed above his desk where a flimsy copy was stuck to the wall. "Apparently it recently had some kind of revolution, gained independence, that sort of thing. No one knows anything about it." He laughed. "Not that that's at all unusual in this business. Makes your job a walkover. Invent anything you like."

The door opened, and a woman staggered in with an armful of papers.

"Donald, here's the bumph you wanted on RR 001," she said breezily, depositing them on his desk. "Oh hello," she said, as she noticed Christopher. "You must be the newbie?"

Christopher got up awkwardly. "I'm afraid so."

"I'm Cynthia," she said. "I'll be your contact here should you need any help." She looked him up and down. She was tall and intimidating, with a mane of glossy red hair flaming down her back. It curled slightly at the ends and she was wearing a pale yellow cashmere jumper with a string of pearls. The whole effect was handsome rather than pretty, reinforced by a striking, almost masculine nose. Early thirties, guessed Christopher.

"Thanks Cyn. With luck he won't need you."

The woman raised her manicured eyebrows a fraction. "Are you jokey-poohs? This one's literally going to be a nightmare." Unexpectedly she let out a high pitched screech, that rose and fell and rose again – like a hyena. Christopher stared at her.

"But heaps of fun," she screeched, before quickly composing herself.

"Now this is the first batch. I'll have the rest for you in ten minutes. Itinerary," she began peeling off the layers of documents one by one, "rooming lists, hotel and restaurant vouchers, insurance forms, luggage labels, coach signs."

"Ignore John Sutton," interrupted Donald. "He was supposed to be the tour manager. Dropped out yesterday afternoon. You'll be travelling on the spare visa. How are you doing on that Cyn?"

"Ten mins, Donald."

"Because I expect you'd like to get going, eh, Wainwright? Got a few things to buy before you go? Get prepared and all that? Oh, and one other thing. There's a Joseph Spinelli marked with a star. He's the Universal rep, VIP status. Whatever else you do, treat him with kid gloves."

Christopher gulped. "What time's the flight?"

Donald looked at Cyn interrogatively. She consulted her clipboard. "RR 001? London Heathrow to Vienna, 13.10. In six hours."

"Six..."

She swished out.

"Cynthia," winked Donald, by way of explanation. "A word of warning. She's the one who really matters around here. Be nice to her and she'll make it happen for you. From Scotland."

"Scotland? Doesn't sound like it."

"Well, you know, her family owns half of it, they don't actually live there. Good God no. But if she manages to bag her Earl we'll miss her. Frightfully." He burst out laughing.

But Christopher had stopped listening. He was in overload. He picked up the first of the mass of documents, panic rising. *'Accident and Emergency Report,'* it was headed. *'Delete where applicable: Death. Sudden collapse. Injury/Broken limbs. Other.'* At the bottom it said in red letters: *'Tour Directors are strongly advised not to touch a client under any circumstances. If in doubt, call a doctor.'* Someone had scribbled at the top *'RR 001 - The Land That Time Forgot - TD please note: pax 17,18, 21 & 22 are over 75. Collect Medical Certs on arrival.'*

Christopher looked up anxiously.

"How am I going to be ready in four hours? And what's all this? People in their seventies?"

"And their 80's and 90's," said Donald, puffing heavily himself. "Half our clients are on their last legs. They're the only ones who can afford it. Spending their savings like crazy so they don't have to pass it on."

"I.."

"Now, got a pen? Right. Make a few notes. I'll give you some background on how you can run this tour. Shouldn't take more than half an hour." He looked at his watch. "Shit, is that the time? I've got a meeting in fifteen minutes, we'll have to cut it to ten."

"Ten minutes? To go through all this lot?"

Donald got up and put an arm on Christopher's shoulder.

"Don't worry, Chris, you'll manage. One always does. You'll panic for the first two days, but after that it's a piece of cake. Now," he started pacing around the room. "Let's begin with their arrival. You'll be flying to Vienna where you'll be meeting ten people off AA 452 from Chicago - these are marked as group A in the blue felt tip - at 18.55, seven people on AA 567 from San Francisco, red group, 19.10, and a further four, marked as yellow, from JFK on AA 45 at 21.00. Here's your first problem. The two earlier groups aren't going to want to wait, but I'm afraid…"

TEN MINUTES LATER THEY'D BARELY GOT TO THE PEOPLE'S Republic - after a two day whistle-stop 'acclimatisation' in Vienna - and Christopher's head was fit to explode. Cynthia waltzed in again and laid down a new pile of papers, tags and computer print-outs in front of him.

"Passport details, coach breakdown forms, mileage chart - make sure you fill that in, won't you? Otherwise you'll be paying the mileage yourself - credit card record forms - Amex, MasterCard…"

"Credit cards? What are those for?"

"Health declaration forms, evaluation sheets, refund

vouchers, internal airline tickets, Zenda welcome drink vouchers, visa list." She paused for breath. "Now listen carefully, this visa list is very important. You'll have to check the group through as a whole and in visa number order at Zenda customs on arrival in Ruritovia."

"Ruritania," corrected Donald.

"Whatever."

"But you haven't even had my passport yet! How can you have got me a visa?"

"Excuse me folks, I really must be off," interrupted Donald, hastily making for the door. "If you only remember one thing, Chris, it's to look after your clients' happiness." He shook Christopher's hand with the air of bidding farewell to someone about to follow the brave Captain Oates out of Scott of the Antarctic's tent. More a case of 'Adieu' than 'Au revoir'.

He hesitated on the threshold. "Oh, and one last thing. I suggest you pick up a copy of that book 'The Thingy of Zenda' before you go. Useful background reading. Best of luck old chum."

"But…"

But Donald was already out of the door.

"That's just the point," resumed Cynthia. "You're travelling on a spare visa. Under a different name."

Christopher returned to her. "Whoa! Wait a minute! D'you mean to tell me…"

"Hey, calm down!" she screeched. "Don't panic. This is absolutamente standard procedure, I can assure you, we have a spare visa made out for this chappie on every tour we run, just for such an eventuality. We call him The Spare."

"What eventuality?"

"For when a tour director drops out at the last min. Means we can replace him straight away without going through all the messy-poohs of reissuing visas, they sometimes take weeks and weeks. We get a multiple-entry visa for this chap issued for every country that needs one, each season, just in case. 99 times out of a 100 it's never used, it's simply cancelled on arrival. Another no-show."

Christopher was beginning to feel sick. "But not in this case," he said.

"Not in this case, no. But we've done it dozens of times, there really shouldn't be any problemos."

"Shouldn't," he echoed.

She bared her teeth at him. "Immigration chappies in these third world dumps don't give a Johnny-two-shoes, all they want to see is a name on a visa list matching a name in a passport. The visas are issued as a group – it's just a list of names. There's nothing showing in the actual passports."

Johnny-two-shoes? Christopher was beginning to get angry. "Well that's just it, isn't it? My passport, in case you hadn't twigged, is made out in the name of a character, God knows why, called Christopher Wainwright."

He crossed his arms triumphantly. Cynthia looked offended. She tossed her flaming mane behind one shoulder with an angry little flick. "Now there's no need to get all sarky on me, new boy. We're not intending to send you out without the relevant passport. You'll get a dummy. Just in case, for the purposes of their visa authorities, that is. Highly unlikely they'll actually want to see it. You'll use your own at immigration of course. No one ever matches these passports. If they do, you just send the lot, together, and switch yours with Roddy's – no risk whatevs." She bared her teeth a second time, licking around the edges with her tongue, carefully so as not to smudge her lipstick. "Now, all we need is an image of your mug."

Christopher's arms flew apart, aghast. "You mean to say…"

"Got a spare passport size photo with you, by any chance, or should we get you down to a booth?"

Reluctantly he opened his wallet. It was a mistake. She was on it in a flash, retrieving the small headshot that was poking out of the plastic window with her long, glinting, manicured nails.

"Bit creased isn't it?" she said dubiously, holding it up to the light.

"Oh yes, far too manky."

"But I suppose it'll do. If they're anything like those Russians they won't give it a second glance." She grinned, enjoying his discomfort. "Now, you sure you got everything you need?'

She scribbled a number on a scrap of paper and handed it to him.

"If you've got any questions, call my mobile. But I'd rather you didn't," she added hastily. "Company pol is…well, to be absolutely franky-poohs, you're on your tod. You certainly make enough moulah."

"Well that's another thing. How do I make…*moulah*, as you put it?"

Cynthia developed the look of a girl who's boyfriend's car has ground to a halt on Bodmin Moor, with her in it.

"You mean you don't know?"

"That's what I've been trying to tell everyone! No, I haven't a…"

She waited for him to say what he hadn't got, as he teetered on the edge of a string of profanities.

"A fucking clue?" she ventured.

She was silent for a moment, steepling her fingers under her chin in an attitude of contemplation.

"I tell you what. Talk to Rog."

"Rog? Who's Rog, for God's sake?"

"He's taking a tour into Hungary. You'll see him at Vienna airport tonight, he's meeting his group off the same flights as you are. Have a chat with him, he'll help you out."

She smiled icily. "Now, off you toddle! I've got a dins to go to!"

Chapter 12

The Plan

"Greetings Annie!"

The woman looked bemused as a man in a pressed check shirt with an eccentric looking ginger moustache hurried over to say hello.

"Oh…" she said.

The stranger clasped her hand and kissed her on both cheeks. Her make-up was discreet and her hair just-so. She disliked spontaneity.

"Horst," he prompted her, "Bangermann. We met in London, remember, in February? You were with…" Horst cast his mind back "…Johnny Featherbright. if I'm not mistaken."

"Johnny Featherbright…." she repeated warily, still none the wiser. But she was used to this sort of thing as an art critic: all kinds of unlikely people who you'd never met suddenly claimed you as their friend, especially in these meccas of the art world.

"I was over buying fabric. For the uniforms."

"Ah…" she said, grateful for the handle. Over from where? What uniforms? He was doubtless a wardrobe man for some musical or other. So long as he wasn't another of these 'New

Wind' artists from one of these oddly named new republics looking for international representation.

"You're a costume designer, then?" she countered, hopefully. As she said it she noticed Alex Delamaine wander into view. Her eyes darted towards him.

Delamaine was an important man. He was not only an influential dealer, but also one of the first to champion modern Balkan art. A pioneer, they called him. He'd staged exhibitions in his galleries in Paris and Edinburgh; organised art tours to Prague, Tallinn and Sofia; found sponsors, buyers, patrons. It was he, too, who had coined the term 'New Wind', and God knows, the art world needed a breath of fresh air just then. Personally she'd always thought of this strange little country's art as totally beyond the pale, but if Alex Delamaine was here, well then, it meant that Ruritania was on the map. Seeing him, she felt justified in spending the three thousand dollars it had cost her to come.

Delamaine passed on, and she resumed her concentration on Bangermann. He was in the middle of saying something about the Paris fashion show, and what he said, if she wasn't mistaken, ended in an interrogative. She gave him her deep-in-thought expression, desperately trying to dredge up a clue to the piece of information that she'd missed: the beginning of the question.

"It all depends," she said finally, smiling at him sweetly. It invariably did, in her experience. "But I'd love another drink, wouldn't you?"

THE ROOM WAS BECOMING CROWDED. THERE MUST HAVE BEEN at least six hundred people crammed into the Long Gallery of the People's Palace. Most of the government were present, the Diplomatic Corps were there, the arts journalists were gossiping, a smattering of foreign buyers and dealers were exchanging anecdotes, the sponsors were being looked after, the Foreign Minister of Turkey, in the middle of a state visit, was bemused and, of course, the artists themselves were in attendance, though they were, for the most part, ignored.

The event had been arranged for two reasons. First, to celebrate the Long Gallery's recent refurbishment, and the hanging of twenty-eight of the president's by now famous 'Blue Circle' works in place of the dusty portraits of dukes, arch-dukes and grand-dukes, now relegated to the Strelsau Historical Museum; and second, as an opening for the Ministry of Culture's ambitious 'Installation 2' project. Its culmination could be viewed from the large floor to ceiling windows: the West Tower had been covered in swathes of white bandages by a young Ruritanian artist. The whole thing sponsored by a major pharmaceutical company based in Basel. The title? '*Sore Thumb.*'

A few metres from the female art critic Rupert Hentzau was busy slagging it off to a member of the TV Regulatory Committee.

"What does it mean, could someone tell me?" he said, sipping on a glass of sparkling Chateau Tarlenheim.

"Damned if I know," exclaimed the red-faced Committee member blousily. "But I suppose it puts us on the map."

"Puts us on the map?" Hentzau was indignant. "Ha! Not a map, I submit, that we even want to be on. We might be fashionable for a while amongst all these..." he looked around with distaste "...arty-farty riff-raff, but for the rest we become a laughing stock." He lowered his voice. "Blicker's circles are bad enough, without that...that...*thing* over there."

He drew breath to look at it one more time. It was not just incomprehensible, it was outrageous.

"Mind you," he went on, "you can't help but feel a sneaking admiration for the fellow. You know what he's doing, don't you? Taking us all for a ride. Got us paying him double welfare to produce a piece of meaningless rubbish."

He tossed his head back dismissively and looked around for a waitress.

"Not to mention all this lot," said the Committee member, gesturing airily around the room. "I thought we were hard-up."

Hentzau watched him. The man was plastered. Not the ideal moment to broach the subject, but then he was painfully aware that there probably wouldn't be another opportunity before the Committee meeting the following week. Besides, he was expecting his son to arrive at any minute. He could see the photographers he'd booked, lined up and waiting. He decided to risk it.

"We are," replied Hentzau. "Which is why I wanted to talk to you. You've presumably heard of Globalny Foods Inc?"

The member confessed that he hadn't, so Hentzau explained: about the five thousand TV Eezy-Cooks, the Nevsky Prospekt TV reality show, the generous offer, the financial scenario. Or rather not the entire scenario, for Hentzau was careful to omit the not inconsiderable involvement of Globalny Foods in the refurbishment of Zenda Castle in time for the tourist season. But he was determined to put his case to as many sympathetic Committee members as he could before the meeting, for contracts had to be signed, and he didn't relish further irate demands from Yuri Lougouev.

As for the Committee member, he was getting confused. He'd already had a long and incomprehensible conversation with a Mr. Delamaine about the luminosity of blue and the power of the circle as a universal archetype. And now this: what the hell was a TV Eezy-Cook? But just as he hadn't queried Mr. Delamaine too closely, so he was careful not to ask Hentzau the obvious. For he was a Committee member, and he knew only too well the dangers of sticking your hand up. Instead he nodded. Practically off to sleep.

"I THINK THIS SHOULD SECURE US CONSIDERABLE COVERAGE," the Minister for Culture was telling President Blicker in another part of the crush. "Have you seen the journalist from Art International? She's here, over from New York. The International Herald Tribune, they're here. Oh, and have you seen Alex Delamaine?"

Blicker had seen Alex Delamaine. Or rather Alex Delamaine had seen him, been tripping over himself to see him, in fact, from the moment he became president. An attitude which contrasted nicely with his former hauteur.

"Ah, now I'd like to introduce you to this gentleman, Mr. President," the Minister continued, relapsing into the more formal mode of address as he brought forward a short fat swarthy man in a pale suit who'd been hovering nearby.

"John Bigelow from Los Angeles. He's a film producer. He's making a film up at Zenda over the next couple of weeks."

Really? That was news to Blicker. Something Hentzau had organised, no doubt.

"John H. Bigelow," boomed the visitor. "Pleased to meet you Mr. President, sir."

Blicker looked down at him sceptically and shook his hand. It proved to be pudgy and faintly moist.

"I just love this country of yours," bellowed Bigelow, his hair bouncing up and down, his face uncomfortably close to the president's "…just love it, Mr. President. I believe we create a lot of awesomeness here, I sincerely believe that. For example, let me illustrate the point…" Blicker would rather he did not. The man reeked of shampoo, of some strange fruit variety, and he began to feel dizzy.

"You have unbelievable infrastructure for movie-making here. You have landscape, you have historical buildings, you have economic labour conditions, economic materials. I mean you could be anywhere, Mr. President, really anywhere. You could be London before WW Two, you could be eighteen century France, you are peach Dracula country, you could…"

"Is that what you're doing up at Zenda?" interrupted Blicker, in an effort to maintain his concentration.

"No, no, that's just a sequence, Mr. President, small stuff. But for the next one…"

It was not for nothing that Mr. Bigelow was known as 'The Mouth' in the canyons and condos of Hollywoodland. He was one of the deftest and nimblest practitioners of the elevator pitch anywhere. It transpired, before his sixty seconds were up, that he had a 'package': he had a script, he had a director, he had two stars. The storyline was 'high concept'.

"Now let me give you the elevator pitch…"

Blicker drifted off. He'd never been one for receptions, and now he was President they had become his worst nightmare. All kinds of people opportuned you.

"…rescues the kid and gets honoured by the president. So what do you think, sir?"

Blicker stared at him and tried to focus. It was that hoary old dilemma, honesty versus an easy life. But he was saved by a sudden commotion at the far end of the room. Flash bulbs started going off in all directions, ambassadors turned round, conversations trailed off, and the noise level seemed to drop several decibels. Who was it? Who had arrived? The President was here. Alex Delamaine was here. Who could it be? The Mouth scented glamour. The hair quivered.

"So there it is Mr. President, and I appreciate you're a busy man and I thank you for your time." Blicker found a card being pressed into his hand. "If I may, I will call your office

The Spare and The Heir 91

tomorrow to fix up a meeting with one of your team." A hand appeared to be shaked.

"Yes, of course," muttered Blicker distractedly. He had hardly released the Californian's small fat digits before he was off, like a lizard. Blicker turned to a subordinate.

"Looks like Hentzau's son, sir," answered the man to his query. Hentzau's son? For a moment Blicker didn't understand. But then the crowd parted for an instant, and he caught a glimpse of Hentzau steering a glamorous couple into the throng.

Andrew was dressed in a smart dark blue suit and a tasteful salmon pink tie. He looked very different from the sullen playboy the clubs of Strelsau were accustomed to. Someone had clearly done a makeover job, and in a hurry. His square jawline was well accented by a high white collar and a light tan. His mop had been cropped and his ear hairs lopped off. Even his eyes were bluer, on account of an expensive pair of shaded contact lenses. He was still a little overweight, but no one expected miracles overnight. As he approached, someone whispered in Hentzau's ear:

"Wow, they've done a great job. He looks a thousand dollars."

"Ten thousand, four hundred and fifty two," hissed Hentzau as he moved forward in his own expensive tailoring to greet them.

"You look beautiful, my dear," he said, bowing gallantly to the woman on Andrew's arm. She was wearing a low-cut black halter dress and diamonds sparkled in each ear. "As always."

But why was she wearing dark glasses? It was insufferably pretentious. And then it clicked. It wasn't Rose at all.

"Who the hell is this?" he hissed to his son, pulling him aside.

Andrew hopped from foot to foot uncomfortably. "Erm.

I'm afraid she's being difficult." Flashes were going off left, right and centre. It was a disaster. "She refused to come."

His father glared at him. What was the matter with the boy? Did he want to sabotage everything? He grabbed the girl and hustled them both out of the room. A murmur of consternation followed them.

"People will see you together," he barked. "Get her out of here!"

"Chill out Dad, now one even knows what Rose looks like. They won't know the difference. Mandy's not a bad double actually."

"Don't be so simple. You're lucky those photographers are ours. Otherwise…"

"Look up, my dear, look up," boomed a voice. "Always make love to the camera!"

A flash exploded, and the Hentzau family grouping, plus unidentified woman, found themselves looking down at the small squat frame of John H. Bigelow.

"What's your name, sweetie?"

"Rose Elphberg," said the girl as she'd been told to do, and before anyone could stop her.

Hentzau groaned. Bigelow scribbled something in a black crocodile leather notebook.

"I'm making a movie, and you've got just the face I'm looking for. I'll be in touch," he called over his disappearing shoulder.

"*I mean Mandy Stein!*" cried the girl, seeing her one chance of Hollywood fame disappearing with it. She lunged after him but Hentzau restrained her.

"Now scram!" he spat.

A SHORT DISTANCE AWAY AN ASSISTANT WAS WHISPERING something in Blicker's ear. The President excused himself to the Indonesian military attache and strode out. His secretary was waiting. She handed him an envelope.

"We've just decoded it, Mr. President. It's from London. For your eyes only." Blicker's face lit up. He ripped open the envelope, and read:

'For the president's eyes only: 10.00 hours GMT. London 21/7
001356 PEOPSPAL
Positive ID on potential heir:

Adoption of Elphberg orphan by Angus MacHuff of MacHuff in 1895, named Roderick. Almost certainly the son of Queen Flavia and Rudolf Rassendyll (disappeared, presumed deceased, 1885), who was McHuff's second cousin; married 1917 Lilly Fraser, killed France 1918. Only son, Humphrey Fraser-MacHuff, born 1919; commissioned Flt Lieutenant RAF 19xx; married Angela Dawson 19xx; deceased 19xx. Two children: son, Angus, born 19xx; second son Hugh born 19xx, died 19xx. Angus married Candice Berwin 19xx, one son, Roderick, born 19xx, one daughter, born 19xx. Both Angus and Candice killed in a skiing accident 19xx.

The son, Roderick Fraser, would therefore appear to be the sole great great grandson of Queen Flavia, and by a direct male line. They seemed to have dropped the MacHuff, just called themselves Fraser - perhaps to minimise risk from RUSK.

No records for Roderick found, however, beyond a birth certificate, and the following news clipping from the Daily Telegraph, 6.5.20xx: REUTERS: Twenty seven Western tourists were detained in Alma Ata late yesterday after one of their number, a Mr Roderick Fraser, was arrested for gross indecency by Kazakhstan mounted police. According to one of the travellers, an American who declined to be identified, the train they were travelling on was intercepted after complaints that a naked and inebriated Mr Fraser was harassing the Chinese train staff. Reports that Mr Fraser worked for the London-based company who organised the trip are unconfirmed.

Action: No further enquiries made. Request instructions.'

Blicker couldn't help smiling. At last. He couldn't wait to

see the look on Hentzau's face when he proposed a Restoration, and, what's more, one that didn't include Rose Elphberg. Hentzau would protest, of course. And he'd be right: going on all normal criteria, Elphberg was a far more suitable candidate than this character appeared to be. Assuming it was the same person, that is. But Hentzau wouldn't be able to protest too much, bearing in mind his not inconsiderable vested interest in Rose's claim.

Yes, Blicker told himself, he would relish every minute of his squirming dilemma. He could see it now. He'd shrug regretfully, explaining that, unhappily, the president's hands were tied. The bars of gold in the vaults of the Bank of England depended on a watertight and direct bloodline. As did the whole success or failure of the Restoration. Illegitimacy had never been an issue according to Ruritanian custom. It was the most direct bloodline that counted. A shame, he'd argue, because Rose was a lovely girl. But there it was. Fraser's great-great-grandmother was Queen Flavia, and what's more he was the result of her grand passion with the former Kingdom of Ruritania's erstwhile British hero, the glamourous, good looking Rudolf Rassendyll of legend. It was perfect. So romantic. So scandalous. The People's Republic - soon to be the People's Kingdom - would love it.

He couldn't wait to tell Boris. He found him alone, smoking what smelt suspiciously like a spliff on a balcony overlooking the palace forecourt.

"What are you doing Boris? Is that legal?"

Boris grinned. "Sorry Boss." But he showed no signs of stubbing it out.

Blicker glared at him, but decided against a confrontation. There were more important issues to focus on.

"Listen," he continued, "I need you to concentrate. I've just received word from London that we've found an heir."

"We have?" smiled Boris. "You mean the rumour was

true?" Blicker nodded. "Why, that's fantastic. Who is it? Male, or female? Black or white?"

"Don't be flippant, Boris. I'd like to know what you think. My God, what was that?"

A strange noise had suddenly become audible from somewhere beneath them, like a chant starting up. Blicker rushed to the parapet. Far below in the forecourt a tight knot of people were waving placards at departing guests. Blicker was just able to make out what one or two of the words:

'Down with... organic...rubbish. School Burgers OK.'

School Burgers OK? What in God's name did it mean, a startled Blicker wanted to know. Boris shrugged. He clearly wasn't in much of a state to draw conclusions. Blicker had a closer look. Whatever it meant, he couldn't have them there. What the hell would all the ambassadors be thinking?

"Ten to one it's another of Hentzau's little agitations," he said anxiously. "We can't hang about a moment longer." He turned away from the window. "Boris, here's what I propose."

And he outlined his plan.

Chapter 13

The Spare

The plane was delayed, it was nearly three in the afternoon before it took off. Christopher wondered what all the people he was supposed to be meeting would actually do if he wasn't there to collect them off their flights in Vienna airport. They were depending on him. He was taking twenty-five people he'd never met to a place he'd never been. Christ.

He glanced once more at his phone, and the messages of good luck he had received from his family. His mother's text said to be careful. Max, his 14 year old little brother, had messaged on the 'Bros' WhatsApp group, and was equally practical: he wanted Christopher to bring him back a packet of 'Mozart balls' from Vienna. What the hell were 'Mozart balls'? thought his elder brother.

Then he noticed a new message. It was a voicemail, timed just after a missed call. With a sinking feeling he opened up the call screen and, sure enough, there it was, that 0151 number from Liverpool that he recognised it all too well. They'd be wanting to know when he would be transferring the money. He felt a sudden lump in his throat and, swiping to delete the notification, he flipped open up his briefcase.

The Spare and The Heir

It was crammed with papers. He'd already made a start in the departure lounge, skimming over a potted history of Ruritania that he'd picked up at Smith's at the airport. It had not really enlightened him - it was all about some King of Ruritania in Victorian times who had been drugged on the eve of his coronation, and some Scots dude on holiday in the country, who coincidentally looked like the monarch, who had been persuaded to step in for him to avoid an anti-monarchist coup. Fairytale stuff. No wonder it had been put in the fiction section.

He ordered a vodka and tonic from the steward and started on the brochure. It was entitled *'The Land That Time Forgot, organised by special arrangement with Universal Foods Corporation. Milwaukee.'*

'The former Kingdom of Elphberg,' it began, *'the People's Republic of Ruritania, country of romance, literature, and fairy-tale castles, welcomes you with open arms. Whether you're a first time visitor to Eastern Europe or a seasoned 'regular', you'll find the excitement of this ground-breaking tour to 'The Land That Stood Still' irresistible. This sixteen night vacation starts in Vienna, magnificent former capital of the Habsburg Dynasty and Gateway to the East…'*

Christopher paused. He'd always thought Istanbul was the gateway to the east. Or was it Venice?

'…and continues, after a number of exciting Alpine excursions, by air to Zenda, capital of the northern provinces. Experience the thrill of Dracula country, the magnificence of Zenda Castle, and the picturesque costumes of local people. From there we travel by motorcoach…'

Air-conditioned? He scribbled a question mark in the margin to ask Cynthia later.

'…with a visit to the world renowned Rosewater Factory at Felixtown if we are lucky, through forests redolent of the Dark Ages…'

Oh, please.

'…to the country's ancient Capital. Here you will view the majestic National Art Institute and be amongst the first to visit the world famous

Royal Apartments of King Rudolf and Queen Flavia of 'Prisoner of Zenda' fame. You'll also marvel at the incredible array of other monuments to Ruritania's history. With lots of time to explore on your own, and at an unbeatable price, we guarantee you the time of your life!'

Below this blurb was a section entitled *'Your Holiday Includes:'*

'Accommodation: specially selected, mostly first class hotels with private shower or bath.'

There didn't appear to be a comma between 'hotels' and 'with'. It took a hard-bitten telesales exec to recognise loopholes like that.

'Transportation: air; Gateway city: Vienna; Vienna-Zenda; the Capital- Gateway city; de-luxe motorcoach; optional excursion on a steam train. Board: All breakfasts (continental with juice) and dinners (minimum two courses) included. Selected optional lunches featuring regional cuisine.'

He laughed out loud.

'Welcome drink at the four-star Hotel Ramada in Vienna.'

Four blocks from the two star Mozart where we're staying, I bet, thought Christopher.

'Welcome roochi in Zenda.'

Christopher gazed out of the window. Now what the hell was a roochi? A local Morris dance? Some kind of fondue?

'Farewell drink at a location to be arranged in the Capital.'

What was all this crap about 'The Capital'? Surely it had a name?

'Services: Orientation sightseeing drive by Tour Manager in Vienna.'

His heart skipped a beat. He read it again, just to make sure. FFS. Donald had said nothing about this. He'd never even been to Vienna, so how the hell could he be expected to do an orientation tour? Local guides, Donald had said. He would have to cut it out, make up some excuse. 'Major multiple pile-up outside the Opera House', something like that. He read on.

'...followed by full-day's sightseeing by local guide. Services of local

host/hostess during your stay in Ruritania. Plus the services of a full-time multilingual Tour Manager throughout.'

Multi-lingual? Ha, that was a joke.

'Drink, sir?'

The steward had appeared at his elbow and he ordered another vodka. He put the brochure back in his briefcase and pulled out a copy of the rooming list, trying to visualise what Martha Fierstein would look like, or Mike Williams, or Henry Finkelburger - God, what a name - or Roderick Fraser. But however much he tried, he couldn't begin to. That was the thing about this trip. He had no fucking clue.

He downed the remains of the vodka and went to the toilet. Once inside he put down the seat and sat on it, his head in his hands. The whine of the aircraft and the hiss of the cabin air made his head spin. Holy shit, he thought, what have I let myself in for? For the first time he realised the enormity of what he was about to embark on. In TravelCo's offices it had seemed so far away, so remote. As for yesterday…yesterday he'd been safe behind the end of a phone line. What had he been thinking? He must be mad.

He got up, straightened his blazer, and examined his face in the mirror. He could have sworn new wrinkles were forming.

"Hi," he said out loud, forcing a smile at his reflection. "How d'you do? I'm Christopher, your tour director. How nice to meet you." He varied his smile. No, on second thoughts, too toothy. Besides, these people might have had a gruelling journey. The last thing they wanted to see was him grinning like an ape. He ran it again.

"Hi. The name's Chris." It was tight, professional, reassuring.

By the time he arrived at Vienna International Airport Christopher's nerves had cranked up a notch or two, despite two more vodka and tonics. He was uneasy for another reason, too - the second, false passport they'd given him in the office. Least he assumed it was there, because he hadn't even had time to open the sealed manila envelope he'd come away with, such was the weight of documentation he'd needed to plough through.

The immigration officer waved him through without a murmur. The customs officials were more careful. A tall thin one with a close-shaven baby face beckoned him across. Behind him, a large black Alsatian sat panting on a leash.

"Who, me?"

"Ya, you."

Christopher hoisted his large yellow duffel bag, together with an item of hand luggage, onto a kind of gridded bench. "Just ze two bags?"

"Just the two bags."

"Open them please."

Christopher opened them and winced. The holdall was jammed full of dirty laundry. At four hours notice he had little option - it would have to be done in the hotel. It had been bad enough on the floor of his bathroom in Stoke Newington, heaven knew into what state it might have fermented now. But he didn't have long to find out. Baby-face delved into the smaller bag first, and visibly recoiled.

"Purpose of visit?"

"I'm a tour escort."

Baby-face looked up. "Say again?"

"Eine Reiseleiter."

"Ah, sprechen-sie Deutsch?"

"No."

"You don't live here?"

"I live in London."

"Then what is zis?" he said, holding up a stray sock at the end of the aerial of his walkie talkie. The dog sat up, scenting something. "You are coming home to Mutti, no?"

Christopher coughed nervously.

"No, that's not it...um...I always bring a certain amount to do in the hotel. I travel a lot you see."

The man looked at him, no doubt weighing up the likelihood of Christopher having hidden a stash of marijuana in the hardened crevices of a soiled pair of Y-fronts.

"Fritzi," he barked.

Fritzi bounded up to the bag, gave it one sniff, then slumped on its haunches, emitting a kind of whining noise like a congested hoover. Baby-face hesitated. Finally he motioned Christopher on with a dismissive wave of the hand. Supercilious bastard, thought Christopher. Supercilious hound. He hurried on, conjuring up libellous thoughts on the unnaturally high proportion of Austrians in the Waffen SS.

TWENTY MINUTES LATER HE MADE IT TO THE '*BRIEF Encounter*' lounge. It was here, Cynthia had told him, that he was likely to find the man called Rog. He scanned the room. There was no one who looked even remotely like a Rog – or a tour director, whatever they were supposed to look like. He sat down and, retrieving a glossy blue and white TravelCo badge from his briefcase, furtively pinned it on the lapel of his blazer. He straightened the polyester red and yellow striped tie that Donald had given him and checked his watch: 6.30, twenty-five minutes till the first plane landed. He sat back and waited, his stomach beginning to churn.

He hadn't been waiting long before a gruff voice butted into his consciousness.

"I should take that off if I were you, mate."

Christopher turned. The man looked about his age, with a tanned, weather-beaten face, and was jacket and tie-less. Slung around one shoulder was a garish lime and yellow nylon satchel.

"I'm sorry?"

"You must be the new boy. The tie. And the badge. Lose it."

"But I'm the TravelCo rep," protested Christopher, "I'm meeting my group off a plane from Chicago in twenty-five minutes."

The man shrugged, and slumped down beside him. Something glinted on his wrist: a gold Rolex, studded with tiny diamonds.

"I know exactly who you are. But please yourself. Me, I prefer not to look like a prat."

He began to run a battered comb along his receding hairline. Christopher eyed him.

"You're not Rog by any chance?"

"Rog-*er*, if you don't mind."

"Sorry, only Cynthia told me…"

"That Henrietta? The sooner she snaffles her Rupert the better it will be for all of us."

"Her Rupert?"

"Her Viscount, Duke, Count or whoever it is she's planning to hitch up with. They're all called Rupert, didn't you know? And you are?"

In Christopher's limited experience they had names like Zac and Cosmo these days.

"Christopher. Christopher Wainwright." He tittered nervously. "This is my first tour of duty."

"I can see that. What are you on?"

"I beg your pardon?"

"Which tour you doing?"

"Oh…it's called 'The Land That Time Forgot'".

Roger stopped his combing abruptly.

"The what?"

"It's a corporate special." Christopher explained where it went.

"Jesus. Where's that?"

"Exactly."

"Typical!" scoffed Roger. "Last year Donald laid on a tour to some place in Central Asia only to get reports back when they arrived that it was under martial law, dusk to dawn curfew. But, as we say in this business," he added, pulling a camp expression, "that's life in the tropics, darling!"

"Oh no," said Christopher. "I don't think this place is like that. They've apparently just had some kind of a democratic revolution."

"Uh-oh. That spells food and petrol shortages." Roger grinned. "Rather you than me, old mate. Shit I feel awful, got an aspirin?"

Christopher shook his head.

"So let's have a look at your list then." He held out his hand. "Your rooming list. See what talent you got."

Christopher hesitated. The hand flapped impatiently. "Come on, cough it up, you want some tips or don't you?"

Somewhat reluctantly he fished it out of his briefcase. Roger scanned the names hungrily.

"Finkelburger, Henry and Mary. Jesus, what kind of a name's that? Hershey, Bob and Barbra. Could be the chocolate people with any luck. Brown, Hilda and Woods, Rosa-Lee." He paused, and looked up. "Two chicks rooming together. Looks promising. Mind you, I'm not sure. Hilda and Rosa-Lee are kind of boomer names, wouldn't you say?"

"I've really no idea."

"I'd say they were. More likely to be old bats. Better for the money though." He winked. "You'll learn that about this business. It's a trade off between money and sex. If they're all young, you get plenty of sex but they don't spend anything. If they're older you make lots of dosh but they're not so fit. Know what I mean?" He gazed into the distance, as if imagining something. "In most cases."

"I…"

"Fuck me, what's this?" he gasped, snapping his attention back to the list. "Seven male couples? A work trip? Leroy, Hank, Joe. Sixteen of them. Maybe high school kids. Or God forbid, maybe they're senior citizens, here to trace their European roots before it's too late. That would be typical. These people never seem to understand that adventure tour means adventure tour, that sometimes they actually have to get out of the effing bus. I've seen it happen countless times." He mimicked a Midwestern accent: "*Whaddayamean we gotta walk? There's nuttin' about walkin' in the broch-ua!*' Nothing about breathing, either, Mr. Menkelschrump."

Christopher laughed uneasily.

Rog's eyes lit up. "Ah, this is more like it. Two singles, and both female. Elizabeth Kigovski and Martha Fierstein. Start praying…"

"Well, I.."

"…that they're under forty. Let's see now," he half closed his eyes, trying to imagine them, "Martha Fierstein will be East Coast, rich but neurotic. Kigovski sounds Polish. Dark, passionate, slightly tragic. She too will be returning to the continent of her ancestors. To the roots of her turbulent history. Fierstein you take shopping. Kigovski," he said, jabbing Christopher in the ribs, "you take to bed." He handed the sheet back with a grin. "Mind you, two out of twenty-five is nothing to write home about. But then you can't expect miracles on your first tour."

This was an angle that Christopher had not considered. The tannoy burst into life with the news that flight AA 452 from Chicago had landed. Christopher hurriedly snapped his briefcase shut and leapt up.

"Whoa there, cowboy!" cried Roger, pulling him back. "Not so fast. Bags are not even in the halls yet. They'll be at least half an hour."

"But shouldn't we be there? Just in case one of them comes through early?"

"What you trying to do, win an award? So fucking what? They'll be running around like some headless turkeys then, won't they?" He eyed Christopher suspiciously. "Listen, a word of advice, mate. Stamp your authority on them early. They've gotta realise early on that they can't function without you. You'll get managing directors, I mean we're talking high powered people here, CEOs, government employees, Mafia boss-men and their dolly-bird wives, retired generals. All of them - without exception - are used to giving orders. This is the one time they want to get away from all that. Believe me, they want you to boss them. Cos if you don't, God help you. Can you imagine, twenty-six leaders, leaderless? Recipe for anarchy. Absolute fucking pandemonium. So let them run around and panic. Drum it into their little pea-brains early on. You're all they have between order and chaos."

"It sounds terrifying."

"Exhilarating, I call it."

Christopher hesitated, unsure of where to begin.

"Cynthia in the office told me you might be able to help me out with something."

Rog raised an eyebrow.

"She said you could fill me in on how you - we - make money on these trips." He coughed. "I need to make some, and fast."

Roger burst out laughing.

"What, you mean you don't know?"

Christopher shook his head. There was a moment of silence. When Roger spoke again it was in a lower voice.

"How long you going to be in Vienna for?"

"Two nights. We fly out on Saturday."

"And you're in the Hotel Mozart, right?"

Christopher nodded.

"Leave it with me mate. I'll show you the ropes."

HALF AN HOUR LATER THEY WERE STANDING TOGETHER AT THE gate waiting for their arrivals. Roger was droning on to Christopher with his tales of derring-do. Christopher was barely listening.

"Most dangerous combination is a mother and daughter, in my experience, Chris," he was saying, now chewing gum and holding up a cardboard sign with '*TravelCo / Roger and Chris*' scrawled on it. "I remember one time, God this takes me back, I was fucking the brains out of this one young lady, can't have been more than nineteen, and her mother keeps asking me up to her room to discuss her daughter's wellbeing. Young Bella, it seemed, had skipped a couple of city sightseeing tours and Mom was afraid she was missing out. My foot. Jealous of her daughter, was all! There Mom reclined, one leg on the bed, one on the floor, chiffon night-dress showing just enough thigh to arouse the most restrained of blokes…"

Christopher scanned the sea of faces just then beginning to emerge from the arrivals gate. He could feel his heart thumping furiously.

"I wanted to fucking reassure her," continued Roger blithely. "Young Bella wasn't missing out. She was being rogered stupid, ha-ha, by her handsome tour director between the hours of nine and twelve every morning on a sightseeing tour all of her own." He threw his head back and laughed, loudly, revealing a glint of gold in his upper molars. Christopher joined in politely, coughed, and said,

"I think they're coming through now."

"Don't you want to know how it ended? I had to lean on the frigging fire alarm. I hate to hurt people's feelings. Refusing a woman is one of the most painful aspects of this job. I mean listen mate, they have, after all, travelled over three and a half thousand miles to get here."

"Hi, I'm Christopher, welcome to Europe!"

An elderly lady stood behind a trolley looking at them both through a pair of ancient spectacles.

"No thank you," she said, moving her trolley along. "Come along Hild."

Hild struggled behind with her own overburdened chariot.

"No, no, you don't understand," said Christopher, breaking away. "We're from TravelCo. You're with me, I'm your tour director, I noticed your luggage label. Here, let me help you with those." He made a move towards Hilda's trolley.

"Hey! Stop that young man! Out of ma way!" she screamed.

Rosa-Lee bustled up, flustered. "He's our tour escort, Hilda!" she shouted, "from TravelCo!"

She turned to Christopher apologetically. "Gee I'm sorry 'bout this, she's a little deaf in the ear."

Hilda, urged by Rosa-Lee, allowed herself to be directed to a seating area a few yards away, while Christopher, considerably shaken, went back to the arrivals gate to rejoin Roger.

"My first arrival," he explained apologetically. "I noticed her luggage label."

"Fucking hell mate," hissed Roger. "You wanna win a medal, or what?"

"Just trying to be friendly. Give them a good welcome."

"Remember what I said," he muttered darkly.

Shortly a group of four young women, West Coast types, all teeth, tans and curling tongs, swung through with two trolley loads of matching luggage. Christopher felt Roger stiffen beside him, his eyes swivelling to watch their progress. He was on the point of idling over to accost them when a burly chauffeur, in peaked cap and uniform, elbowed his way towards them. Roger eased back, visibly deflated.

"Bollocks, thought those were with me," he said. "I've got four women in two doubles. God, I hope this lot aren't mine," he added, as a string of enormous men in bulging t-shirts and trainers started spewing into the Arrivals Hall. One of them came skidding through the double doors on the front of a trolley, propelled by a seven foot giant.

"Hey, Johnny, quit!" yelled the man on the trolley. "Quit, I tell ya!"

The trolley raced past the barrier and disappeared into the crowd beyond, accompanied by the cries and oaths of outraged bystanders.

"Some sports team, looks like. I had one once." Rog visibly shuddered. "Never again."

As he said it a large gold signet ring with a diamond in the middle on a thick finger rapped him on the shoulder. It looked like some novelty cigar that you buy for the man who has everything. Roger turned round, and started.

"Which one of yose is Chris?" boomed the owner. Roger's face was suddenly wreathed in smiles.

"That one," he said gleefully, slamming a hand onto Christopher's shoulder. "Be my guest."

"Name's Jackson!" He stuck out a hand which Christopher reluctantly took. "They call me Coach!" He emitted a kind of deep throated roar.

Christopher rescued his hand and flexed his fingers.

"Hi..."

"I'm in charge of this rabble," he grinned, revealing a glint of gold, and indicating a group of sixteen large young men. None of them were under six foot two as far as Christopher could tell. "We're with you, I believe?"

Christopher took a deep breath. They all had eyes that seemed to suffer from some form of hyper-active condition:

thirty-two of them were darting all over the place, each in syncopation with a knee joint.

"You're with the Universal corporate tour?" he said. "The Land Where Time Stood Still?"

"Right, that's the tour, that's it. An' I've got two arriving on a flight from JFK at nine. Know about them?"

Christopher knew all about them. Somehow he had to get his group to wait around in the terminal for two hours until the other two arrived. Why the hell couldn't Donald have organised a taxi, he thought bitterly? What a way to start a tour.

"You mean we gotta wait around for two hours?" exploded the man menacingly after Christopher had explained the situation. "Can't you put us in cabs?"

Christopher sheepishly explained he didn't have authorisation to spend that kind of money. The coach wasn't booked to pick them up until the last two had arrived.

"Holy shittin' Moses, I ain't believin' this…" he went off muttering.

Christopher bit his lip.

"Donald stuffed you, huh?" commiserated Roger. "Bad luck. The guy's so tight you couldn't fit a pin up his arse."

Close behind came the Finkelburgers, a middle-aged couple from Idaho, blinking uncertainly. After pointing out the money change and toilet facilities, he returned to his position. Twenty down and six to go. It was not good. Sixteen American football players called the Arkansas Angels, sponsored by Universal. They were already angry, and ordering extra breakfast before they even got out of the terminal building. He wondered idly if they had any conception of what 'Continental with juice' actually meant. Then came Martha. She wore shoulder length mousy hair, fake leopard skin pants and a day-glo orange T-shirt cut away on the shoulder.

"Way to go, what a flight!" She giggled nervously. "We've had a trip you would not believe!"

"Oh really?" said Christopher as he steered her towards the rest of the group. "I'm sorry to hear that."

"Totally wild! First there was a bunch of French Canadians who grabbed all the aisle seats, then there was this crowd of kiddos who screamed all the way through the movie, oh and the movie!" She laughed again, more loudly, revealing a whole canteen of dental work. "It sucked! It was called '*Dad What Have You Done To The Cat?*' You seen it?"

He confessed that he had not.

"It was about this cat, right, and…"

"Excuse me for one minute," interjected Christopher and returned hastily to the barrier. OMG, sixteen days with this lot? Next came the Hersheys. Both were, he guessed, in their late forties or early fifties, dressed in a combination of matching tracksuits, dark glasses and headbands. They sported identical badges: '*I love Universal!*' He vaguely reminded Christopher of a Julio Iglesias look alike while she could have been Kim Cattrall's twin sister. They took in their surroundings disdainfully, as Christopher stammered out directions to them to change money, go to the bathroom, and be back in ten minutes for 'further instructions.'

Finally a man and a woman brought up the rear. As the woman emerged Christopher couldn't help doing a double take. Could this be one of his? He was still missing Elizabeth Kigovski. He remembered Roger's analysis. She came towards him, flushed and laughing as she tried to control her trolley, and charmingly ran over his foot. The girl was an angel. Her face had the complexion of peaches, her hair was long and dark, her eyes the colour of cornflowers. This was what he had been looking for, been missing, for so long.

"Hi, welcome to Europe!" he beamed, with every ounce of charm he could muster.

"Hey I'm sorry...oops...your foot!" she giggled.

"Here, let me help you. That looks heavy."

"Oh. Thanks," she said, blushing, and graciously ceding her pile of Ralph Lauren travel accessories to Christopher's more capable steerage. A man in a black leather jacket and shades tagged along behind, wheeling a trolley the size and complexity of an aircraft carrier.

"So, how was the flight?" Christopher smiled at her. "Good movie?"

He smelt a whiff of something warm and floral, with an undertone that sent his pulse racing.

"The movie?" She looked puzzled. "Oh, sure…"

"About cats, I hear," he pursued.

"Cats? No...I don't…"

"Excuse me." The voice was slow and imperious. Christopher turned round to find another old lady peering up at him. "Are you the representative?"

"Er...yes." He stared at her. Who was she? She wasn't with him, he'd got everybody he was meant to have, bar one man. "But I think you're in the wrong group. You're not with me, you must be…"

"Excuse me the lady is with you," said a man labelled United Airlines, lumbering up behind, "cos she's with me."

"With you?"

"Yeah. I brought her through accompanied."

Christopher stopped, relinquished the Ralph Lauren fashion items, and went down his list. Could they have added an extra without telling him?

"Well, in that case, glad to have you aboard. They don't seem to have updated me, but don't worry, just a small administrative thing." He was already beginning to calm down. He had a warm feeling inside. "Can I have your name, please?"

"Kigovski."

Christopher paused for a moment.

"Ah. You must be with Elizabeth." So she'd brought her grandmother along.

He turned and winked at Elizabeth, but the wink floated off into space and startled a security guard. She had disappeared.

"I'm sorry?"

"You are a relation I presume?" repeated Christopher. "Of Elizabeth's?"

"You mean there's another Elizabeth Kigovski?" croaked the old lady, startled.

Christopher stared at her grimly, and then took a last, desultory look around. He kicked himself. Fuck.

"No, no, I'm sorry, my mistake." He sighed. "Follow me."

Of the other woman, the girl with the long dark hair, the cornflower blue eyes, and the skin the texture of peaches, there was nothing to be seen. She had merged seamlessly, along with her stack of Ralph Lauren vanity cases and exotic floral undertone, into the great mass of travellers who were on the move just then. Like a trolley in the night.

He had never spoken to a large group before, and as he addressed their expectant, weary, upturned faces, he began to understand what Roger had been talking about. They depended on him. It was an odd feeling. He introduced himself, then checked them off his list. One man had failed to turn up. He left the bad news to last. They had two hours to kill. They stared at him in disbelief, but he didn't give them a chance to complain, he just pointed out the rendezvous and fled to Roger. He caught him as he was pointing two blonde women to the bus parking lot where his coach was ready and waiting.

"What do I do if someone doesn't show up?" he said breathlessly.

"Text London with a no-show. Who is it?"

"Guy called Roderick Fraser."

Roger stopped in mid-stride and laughed.

"Oh don't worry about Roddy, he won't be showing up."

"Why ever not?"

"Because he's dead."

Christopher looked aghast.

"Look mate, it's too complicated to explain now. He's one of Cynthia's…" Roger trailed off as he watched his two blondes boarding his coach, giggling.

Christopher started after him, and then it dawned on him. He'd been in such a hurry he hadn't even had time to look at his fake passport. Roderick Fraser was The Spare.

Chapter 14

The Monstrance

"Roderick Fraser."

"Speak up," shouted Boris, on a weak mobile signal from Paris. "I can't hear you."

Blicker raised his voice so that his secretary, who was just then pouring him out a cup of coffee, looked up, startled.

"Roderick Fraser!" he shouted. "The heir! We've found him!"

"That's better." The line was suddenly much clearer. "But you already told me he's the heir, what's new?"

"What's new, my dear Boris, is that we've tracked him down. Remember that incident on the train I was talking about? My friend the President of Kazakhstan looked into the case personally, and was able to give me his address from the old visa application. It's in Covent Garden, London."

"So what are you saying? Be quick Johann, I've got to leave for my meeting with the Chinese in ten minutes, and I'm not even shaved."

"What time's your flight back?"

"Nine."

The Spare and The Heir

"Good, because I want you to meet Horst at Cartier. He's choosing something to present to this fellow."

"What sort of something?"

Blicker could hear the suspicion in Boris's voice.

"Oh...a little bauble. It's not as if we have any crown jewels left, is it? We'll need a gift."

"Oh I get it. We offer the guy the throne, a sackful of gold bars and a 'little bauble' from Cartier. Where do we find him, in a manger?" He hooted with derision. "How much is this all going to cost, if you don't mind my asking?"

Blicker pulled a face at his secretary.

"What are the odds of landing the Chinese deal?"

Boris was in Paris for a few days at an international gathering of Finance ministers, and had managed to fix up a bilateral with the Chinese delegation.

"What's that got to do with it? A fraction of what the IMF was offering. They're interested in our garment factories."

"Good. That means we can afford a little bauble. Besides, think of the rest of the gold."

"But boss…"

"Boris! that's my final word. Just get on with it."

WHEN BORIS ARRIVED AT CARTIER'S RUE ROYALE BRANCH later that day, the store was packed. The mid-summer sale was on, and the normally calm and deferential atmosphere that pervades the smartest jewellery store in the world was punctured by outsize ladies trailing chauffeurs, and bustling groups of Chinese in smart suits. Large and grotesque egg-shaped things in gold and platinum were being snapped up by powdered milk heiresses, and 10,000 Euro discounts on jewel-encrusted motorcars - not to scale - were being rapidly converted into Rials, Roubles and Yuan.

Boris felt like throwing up. He burst out into the street

gasping for air, then hurried the hundred yards to the bar where they'd agreed to meet. He found Horst carefully wiping the last remains of a mille-feuille from the wisps of his moustache.

As soon as he spied his countryman he burst into song.

"Paris, in ze spring time…"

"Hello, Horst."

"…iz ze finest place I know." He broke off, inhibited by Boris's scowl.

"Isn't it gorgeous here? Care to join me for a sticky?"

Boris glanced at his watch impatiently.

"Let's get this over with, shall we?"

He watched as Horst downed the last of his coffee, struggling to get up. "What's the hurry? Cartier doesn't close until six."

"I've got a plane to catch."

"Rush, rush and more rush," muttered Horst, grappling with a clutch of shopping bags deposited under the table.

"Good God," exclaimed Boris, peering inside the one emblazoned Armani. "What the hell have you been buying?"

"Oh, nothing really. A few samples, bits and pieces."

"That's crazy. Most of them are made in our factories. Surely you can get all this stuff at home?"

"Tut tut Boris, you know as well as I do they never give us the best lines to manufacture."

Boris pulled out a sleek linen jacket wrapped in fine tissue paper. He was conscious of an almost audible intake of breath at neighbouring tables as the clientele admired it.

"And this?" he said accusingly.

"Giorgio designed it personally."

"For what? Casual sportswear?"

Horst looked hurt. "I've got to look the part when I meet His Royal Highness. We don't want him thinking he's inheriting a country of dowdy provincials now, do we?"

There was hardly any danger of that, thought Boris to himself. He tried to smother a smirk.

"Now there's no need to be like that," Horst sniffed. "Oh come on, don't be a spoilsport. I can recycle it. It'll do nicely for one of the footmen. Have you seen what some of them look like? It's a scandal." He paused. "It's just simple PR, that's all."

"In that case take it out of the simple PR budget," snapped Boris, dropping it back in the bag. He grabbed another labelled Fauchon and strode out.

Ten minutes later they were battling through Cartier. It was astonishing, thought Boris, there was meant to be a cost of living crisis and the rich just went on spending. Or perhaps that was why – no longer comfortable putting their money in stocks and bonds, they were stuffing it in portable assets: in art, antiques and glittery gewgaws. He halted in front of a display cabinet.

"My God, what is that thing?"

Horst followed his gaze. There, on a cushion of deep blue velvet, protected by bullet-proof double-glazing and covered by a security camera all to itself, was a crystal paperweight embedded in a mass of rubies.

"Oh my goodness. They can't be real."

"No? Take a look at the price tag." He peered at it - 55,000 EUR - straightened up and turned to Horst.

"What the hell are we looking for exactly, anyway? How did I ever agree to this madness?"

"Something...appropriate. A decoration...or a chain, or …"

"Why we can't find something at home beats me."

"Because there's nothing left, that's why. It all got turned into corn for the peasantry."

"Don't give me that."

"You don't believe it?"

"Of course I don't believe it. Don't you remember that

story about Mrs Stalin turning up wearing those ear-rings made up from two of the Elphberg marbles? That Stalin was incredibly insensitive." Boris paused, as if reviewing the whole catalogue of the man's thoughtlessness.

"Now. What about this…" he said disgustedly, gesturing at a vulgar piece of bejewelled engineering that vaguely resembled a crown. "A mere 89,550 Euros. Why the fifty? Yuk."

"OMG," swooned Horst. He turned pleadingly to his Government colleague. "Boris…"

FORTY-FIVE MINUTES LATER THEY EMERGED INTO THE PLACE Vendôme with a large pink box wrapped in red ribbon. Boris was muttering under his breath.

"The boss is mad. You're all mad. Here, take your packages. It's time I went to the airport."

"How am I going to manage all this stuff?" whined Horst, his arms bulging.

"That's your problem. And don't forget to keep the receipt. If this heir turns out to be unsuitable I want my money back." He paused. "Oh, and Horst?"

He pointed an accusing finger at Blicker's artistic director, now so laden down with shopping that he looked, with his ginger moustache poking out above a Ralph Lauren box, like a fairground clown.

"That goes for the jacket, too."

∼

BACK IN CARTIER A MAN WAS ASKING QUESTIONS WITH A ONE hundred euro banknote. The sales woman was drawing an artist's impression. The man was visibly shocked.

"What, they bought that? What for?"

"Look Meester," retorted the woman haughtily, "don't you shout at me. How should I know?"

The man rubbed his temples hard. He was beginning to get a headache. He'd been trailing Blicker's emissaries for nearly a week now, on a mission for his boss, Rupert Hentzau, and he still didn't have a clue what they were up to. Or rather he couldn't help feeling that somehow he did now have a clue, but it was a clue he could make no sense of at all. It was the most outrageous piece of shopping that he'd ever witnessed, and that was saying something, considering the missions he'd run for Hentzau in places like Dubai and Singapore. It resembled one of those garish Monstrances that were on display in the Treasury in St Felix Cathedral. And all on the National Government of Reconstruction's American Express card. Hentzau would soon see what a hypocrite that Boris was.

He took a snap with his phone of the artist's impression he was clutching, and strode out into the street.

Chapter 15

Schools out

Hentzau was sitting at home eating breakfast in his study with his Chief of Staff when the image pinged through on WhatsApp.

"I don't like it," said Hentzau, sweeping his hand through his blond locks, nervously. "I don't like it at all. Blicker's up to something."

"He's always up to something, sir. Are we surprised?"

"Yes, but this is different. His agents have had meetings at the US State Department, they've broken into the London offices of the Ruritanian Trade Association, they've even had dealings with the President of Kazakhstan. And now this." He handed the phone to his staffer. "Apparently Horst just spent government funds on this in Cartier."

His deputy examined the magnified image. "Good God!" He looked shocked. "Is it a bribe?"

"A bribe?" snorted Hentzau. "Who on earth would accept that as a bribe? And what for?"

"Well, let's look at this rationally, sir," countered the deputy. "Why would Horst spend three days going to museums and shopping in Paris?"

"Well, he is the artistic director."

"Yes, but three days, sir? With whose money? And in work time? I reckon they are looking for something. Perhaps it's about paintings the oligarchs looted and sold to museums, which Blicker wants back, hence the meetings at the State Department, and the business at the Ruritanian Trade Association."

"But why break in?"

"Perhaps they didn't want to let on, sir," replied his deputy, "didn't want to tip them off." He paused. "So maybe they finally found some of the stolen art. But then comes their next problem, you see, sir: proving they are stolen is only half the story, they need to get the museum director on board. How do they do it? Simple, sir. They find out his wife has got a weakness for this kind of thing." He waved the phone at arms length, as if it were contaminated.

"A very pretty theory, Chief," said Hentzau. "But somehow I don't quite buy it." He frowned. "Oh, well, what does it matter? Very shortly we'll have the monarchy restored, and then all this will be forgotten. Who cares about Blicker's little games? Now, what are we going to do about the Felix Stone? Had any more ideas about that?"

"I've got some pictorial references, sir." His chief of staff went over to open his briefcase, and dug out some photocopies of old engravings. It was round and smooth and looked rather like a fossilised dinosaur turd. Traditionally it was knelt upon by monarchs at their coronation, but in the years after 1927 it had gone missing from the Cathedral. "We still don't know what happened exactly, but the last trace of it we have was a delivery to a sculptor's studio."

"Oh my God! Do you suppose…"

"that's exactly what I suppose, sir. It's probably sitting in some sculpture park right now, retitled 'Wind and Rain' with a couple of holes bored through it."

Hentzau suddenly roared with laughter. His deputy certainly had a very good way with words. He had the president spot on.

"Very funny, Chief," said Hentzau. "So I suppose we'll have to make a replica. No one will know. We can announce we've found it, and return it to the Cathedral. Just wait. Everyone will see it as an omen." He glanced at his watch and got up. "8.30, news-time. Incidentally," he said as he flicked the remote, "how are the roses coming along? Because I've been thinking: we need to start no later than the end of next month."

"Bad news, I'm afraid, sir. There's nothing. I've ordered carnations as backup." Hentzau swivelled.

"Carnations? The people will never swallow that. It's traditional to acclaim a new monarch with roses, come on Chief, you know that! Can't we import them from somewhere?"

"We can, sir, but it all costs money."

"Money, money, money," sighed Hentzau. "When is it not down to money? Answer me that?."

He switched on the television breakfast news, halfway through a bulletin from the previous evening. News had never travelled fast in the old Ruritania and things had not changed much, even now.

'The children, all aged between ten and fourteen,' the anchor-woman was saying, to pictures of pint-sized bodies battling with truncheon-wielding policemen, 'were hustled into police vans and driven away to be cautioned. Two twelve year old girls were accidentally hurt when a police dog broke its leash and are now in hospital, and said to be in a stable condition.'

"Is something the matter, sir?" said the Chief of Staff, noticing the horror on Hentzau's face.

"It can't be…" he murmured.

'Civil Rights activists have called for an immediate inquiry…' continued the bulletin.

"Tilly!" bellowed Hentzau. He got up and strode into the hallway. His deputy made to follow, then thought better of it. He'd had experience of these Hentzau family altercations in the past.

"Tilly! Come here immediately!" boomed Hentzau towards the kitchen. After a few seconds a pair of pig-tails and a mouth full of pop-tarts poked their way round a door at the end of the corridor. Hentzau marched towards her.

"Now listen here young lady! I want an explanation from you!" She retreated back into the kitchen. "Was I mistaken," he continued, following her inside, "or was that Miss Matilda Hentzau waving a banner saying 'Down with low productivity' on TV just now?"

Tilly eyed her father from the other side of the kitchen table, her mouth working steadily to finish the remains of her breakfast.

"Well? Mmm?"

"Mmm," she replied, pointing a finger at her rippling cheek. "Mmm."

"What the hell did you think you were doing?" exploded Hentzau.

"Papa!" she said, swallowing the last of the pop-tart. "Just wait will you!" She wiped the crumbs from her face and sat down. Hentzau glared at her. When she was finally ready to answer him there was a gleam in her eye.

"What, you mean we were actually on telly?"

"You should be in prison by the sounds of it!" retorted her father. "Lucky you weren't attacked by those police dogs. Two girls are in hospital."

"I know. Weren't they brilliant?"

"Now listen, just answer my question. What were…"

"It's called direct action, Papa," she said, nonchalantly buttering a piece of white toast.

"What do you mean, direct action?"

"Oh come on, Papa! Revolution is not a dinner party, you know."

He exploded. "I can do without the Mao quote, thank you very much!"

"To change things you need action, not just words. So, what we did was, we got together a few of us to complain about the new food they're making us eat, we made some signs, and we went outside the castle to show everyone what we felt. Simple really." She finished her buttering and took a large bite. "You ought to be proud of us," she continued, munching. "It all went according to our plan, especially when the police…"

"Look, it's all very well those teachers indoctrinating you with all this lefty rubbish…"

"Lefty?"

"Fascist then…"

"Fascist, Papa? What's Fascist about direct action? The Bolsheviks used…"

"Centrist then!" Hentzau was exasperated. "I don't care what you bloody call it. But what I do care about is you. And putting your class out on the streets is not the way to change things. Besides, I'm not having you mixed up in it."

She started to protest.

"Children, bloody hell!" he snorted. He drew up a chair, leaning across the table towards her.

"Now listen," he began, in a more conciliatory tone, "I know you want to get involved. And I promise you, there'll be a lot for you to get involved in soon. You have my word on that."

She dug a scoop of ice cream onto a plate. Did the girl never stop with the sugar? It was all because she didn't have a mother, he reflected sadly. If she did, she might have had some supervision. A thought struck him: perhaps she didn't get enough recognition?

"And don't think I don't appreciate what you've achieved at Zenda. You and your friends are doing a marvellous job with the moat, you really are, and your *Zenda Experience* performance is really coming along well. But if you get locked up in prison, that will really put a spanner in the works. We have our first tourists arriving this weekend, remember? The American tour group. I am relying on you to give them a good introduction."

"Papa," she said, ignoring him, "I suppose you think that demonstration of ours was all about school food, don't you?"

He raised his eyebrows at her.

"You really don't understand, do you, you have no clue?"

"Don't talk to your father like that!" he snapped angrily.

"Sorry Papa, but I'm not going to sit here all morning arguing with you." She got up hastily, shoving the uneaten ice-cream aside. "I'm late. You go back to the capitalist-roaders of your Government of National Reconstruction or whatever you call it and play your counter-revolutionary games and I'll get on with doing something about it. I'm off to school."

She grabbed her satchel and marched out.

∾

ONCE OUTSIDE, TILLY TOOK A DEEP BREATH. SHE HATED arguing with her father. But he really was very stupid sometimes. He just didn't get it. He was almost as dense as her brother. Didn't he realise that something had to be done? It was no good just expecting everybody to welcome the new Queen with open arms. There was more to it than that. For a start, they had to begin making the National Government of Reconstruction as unpopular as possible. There were thousands, no, millions, of people around the world who would have given anything for pictures like that - of policemen beating up on kids. He ought to be proud of her.

Who did he think had unleashed those police dogs in the first place? The police? She felt sorry for the two little girls, but, well, there were things more important than the individual. Sometimes she wondered whether her father really had what it took.

She stuck her nose in the air, smelt the flowers in bloom in the manicured gardens beside the road, and felt a sudden adrenaline rush. It was brilliant to be alive, it really was.

She couldn't wait to grow up.

Chapter 16

Rosie

The long dark hair was up and wrapped in a towel, and the cornflower blue eyes were obscured by steam. All around, the skin with the texture of peaches was getting a little rejuvenation.

"Dior, Chanel, Aveda," intoned a female voice in the adjoining room. "Rosie, you must have spent a fortune in Vienna!"

Rose Elpberg – Rosie to her friends - rubbed the steam off the mirror with the palm of her hand and stared at her reflection. Gently she wiped the remnants of the cucumber cream from the edges of her eyelashes. Wrapping a dressing gown around her, she returned to the bedroom. Her friend Sophie Bernenstein, a PR assistant and 'influencer' in the National Government's Ministry of Communications, was sitting at an antique walnut dressing table, sniffing bottles.

"It's not my money."

"Bet you had a good time."

"Oh, sure. Great. You don't think he let me go on my own, do you? I was frog-marched down the Kartnerstrasse by one of his deranged minders. I suppose after that business with Andrew at the art show he wasn't taking any chances."

She went to the window and drew back the corner of a curtain. A car idled on the corner of the street. "See down there? That's probably two of them watching me now."

Her friend carried on lifting bottle stoppers greedily. "Mmm, number 19." She inhaled. "But what I don't understand is why?"

"that's what I was hoping you would tell me, Soph. It doesn't make sense."

"No, I mean, why don't you want to marry him?" Sophie gave her friend a look. "It's not like he's not fit."

"Sophie! He's a creep! And that little vixen Tilly for a sister in law."

"How long have you been engaged now? Two years?"

"Three," replied Rosie despondently, feeling the smooth skin of her shoulders beneath the towelling.

"Well - can't you get out of it?"

"My parents, Sophie, you don't understand. They owe him everything. If I let them down now…" She sat down heavily on the edge of her bed, thinking of her adoptive mother and father. "I can't, Soph, I just can't."

She was on the verge of tears. Sophie went over and put her arm around her. Awkwardly, since Rosie was a full six inches taller. And now, sitting next to her, Rosie was reminded of the difference in the size of their breasts.

Sophie had once told her she was a C Cup. No Sophie, you're not a C.

"But why now? Why the hurry? He's paranoid that I'm going to make trouble. All these outfits he sent me to buy in Vienna," she gestured around wildly "with those security people of his; the courses of beauty treatment; the Ciao Magazine article… d'you think I asked for all this?" She sniffed. "It's almost like they're grooming me for… God, it doesn't bear thinking about!" She turned to her friend and looked her in the eye. "Listen, Sophie. This is serious. Is there anything going on I should know about?"

She could normally rely on her friend for titbits of gossip from the inside of Government. Though she was not close to any of the ministers, she was very good at keeping her ear to the ground.

"Oh darling," she said. "I'm sorry."

It irritated Rosie when Sophie called her darling. It didn't suit her. She sighed. "I suppose if you knew you wouldn't be able to tell me. Official secrets blah blah blah."

"You know I would always tell you everything. Anyway, it's not like I know much. I'm just a humble PR person."

Oh right, sure. If anyone knew what was going on, it was Sophie. She was a notorious flirt, and trader of gossip. Rosie often wondered why she still kept her on as a friend. They had grown up together, gone to school together, and somehow Rosie had never had the heart to dump her.

She laughed. "There's no such thing as a humble PR person."

"Still.." said Sophie, "I really don't think it's that."

Rosie spun round. "You don't think it's what?"

"I...I don't want to disappoint you, Rosie, but there is something you really ought to know."

"Oh?"

Her friend bit her lip. "I don't think you ever will be Queen."

Rosie caught her breath. "What makes you say that?"

"Well.." Sophie hesitated. "Shouldn't be telling you this. But.."

"Go on!"

"They want to offer the throne to someone else."

"They do?"

"'Fraid so."

A smile crept across Rosie's face.

"Why, that's fantastic!"

"It is?" Her friend looked confused.

"Of course it is! It means I'll never be Queen!"

Sophie eyed her friend in alarm.

"You mean you don't want to be Queen?"

"Fuck no!"

Sophie fiddled with her blond hair, feeling the sharp wedge cut at the back of her neck.

"I mean, would you?" continued Rosie.

"Mmm..not sure." Sophie twisted her head to give herself a three quarter profile in the mirror, and lowered her chin. She hastily lifted it again. "Wouldn't say no."

"But hold on. If they're going to go through all the hassle of getting the monarchy up and running again, who do they think they're going to offer it to, if not me? That's crazy!"

"Can't tell you that. Told you far too much already."

"It doesn't make sense. I'm the one with the best claim. Unless it's cousin Joey." She started giggling.

"It's not cousin Joey."

"Then who on earth is it?" She stared at Sophie, but Sophie's lips were pursed. "Oh who cares! I don't want to know anyway." Then, suddenly, she jumped up. A truth had suddenly dawned on her.

"Wait a minute! If it's not me, then Hentzau won't want me anymore! Everyone knows I'm his insurance policy. But I'm worthless if someone else is on the throne, aren't I?"

"You are?"

"To him, yes!" God, Sophie was slow sometimes. "Does he know?"

"I don't think so."

"In that case someone ought to tell him. So we can break off our engagement."

Sophie got up and walked to the window, fingering her hair nervously.

"I don't think that's a very good idea."

"Why on earth not?"

"If you tell him that, they're bound to trace it back to me."

"Don't be idiotic. How can they possibly do that?"

"Because it will be obvious," She sighed. "Oh shit. I knew I shouldn't have told you."

"But Soph...he's got to know!"

"He will eventually."

"'Eventually' might be too late! He wants us married in four weeks!"

Sophie stared out of the window.

"Can't you stall him?" she said finally.

"You think I haven't tried?"

"Then disappear," said Sophie. "Then I promise we'll get the news out somehow. By the time you reappear it will all be over!"

"Disappear to where? And how? Look out the window at those thugs down there. Besides, you need money to disappear."

"What about your other friends?"

"They're all terrified of him too."

Sophie didn't like the 'too', although it was gratifying that Rosie's 'other friends', whose existence she scarcely acknowledged and of whom she was intensely jealous, might have this flaw.

"I mean, would you hide me?" Sophie didn't answer. "There you are, you see!"

Rosie went back into the bathroom and began wiping off the cucumber face pack. She felt considerably better now. The panic of half an hour ago had subsided. Yes, she had to protect her friend. But really, she was being over-dramatic, as usual. Poor old Sophie, she'd always been a bit of an airhead.

She smiled at her reflection: perhaps that's why she had kept her as a friend. Every girl needs someone who looks up to her. Preferably one who's not as pretty as you.

She scraped her face clean. Her cornflower eyes sparkled back at her as she unwrapped the towel and shook out her hair. A face that was made to love, not to waste itself on a jerk like Andrew.

Unexpectedly, an image popped into her head. The boy at the airport in Vienna. He really had been very cute. She wondered where he had been going. What he was doing. If only she hadn't had that minder with her. Because she was sure she glimpsed the word 'Ruritania' scribbled on a label on his briefcase. But then again, maybe she'd been imagining it.

"Got an idea!" her friend called out from the other room.

She snapped out of her reverie. One day she'd have a boyfriend who she chose, not who chose her.

"Oh yes?" she said absent-mindedly.

"How about a temporary job? A job which involves a lot of travelling?"

Chapter 17

A Tempting Offer

Horst found his way to Covent Garden on google maps. He straightened his jacket in a shop window, checked the top button of his shirt was done up, and marched purposefully down Long Acre.

As he looked around him he told himself how wise he had been to invest in the Armani. It was lunchtime, and the streets were throbbing with them.

"Come on, boys," he said, as his two acolytes struggled behind him, "not far to go now." One carried a suitcase of Felixtown Rosewater, the other the thing from Cartier. He'd engaged their services via the Ruritanian Trade Association, which doubled as a social club for exiles based in Ealing. They were two good-looking actors, currently resting. Well not today, smirked Horst to himself as he clutched the briefcase Blicker had given him, with a scan of the letter from the Bank of England.

They turned into Floral Street. After fifty yards he stopped abruptly.

"Ah, Paul Smith," he said with surprise. "Good, we'll come here afterwards to celebrate."

Four doors down a small buzzer said 'TravelCo'. Horst pressed it hard, and waited.

Donald was licking his fingers, finishing the remains of a chocolate cake at his desk when Cynthia came bustling in.

"Look I know it's my birthday, Cyn," he protested good-naturedly, "but are you ever going to learn to knock? I might have someone in here."

"Don't be ridiculous Donald. I can see you haven't through the glass partition. Listen, there's some chappie downstairs who says he wants to see Roddy."

Donald stopped mid-mouthful, the last morsel of chocolate poised mid-air.

"Shit! Why can't these people email? Are you sure?"

Of course she was sure. She was worried. What did he want to do about it?

"OK, get him up," he said, popping it in. "You'll have to stall him in reception. "When did we last activate Roddy? Poland wasn't it?"

"We're literally using him now, remember? Wainwright."

"Well it's hardly likely to be about that, is it? If it's an irate client, tell him very sorry, Roddy's out on a trip. If not..." He sucked his teeth thoughtfully. "Unless he's from one of the embassies."

Cynthia looked nervous. "That would not be helpful." She came back shortly. "He's not letting on. He says it's a confidential matter. He's very insistent."

"Really? Perhaps he really is after young Rod," suggested Donald, chuckling.

"I don't think so," she said curtly, astounded not for the first time at her boss's amazing lack of tact, not to mention taste.

He sighed. "OK, show him up."

Horst and his two companions were struggling by the time they reached the fourth floor.

The Spare and The Heir 135

"Lift not working," he gasped to the receptionist, who from that moment was owed ten more pounds by Susie in accounts. There was a running office wager on the comments of first time visitors, and the receptionist was thirty quid up that month.

The two young men staggered in with large packages and laid them carefully on the floor. Cynthia came up to them and stuck out her hand. "Hello, I'm Cynthia, how can I help you?"

Horst straightened up.

"Ah yes. We'd like to see Roderick Fraser."

"May I ask what it's about? Are you a former client of Roderick's?"

Horst peered at her. "A client? What…er…what sort of work is it that Mr Fraser does?"

"Perhaps you are from one of the embassies?" she pressed. Were they about to be rumbled?

Horst's eyes narrowed. "We're from Ruritania," he announced cagily. Cynthia's eyes widened and she excused herself. A minute later she returned.

"If you'd like to come this way."

They followed her into Donald's office. Horst was taken aback. The man before him didn't look at all suitable. He rose from his chair and lumbered around to shake hands. Horst noticed a small crumb of cake stuck to the inside of his sweat stained, open-neck collar.

"Take a pew," said Donald affably. "What can I do for you gentlemen?"

"Can I get you anything?" Cynthia hovered at the door. "Tea, coffee?"

"No thank you."

She left the room. As soon as the door had closed behind her Horst stood up again. His two acolytes followed suit. Donald looked up at them, startled.

"Your Majesty…" began the visitor.

Donald twitched. He pushed away the remains of his cake, suddenly aware of the impression it might be creating. "Come again?"

Horst got out a large sheet of paper and started to read from it.

"We are sent by command of the National Government for Reconstruction of Ruritania...."

"Hold it, hold it!" waved Donald. "Are you gentlemen from the Embassy?"

"No, Your Serene Highness, we come direct from Strelsau."

Your Serene Highness? So he had heard right.

"And we come with glad news. The throne of our sad country, so long neglected, has recently become vacant, and the subject of much speculative comment amongst our people. As I am sure you are aware, your Majesty, our recent White Revolution has at last enabled our sorely tried country to throw off the shackles…"

Donald snapped his mouth shut. What the hell were these men babbling about? He glanced behind them, at the door, firmly closed. They were clearly unhinged. Would they try something? Or was this some University Rag week scam?

"…and after due consideration, and with much sounding of public opinion, it has been decided to investigate the possibility of a Restoration, and it is with humble offerings of gold, rosewater and a small something from…"

"Hey! Hey!" he shouted, raising his hand. "Please. STOP!"

He inspected them more closely. He could smell actors a mile away. If the absurd ginger thing the lead man was twirling was not a stick-on job, he, Donald, was the Pope. Was it one of the breakfast cereal competitions the office girls were always going in for? Perhaps they'd entered Roddy's name as a laugh? Then it dawned on him. Ha, ha, yes! A birthday prank! It was common knowledge he loved charades. They had one every year at the office Christmas party.

He strode over to the door and flung it open so the rest of the office could overhear him.

"Well," he said loudly, laughing. "I am most honoured to be receiving such a high powered delegation from my subjects. As you can see," he flourished a hand at the flimsy hand-drawn map of this weird little country pinned on his noticeboard, "I take a great interest in my people!"

Horst peered at it in some concern.

"That is in Russian, no?"

"Indeed it is, emailed direct from the KGB. Now, what have you three wise gentlemen brought me?" Donald beamed at the boxes the men had deposited on the floor. The office must have clubbed together. How sweet.

"Rosewater? What is that?"

Horst motioned to one of the boys, who flipped open a leather case to reveal three bottles of their most prized export embedded in folds of velvet. Donald raised one and smelt it.

"Cyn?" he called through the open door. "Julie? This a hint by any chance?"

But he was met with blank stares through the plate glass partition. OK, so he'd play the game a little longer.

"We would also like to present you with this, Your Highness."

Not very good actors, Donald thought, as the man bent to retrieve something from a briefcase. Your Majesty, Your Highness. Get it right. "It's the notification of a deposit account in the Bank of England."

"Money? Now we're talking."

"In 1945 it was worth…"

"1945?" scoffed Donald. He guffawed. Cynthia appeared in the doorway.

"What on earth's going on?" she said with a look of concern.

"This your idea?"

"At today's value, Your Majesty, it would be worth…" Horst tapped some numbers into his phone "…in the region of three hundred and forty-two million, eight hundred and ninety one. Pounds sterling."

There was a deathly silence. This was certainly elaborate, thought Donald. He wondered where it was leading.

"In gold," continued Horst hopefully.

"I see. Well, thank you very much gentlemen for coming. I must say I've been considering for some time an invasion to claim my birthright.."

"You have?"

"Oh yes. In fact coincidentally I am on the point of launching a pre-emptive strike any day now under the intrepid leadership of Roddy Fraser, alias Christopher Wainwright." He chuckled. The whole office had now gathered round and were watching the scene with amazement. He was determined to give them a good run for their money.

"You mean you're not Roderick Fraser?" Horst developed a kind of panicked facial tic that didn't fail to impress Donald. Perhaps they were not so badly rehearsed after all.

"Oh no. Rod, lucky fellow, is at this precise moment…" He glanced at his watch, and smirked for the benefit of his audience, "…marshalling his shock troops in Vienna, and in the next few days will take the…er… Republic of Ruritania by storm."

He looked around his staff, beaming. Each thought it might be some funny act organised by one of the others. They burst into a spontaneous round of applause. Donald bowed.

"I beg you to reconsider!" cried Horst.

Donald returned to him, his face hardening. God, how long was he expected to go on? They had work to do.

"Please! I beg you, your…" Horst stumbled. "There's no need for such drastic measures!" He was twirling his moustache furiously. Unwise, thought Donald, it would be bound to peel off. "In the absence of His Majesty I'd like to present you with something for him."

He fumbled with a large pink box that Donald hadn't noticed. Aha, the piece de resistance. He glanced at Cynthia.

"One of you better own up to this…"

"The Order of the Rose, which by command of the President I hereby confer…"

"Get away from me with that hideous thing!" hissed Donald. This was going a bit far. "Oh I get it. A play on me as the dictator, right? Cyn?"

But Cynthia was helpless, her shoulders heaving in uncontrollable mirth, relieved that it was nothing more than a practical joke. Besides, it was the most vulgar thing she'd seen in her whole life.

"OK, fun's over," said Donald. "Off you go now. Scram." He propelled Horst and his team towards the door. "Give it to Cynthia," he added, referring to the monstrosity, "and we'll hang it in the toilet."

"But you don't understand…!"

"Please, enough's enough. Fuck off." He shut the door on them and watched them through the glass protest all the way to the stairwell. Shortly Cynthia returned, her cheeks stained with tears.

"My God," she said, "what was all that about?"

Donald shrugged. "Bloody silly prank if you ask me." He eyed her. "Sure it wasn't you?"

"Swear to God."

"Must have been someone in the office. What did you do with that thing?"

"They took it away."

"Thank God for that. Must have been a prop."

"Must have."

The phone rang and Donald picked it up.

"Yep?"

He listened then held it out for Cynthia.

"For you, and speak of the devil. It's young Roderick Fraser himself."

She bared her expensive teeth. "Already?"

Chapter 18

Cuckoo

"But he's never been to Vienna before!" protested Christopher, eyeing his driver, Michael, in the idling coach through the window of the cafe he'd gone into to ask directions. Michael seemed to be in animated conversation with a couple of the group seated in the front of the bus, and roaring with laughter.

A row of expectant faces peered down at him as he stared back, his phone clamped to his ear. "We're supposed to be following Roger to some cuckoo clock shop on the way to our folklore dinner, but he's shot off ahead, and my driver is going round in circles. Can't you get me a replacement?"

Christopher listened as Cynthia spelt out to him why Michael - a TravelCo regular, apparently - had to stay.

"OK, OK," he muttered, the sweat trickling down his shirt, "just make sure when we get to this godforsaken country he understands where we are going. Can you have a word with him? What's that? Sat nav?"

He told her that the Sat Nav on his phone had been sending them in the wrong direction.

"Well get a taxi, then," snapped Cynthia impatiently. "Now if you don't mind…"

Taxis? How was he to get them all in taxis?

He could also hear Cynthia mutter 'idiot' in the background as she explained the process, before she cut him off.

He hurried across the road back to the bus, stopping briefly to scan the area for cabs. There were none in sight. She might have been more sympathetic, he must say. He got the impression she was irritated he'd called about such a trifling matter. Trifling? A driver and a tour manager who didn't have a clue of where they were going? It was a nightmare.

He clambered aboard and gave Michael the 'let's get going' universal hand signal, a kind of sideways chopping motion with the hand in the direction intended.

"OK, boss," grinned Michael, gunning the coach into action. Christopher, grabbing the microphone, was forced to clutch the luggage rack to steady himself as the coach rejoined the traffic.

When he had recovered sufficiently he announced unconvincingly "No problems ladies and gentlemen. We'll be there in a few moments. Just relax and enjoy the ride."

He sat back in his seat and took a series of deep breaths to steady his nerves. It was all going horribly wrong.

IT HAD STARTED AS SOON AS THEY'D LEFT THE AIRPORT perimeter the previous day. Michael had lost his way, quickly confessing that he had never driven in Austria before. Was it so unreasonable for Christopher to assume that the driver would have figured out at least the first, and shortest, leg of the journey, the one to the hotel? When they'd finally arrived, after numerous embarrassing stops to ask directions, all the best rooms had been taken by Roger's group, so Christopher had spent an hour and a half negotiating changes with a highly uncooperative reception staff. One person was terrified of heights, regretfully unable to accept a room anywhere above the third floor; then there was Martha, who got claustrophobia in elevators, so had to have a room with stairwell access; while the football players from Arkansas demanded rooms side by side, and when some of them turned out to be 'matrimonials', with just bolsters to keep them apart, there was a near riot. He had no idea that checking into a hotel could be so complicated. It took two hours and twenty minutes to get them all settled.

Lastly there was a man called Spinelli. He'd been one of the late arrivals. It was unfortunate that his name was the one with the star alongside it on the rooming list - the V.I.P. that Donald had been so concerned about. His problems had started as soon as he walked through the door.

"What d'ya mean they haven't arrived?" Christopher had overheard him yelling at the reception staff, in the middle of his own argument with one of the older guests about the lack of anti-slip bath mats in the bathrooms. "They were supposed to follow on from the plane!"

"What exactly are they sir?"

"Tell the guy if I slip I'm suing."

"She says if she slips she's liable to take it up with a higher authority."

"They're kinda food samples."

"Excuse me, Mr Christopher, I am not understanding you."

"I'm liable? Hell, they're liable!"

"In a chill box."

"May I help, Mr Spinelli?" Christopher gave up on the anti-slip bath mats. If the receptionist had any sense he only needed to take one look at the lady to realise it was not a matter of if, but when.

"Sure can, Chris, I got a problem here. Shipped some food samples over and they ain't arrived from the airport."

"Food samples?" Christopher realised he was on a steep learning curve.

"You got it. They need to be kept chilled, otherwise they will spoil. They're probably held up in some goddam warehouse." He returned to the receptionist and slammed his palm down on the desk. "Get me the airport."

The receptionist raised an eyebrow at Christopher, as if for confirmation.

"You hev told him there is a MacDonalds on Kartnerstrasse, Mr Christopher?"

It suddenly dawned on Christopher. Roger had told him about people like this. Clients who brought their own supplies, and had to have special meals prepared for them at every hotel and restaurant.

"D'you have a problem with the food Mr Spinelli? I mean are you a vegan or coeliac or something?"

"What the hell are you talking about? I'm Eye-talian!" Delving into a pocket he produced a dog-eared business card. *Universal Foods Corp*, it said, *Joey A. Spinelli, Sales Representative*.

CHRISTOPHER SNAPPED OUT OF HIS RECOLLECTION AT THE sight of a taxi at a cab stand.

"Quick, Michael, stop!"

The coach shuddered to a halt and Christopher tumbled down the stairwell. The door opened. Now what? thought twenty-six passengers, following his every move.

Luckily the taxi driver understood English. Yes, he knew where the Mozart Cuckoo Clock Shop was. In the reverse direction. He was a little put out when no one actually got into his cab - until Christopher explained he'd be following in the coach. The cab driver laughed, Michael did a six point turn, and off they went once more. Christopher squinted at his satnav and checked it off against where the taxi driver said they were. The passengers were beginning to get restless.

"This is fun," said Michael cheerfully..

"I'm glad you think so, Mike."

"Michael, please," he said huffily. "I'm never a Mike."

He eyed Michael suspiciously. There was something unusual about him, he didn't look at all like what he'd expect a coach driver to look like. For a start he was slim, dressed in a pair of Stella McCartney jeans and a tight fitting t-shirt with the legend *'You're talking to a real man'* and he had an earring in one year. Least Christopher hoped it was one ear, as the other ear was out of sight.

"Where did you say you were from?"

"Me? Brighton."

"And you are a full time coach driver?"

Michael flung up his arms. "What are you saying?" he cried in a mock screech.

"For fuck's sake keep your hands on the wheel!" hissed Christopher, nervously eyeing the passengers behind him.

"Hey, what's going on?" hollered Mr Finkelburger. "Thought you said you knew where we were going?"

Christopher fumbled for the microphone. "There's been a gas explosion," he improvised. "Up ahead. Traffic is being diverted."

Worried glances ricocheted around the bus. Beside him, he could have sworn Michael was sniggering.

"What kind of a gas explosion?"

"Shouldn't we go back to the hotel?"

"Are we gonna miss the clocks?"

Then something on the map caught his eye. *Krankenhaus*, it said, coming up on the left. Didn't that mean some kind of hospital? And 'kranken' – he dimly recalled his German GSCE exam. Wasn't kranken something to do with psychiatry? He was on firm ground here, given his BA Hons in Philosophy, Psychology and Scientific Thought. Give them background information, Donald had told him. Keep them amused on the bus. He'd asked Roger - what should he talk about? History, art, culture, Roger had replied blithely. But Christopher didn't know any history, art or culture. None that was relevant, at any rate. He'd never even been to Vienna before. His knowledge extended to the Anschluss, Orson Welles as 'The Third Man', and Sacher Torte. That had taken all of ten minutes, and he'd dried up long ago.

Until now: put 'kranken' together with Vienna, and what did you get? Of course! Sigmund Freud. How could he have overlooked it? Here was his chance to salvage some goodwill.

"Now listen up Ladies and Gentlemen," he began, with renewed confidence. "In a few blocks time, on your left hand side…"

Yes, this was good. Made it look as if he knew the city in intimate detail. He slid the map surreptitiously under his briefcase.

"…you'll notice a large hospital complex. This is in fact the…er…the famous psychiatric clinic where one of Vienna's most renowned sons, Sigmund Freud, trained to be a psychoanalyst."

"How old is it?" asked Rosa-Lee, wheezing like a cancerous alligator. She was wedged into one of the front seats, by her own special request, excused Christopher's rotation system both on account of her medical condition as a compulsive chain smoker, which entailed being near the driver's window, and her fear of getting stuck in the aisle. There had already been several complaints.

"How old is what?" asked Christopher, stalling for time. "You mean the hospital?"

"Yeah," she mentholated. "How old?"

It was rapidly approaching. "Well, over a hundred years

old, at least," he guessed, mindful of Donald's cardinal rule for tour directors: never admit you don't know. "Freud studied here at the end of the last century." That much he was certain of.

The hospital hove into view. All eyes shifted to the left to catch a glimpse of where the man for whom sex was the root of everything had spent his formative years. It looked apt, but unlikely. The place was thirty-five stories of glass and steel. Christopher swallowed hard.

"It's just behind the new accident and emergency wing they've built," he improvised for a second time, his throat starting to dry up. "Just to the...er... left. Oh dear, it's hard to make out."

"Accident an' emergency?" queried Jackson, the Angel's manager, sitting six rows back, with incredulity, his gold medallion flashing by the light of the passing neon. "You mean psychiatric accidents and emergencies?"

"Sure. You know, chronic breakdowns, lithium rushes, that sort of thing." He could have gone on, but thought better of it.

"Gee," purred Rosa-Lee mintily, her eyes wandering up the thirty-five stories. Lithium rushes? She'd only been in Europe twenty-four hours, but already she could see why.

By the time they finally arrived at the Mozart Glockenspielhaus, Roger's coach was preparing to pull out. He hurried over as Christopher's group spilled out into the forecourt.

"What took you so long?"

"You raced on ahead, remember? Michael couldn't keep up."

Roger laughed grimly. "Ah yes, well, you'll get used to that. If I ever get Michael listed on the tour documentation as the coach driver, I refuse the gig. Nice bloke, hopeless driver. No idea why Cynthia sticks with him." He sniffed. "Though the clients seem to like him."

"So where is the restaurant?" said Christopher.

"Top of the hill."

"So we'll follow you."

Roger looked surprised.

"And miss the cuckoo clocks?"

"What's the big deal? Can't they pick some up tomorrow at the airport?"

Roger rolled his eyes. "Are you insane? Do you want your passengers running around Vienna buying up merchandise in any old store?"

"I don't see why not."

Roger sighed. "You really don't have a clue, do you? Go and see Bertrand the manager, he'll sort you out."

"You mean a souvenir? A sodding cuckoo clock? No thanks."

"Give 'em twenty minutes," said Roger. He put his hand up to his mouth, adding confidentially: "And screw the folklore, it's a pile of piss." He scurried off.

"Thanks for the advice," Christopher called after him, not without a hint of sarcasm. He walked disconsolately into the store. The place was a madhouse, a hundred cuckoos chiming simultaneously, in a variety of keys. And then he saw why, as an irate shop assistant chased one of the Angels out of the shop - they'd been setting them off and winding them up.

Elsewhere sales people were bent over calculators as other passengers were faced with the hardest decision of the day - with or without snow?

After ten minutes he started to hurry them along.

"OK, onto the coach everybody. Dinner is waiting."

Nobody paid him the slightest attention. Cash was counted, credit cards flashed. Eventually he had to shout.

"OK, everybody out! Back on the coach, campers!"

Mrs Finkelburger bustled up to him anxiously.

"Oh Chris, I don't know, I really don't, what d'you think, d'you think it's expensive?" She held out a clock where the place of the cuckoos had been taken by a couple in Alpine costumes wielding hammers. She wound it up for him to see, and every third stroke the man's hammer missed the bell and struck Helga in the stomach.

"Don't you think it's doll?" she mewed. "But Henry says we'll find it cheaper at the airport, what d'you think?"

Clever old Henry, thought Christopher. They were allies on this one.

"Definitely," he said, propelling her toward the door. At this rate they'd miss dinner as well. "Your husband's absolutely right. Shall I take it back for you?"

"Well...I.."

Reluctantly she relinquished the aberrant clock and Christopher stuffed it back on a shelf. As he did so he noticed the price tag - 940 euros. Jesus, for this junk? He hurried out, barely acknowledging the staff, and bustled them onto the coach. He was about to board himself when a hand tapped him lightly on the elbow.

"You forgot to collect this," said a voice in a thick German accent, stuffing an envelope into Christopher's top pocket. He turned, but the figure was already hurrying back into the shop.

Christopher opened it. Inside were eight fifty euro notes, and four twenties, and a scrap of paper which read: *'Welcome to Mozart Glockenspielhaus, we hope you will return soon. Total spend: 3200 Euros. Your commission: 480 Euros (15%). Have a good trip!'*

He hesitated for a split second. Then he bounded up the steps of the coach and along the aisle, barely aware of the muffled chimes that were now emanating from the luggage racks.

"Mrs Finkelburger?" he yelped breathlessly. "I've just been informed that it's the last model of that type in the entire country. I should get it if I were you. If you're quick, we'll wait."

"Really?" exclaimed Mrs Finkelburger, her eyes suddenly lighting up and darting from Christopher to her husband and back to Christopher again.

"That's perfectly sweet of you. Hear that Henry?" She returned to Christopher. "D'you really think so?"

"Yes. It's very reasonably priced." He smiled. For the first time on the trip it was easy, relaxed, natural: the smile of the tour director. "*Ab-so-lute-ly*, Mrs Finkelburger. You can take it from me."

Chapter 19

Pre emptive

"He said *that?*"

Blicker puffed nervously on a cigarette while Horst twiddled with his moustache.

"His exact words. Pre-emptive, from Vienna."

"Don't be ridiculous," snapped Boris. "that's absurd. This is the twenty-first century, not 1939."

"So why would I make up such a fantastic story?" cried Horst.

"You said it, Horst. Fantastic." He paused. "Besides, if they were, why would they tell you?" Blicker leant back in his chair. "Yes, I'm afraid Boris has got a point there. It does seem odd, don't you think?"

"Look," bridled Horst, "I'm just reporting what the man said. Pre-emptive strike from Vienna was what he told me. With shock troops. Swear to God. Besides, have you forgotten Ukraine?"

They were silent for a moment.

"But still," said Boris eventually. "Shock troops, really? It's got to be a piss-take, pure and simple."

Horst tossed his head. "Hey, how the heck should I know

what they meant? I listened, I wrote it down. I suggest Johann should be the judge of that."

There was another short silence while Blicker contemplated the glowing tip of his cigarette. A small nugget of ash dropped in his lap. He brushed it off hurriedly and looked up.

"It does seem a little...unlikely."

He rose and went to the window. The streets were quiet, the rooftops of the Capital shimmering in the midday sun. A feeling of somnolence blanketed the whole city. Pre-emptive strike? Could the Russians be mixed up in it? He swivelled round.

"Nevertheless, just to be on the safe side, perhaps we should ask the border guards to keep a look out for any...unusual activity."

"Fat lot of good it'll do against tanks," sniffed Horst.

"Fat lot of good we CAN do against tanks, if you want to know the truth." He turned to Boris. "Is our UN application finalised yet?"

"No idea, you better ask the Foreign Minister. But I still say the whole idea's nuts."

"Mmm." Blicker took the last drag of his Camel and stuffed it out. Then he walked towards the connecting door into his outer office. "What did you say Fraser's alias was supposed to be, Horst?"

"Christopher Wainwright. And I'll tell you something else. Mr President," said his art director, rising to follow him. "I'd like to put on record here and now my...my unhappiness with Boris's attitude and my...my concern for the welfare of our country. I would also like to point out…"

"Horst," interrupted Boris. "You're our art director, are you not? You are not even in the Cabinet."

"And you are the Minister of Economics, Boris," snapped

back Horst, "so I suggest you stick to organic agriculture and then the damage might at least be limited."

"Please, gentlemen!" Blicker's hand hesitated on the door knob. "This is getting us nowhere. We have heard what you have to say, Horst. I thank you for your mission."

He opened the door and beckoned to his assistant. "Make a note of the name Christopher Wainwright, will you? Anyone who enters this country by that name I want to hear about. Or Fraser for that matter."

He returned to his desk.

"But invasion or no invasion - and even if we assume for the time being not - we're still left with the problem of the succession."

"And the gold."

"And the gold." He fired up another Camel. "The fact is, Horst, you weren't actually talking to Fraser in person."

"But I thought I was."

"I know you thought you were," he said patiently, "but the fact of the matter is that it turned out you weren't, hence the man's not unnaturally flippant reaction. What would you do if someone offered you the throne of a country you didn't believe existed?"

"I'd accept."

"You can't be both King and Queen, my dear Horst."

"Oh, ha ha, Boris."

Blicker sighed. "The point is, until we find the real Roderick Fraser, in person, we won't know what the chances of him accepting are. I vote that we try again." He looked from one to the other. "Question is, where is he?"

"At the head of a column of tanks?"

"Thank you Horst," said Blicker wearily. "I think that will be all for now."

Chapter 20

Escape

They eased the window open gently, trying not to make a noise. Rosie climbed out onto the fire escape and beckoned for her friend to follow.

"Why you need me along I really don't..."

"*Ssh*," hissed Rosie, hurriedly shouldering a small canvas bag. She was dressed for practicality - on her legs a pair of tight, faded black jeans and sneakers. Above, a T-shirt with a short, waisted black jacket. Her hair was scraped back into a ponytail. She looked across the rooftops. The moon was up, casting long, silent shadows. A romantic time for an escape in any other circumstance.

They tip-toed down the hard metal steps until they reached the yard at the back. It was enclosed by a high wall, on the top of which was embedded a line of broken glass. A single wooden door led through the wall to the street at the back. Rosie rattled it. "Shit!"

"What's the matter?" said Sophie nervously.

"It's locked."

"That's it then, you can't possibly..."

"I'll have to go over the top!" Rosie threw down her bag

and dug her foot into a hole made by a loose brick. "Give me a leg up, will you?"

"What are you doing? How are you going to get over that? It's broken glass for goodness sake! You'll rip your jeans!"

Rosie turned angrily. "Hey, what is the matter with you? This was your idea, or have you forgotten?"

"Not like this. Not at night. Couldn't you have waited?"

"I already told you, Sophie, I need your help. I can't do this on my own." Her eyes glittered in the darkness. "All you have to do is close the window and leave tomorrow morning as if nothing has happened. Is that too much to ask?"

Sophie looked sulky.

"I need them to think I'm still in there," continued Rosie.

"And when they discover you're not? Who are they going to come running to? Moi!"

"Listen," she snapped. "It's too late for second thoughts now. Help me over." With a sigh, Sophie reluctantly gave a hand.

"Not like that. Clasp them together!" Rosie showed her friend what to do, then lifted her leg to test her weight. Sophie staggered, but was just able to hold her. Rosie took a deep breath and launched herself up onto the wall and over the other side. There was a thud, followed by a muffled exclamation.

"You OK?" whispered Sophie.

But in all probability Rosie couldn't hear her. For the next thing Sophie heard was her light footfall across the street, and then the whistle, as arranged. Then she was gone.

Chapter 21

Inbound from Vienna

Eighteen hours later some last rays of sunshine were clipping the tree-tops as a lone motorcycle messenger wound his lazy way along the approach road to Zenda airport. His destination? An immigration officer in a single two-storey building that served for both arrivals and departures. Zenda had, up till now, been one of the sleepier backwaters on the international travel map. Inside, the immigration officer in question idly swatted a fly, and watched through the window as workmen put the final touches to the new taxi stand. It was Thursday, time for the twice weekly inbound flight from Vienna. But more than that, today was a special arrival, the one they'd all been waiting for. A clutch of photographers from the local press had gathered outside to catch the arrivals, and an odd rag-tag of assorted boot-polishers and purveyors of snacks snuck around the freshly painted pillars.

The build-up had been going on for months now. It had all started, if the official remembered correctly, with the delegation of Chinese, every one of their passports stamped by him personally in the hastily constructed 'VIP' channel. The local big-wig, the Trade Minister and former Count of Zenda, Rupert Hentzau, had accompanied them, and within weeks the first truckloads of construction materials had begun trundling up the road from the Capital. Few had actually seen inside the Castle, of course, but rumour had it that progress, in just three short months, had been spectacular.

The buzzword on everybody's lips was tourism. Without exception they were all, within a forty mile radius of Zenda, looking forward to the increase in business that was forecast for the area. Whilst trucks had come up from the Capital, buses had gone down, as the sons and daughters of the neighbourhood had rushed to the capital to do crash courses in hospitality, marketing, foreign languages - anything, in fact, to help them make a ruro or two from the hordes of foreign tourists who were expected any day now. And for the people who had stayed behind, for the officials and the public employees, there had been the 'customer success course'. It had been most confusing. It felt like they had only just got over the last transformation, when 'foreign imperialist scum' magically turned into 'incoming foreign friends' when the Autonomous Republic of Khomsova had been born. Now someone had decided they were to be called 'customers'.

But the chat in the staff rooms was that it wasn't quite that simple, was it? The previous influx of business people was one thing - smartly dressed, polite, well-spoken, they seemed happy to exchange their money at the new usurious rates and to pay the exorbitant taxi fares into Zenda. But what about the rising tide of backpackers that followed hot on their heels, like seagulls behind trawlers? Rude, aggressive, haggling over the minutest thing, they had flocked in like a plague of locusts, lighting barbecues, swearing and demanding budget accommodation. This tide, since the White Revolution, had become a flood.

Were they to be 'customers' too?

The immigration officer's reverie was interrupted by the arrival of the motorcyclist. He carried a brown envelope marked: '*Circular: For the attention of Immigration at all Points of Entry.*'

"What's this, more junk mail on the new uniform specifications?" chuckled the official. Recently there'd been a forest of missives coming out of the Interior Ministry about proposed 'presentational' changes.

"Could be," yawned the messenger, depositing the envelope on the counter.

"So what's up? Not in yet?"

The official shook his head and stared gloomily across the runway. Then something caught his eye. "Wait a minute."

A small dot was materialising out of the heat haze. The inbound from Vienna! Bearer, so they had been told, of the first of the eagerly awaited third species of customer: the package tourist.

"That's them alright!" he said excitedly. He clambered out of his booth and raced across the smooth tiled floor.

"*Vienna's here!*" he yammered to his colleagues the customs officials, then hurried on to warn the bank teller and the new kid on the block - the purveyor of smoothies, who'd done a roaring trade with the backpack brigade using out-of-date fruit at cut-price rates.

On the way past the taxi stand he noticed a brand new coach blocking the cargo bay. There was a man in the driving seat wearing a pair of Prada sunglasses.

He rapped on the door. "Hey, you can't park here," he yelled. "Move on!"

"You what?" said the driver, in English, as he clearly did not understand Ruritanian. It was Michael, who had driven ahead from Vienna with the suitcases through some of the most challenging mountain roads he had ever encountered. It had taken him two days. The group had had a day off in Vienna before catching up by plane.

The official gave up.

Chapter 22

The Tourism Ambassador

Rose Elphberg sat well back in the shade of a tree and adjusted the scarf around her neck. It had been a busy eighteen hours. The girl - Maria, Sophie's friend - had been most accommodating. No one, least of all her, had wanted the gig as 'tourism ambassador', and she'd only been too pleased to hand it over, especially since Rosie had agreed to let her keep half the fee. The problem was, her office was not to know, so when it was finished Rosie had to hand her back all the papers and the girl would report in as if she'd done the assignment. She seemed to think it would work. Who, after all, was better qualified than Rosie, with her degree in History and Cultural Studies and her near perfect English?

As for Rosie, she didn't care. All she wanted was a week out of circulation, time enough for Sophie to keep her side of the bargain, and to give Hentzau the message that she was going to be as obstructive as possible. The combination of the two *should* be enough to make him think again.

All she hoped was that he wouldn't take it out on her parents. And what better way than to be travelling round the country, staying incognito in hotels, on the road? She almost laughed out loud when she tried to imagine Hentzau's reaction when they couldn't find her. This would be the last place he'd look, hiding in plain sight.

But now, waiting in the shade of the tree, she knew she had to turn her mind to something else. The job at hand. It would only work if she didn't falter. She had to appear confident, otherwise the whole game would be up. For the first time that day she began to feel nervous.

∽

THE PLANE TOUCHED DOWN EXACTLY ONE HOUR LATE. Christopher stepped down onto the tarmac and set off towards the terminal building at a brisk pace, a jangle of nerves himself.

"This is so awesome!" said a voice at his elbow. "It all looks so fairytale."

It was Martha, dressed in a pair of skin-tight leather trousers and a black lycra top. Round her neck was a metal chain, ending in a death's head skull, and she had overdone the mascara. Puffing to keep up with her was Rosa-Lee, who, by the looks of it, couldn't afford to get excited unless she was sitting down. Walking was enough of a physical endurance test without the luxury of emotion. She looked about her dubiously, and said nothing.

"But not for you, right?" Martha stared at Christopher intently. "You've visited here tons of times, correct?"

She's evidently forgotten the literature that had accompanied the brochure, Christopher thought: ground-breaking first-time tour into the '*Land that time forgot*'.

He smiled urbanely. "Well, that's a bit of an exaggeration."

They straggled into the terminal where Christopher halted the group and drew out the Visa List from his briefcase. His heart did another about-turn just seeing it there in print - the last name on the list, at number 27: R. Fraser.

"OK everybody listen up!" he shouted. "To avoid congestion the authorities have requested we go through in visa number order. I..."

"Congestion?" snorted Joey Spinelli. "Place doesn't look like it's had a goddamn visitor in years."

It was true, the place was deserted.

Christopher laughed. "You're right." He was beginning to think that Spinelli was an arsehole. "But nevertheless..."

He explained the system. When they all lined up in their respective positions he led them up to the Immigration desk.

"Good evening," he said to the waiting official who, curiously, seemed to look almost as apprehensive as Christopher felt. "We're from TravelCo and this is the group visa."

"Yes, please, you're welcome, how can I help you?" said the man in a rush. "Name please?"

"Roderick Fraser," he said in as low a voice he could manage without actually having to repeat himself.

"Rod-er-ick Fraser," repeated the official slowly, and loudly, running his finger down the list.

Behind him. Martha said, "I thought your name was..."

"Aagh!" yelled Christopher, suddenly doubling up. "Shit! Ouch! Fuck!"

"What's the matter?"

They were all suddenly there beside him, crowding round, Rosa-Lee, Martha, Mrs Finkelburger, Spinelli, as he bent double.

"It's OK, no problem," he hissed through clenched teeth, grimacing for all he was worth.

"What have you got there?"

"Is it an insect?"

"What's the matter with him?"

"D'you want us to call an ambulance?"

Slowly he straightened up to a sea of concerned faces. "I think it was a wasp."

"A wasp? I didn't hear no buzzin'."

"OK. I see now, number 27," said the official, oblivious to the commotion in front of his desk. He looked up. "You the leader?"

Christopher struggled straight again, nodding lamely.

"OK, you go back of line." He waved him away, beckoning Martha forward.

"First please."

Christopher retreated to the rear, perspiration dripping from his near escape. He found himself next to Joey Spinelli.

"OK buddy?"

"I'm fine thanks," he said. He pulled a face. "A wasp."

"Uh-huh," nodded Spinelli. He dug something out of the inside of his jacket. "Hey, you ever seen one of these before?"

He thrust a small silver package into Christopher's hands. Christopher turned it over absent-mindedly.

"Can't say I have," he said, already imagining how long they would lock him up for travelling on a false passport.

"Guess."

Christopher shrugged. "Looks like an airline meal."

"Not so fast, sonny. We haven't launched yet. It's called a C-CAM."

"A C-CAM?"

"Cook-in-the-Commercial-break-Anywhere-Meal. You know what?"

"No. What?"

Spinelli's voice dropped to a whisper. He looked around confidentially and drew Christopher to one side.

"It's our top secret answer to the Eezy-Cook." They shuffled forward as the line advanced. "A semi-pre- cooked lunch or dinner in 62 varieties programmed to be plugged into an electric socket during one commercial break and whipped out, freshly steaming, during the next; what do you think of that?"

"Impressive," ventured Christopher.

Spinelli did a rapid scan of the concourse then leant right into Christopher's lapel.

"It's gonna be dynamite buddy," he hissed. "Certified effing dynamite. We can produce it twenty percent cheaper for the Ruritonia market on account of them not having no environmental packaging laws on the statute book yet. So long as they don't try to eat the friggin' packaging," he guffawed.

Christopher suddenly remembered what the man was talking about. His samples had clearly arrived.

"Your package turned up?"

"You're kidding! They only flew into Vienna this morning. I told the freight people to forward them on here by special courier. I gave them your name, Chris, so if they call you…"

"You what?"

"Is that a problem?"

"Spinelli!" called out the immigration officer.

"You're on!" hissed Christopher, propelling Spinelli forward.

"*Spin-elli*," repeated the official slowly, flicking through Spinelli's passport. He seemed to take an inordinate time examining every detail, and with each second that passed Christopher's heart seemed to reach higher up into his throat, until he had to breath consciously to steady himself. Finally the official snapped it shut and made a light tick on the list. He looked up.

"Fraser?"

Christopher shuffled forward.

"Ah, tail end Charlie, no?" grinned the official.

Christopher smiled weakly.

The man waved him on.

"Is that all?" said Christopher, incredulous.

The Spare and The Heir

"You important man. We no delay you." He smiled, remembering the script in the manual. "Have a nice day."

Christopher walked through the barrier unsteadily, blinking in the light.

"Mr Fraser?" said a voice.

Christopher didn't react at first. He was so relieved at having got through immigration unscathed that he'd forgotten all about his new persona.

"Mr Roderick Fraser?" said the voice more forcefully.

He stopped, his heart once again skipping a beat. So this was it: handcuffs, special police, imprisonment without trial. He turned around slowly.

His mouth gaped open, involuntarily. It was her. The girl he'd glimpsed so briefly a few days before at Vienna Airport, the trolley in the night, the dark hair, the cornflower blue eyes, the skin the texture of peaches. Could it be? Was it? He peered at her.

"Are you talking to me?"

She too seemed put out. She stammered: "You are... Roderick Fraser?"

And yet there was something subtly different about her. He inspected her more closely. It was her clothes. In Vienna she'd looked like she'd stepped out of a Chanel advertisement. Here she was dressed in a pair of faded black jeans and a white T-shirt, with a white and yellow scarf tied loosely around her neck, the only thing that looked even vaguely like a uniform.

Noticing his unease, she seemed to regain her poise. She advanced towards him and stuck out her hand.

"Well," she laughed, wisps of hair tumbling untidily down about her ears. "You don't seem too sure. In that case I shall assume you are. My name is ... ah... Maria." She smiled awkwardly. "I am your tourism ambassador. To accompany you to the Capital."

He shook himself. Was it his imagination, or had her eyes revealed a flicker of recognition?

"Phew!" he exclaimed. "I mean Hi! I'm very pleased to meet you Maria. By the way," he touched her hand, every ounce of him fighting a sudden, mad impulse to hug her, "everybody calls me Christopher."

Their hands held on for a fraction longer than they might have done. She stared at him. "Christopher?"

"Yes. My middle name."

She retrieved her hand while his own flopped down by his side. There was no mistake this time, thought Christopher. There had been a definite frisson in that handshake.

"OK," she said. "Thank goodness for that, because everyone calls *me* Rosie."

"Is that so?" Just as well, he thought. He'd once had a disastrous affair with a girl called Maria. He dragged his eyes away from her to look around for the coach.

"Is my driver here?" he ventured.

"Yes, over there." She nodded. "Do you have all your hand luggage?"

There was a faint chime in the distance.

"Cuckoo..."

"Apparently so," said Christopher, laughing. She giggled. It was like the crackle of broken ice.

Chapter 23

Alarm!

The Immigration official watched them go with incredulity. That was a package tour? He returned to his booth and prepared to tidy up for the day, stacking the immigration cards neatly for forwarding to the Ministry. He found the messenger in the coffee bar.

"That's your lot. All there. Sorry it took so long."

"Thanks. See you tomorrow then," said the messenger, downing his coffee. He donned his helmet, eager to get back. The official wandered back to his booth. Where he noticed, hidden under a pile of papers, the brown envelope the messenger had brought, unopened.

Unpeeling it, this is what he read:

DEPARTMENT OF THE INTERIOR. URGENT. Re: RODERICK FRASER, male: c. 30 years old. UK citizen. Please notify immediately if seen. Could be travelling under the name of CHRISTOPHER WAINWRIGHT.

The official stared at it for a second, in shock. Then raced for the door.

∼

"What?!" shouted Blicker down the phone.

It was late the same night. Midnight oil was about to burn at the Palace.

"Are you sure? One hundred percent?" He listened intently. "Right, sit tight."

There was a pause. "I said sit tight!" he shouted a second time. His assistant started. Blicker hung up. He looked stunned.

"Mr...President?" she said, a look of alarm on her face.

Blicker stared at her blankly for a second, then picked up the telephone a second time.

Chapter 24

A Decision

The helicopter flew low over the sea, skimming the waves, and banked sharply to the right. On the horizon orange was gradually turning to yellow as the sun rose over the eastern Adriatic.

Strapped in and dreaming of breakfast, the VIP passenger yawned silently. Lougouev's peremptory summons the night before had considerably rattled Hentzau. Who the hell did he think he was, this food magnate, talking to a Minister of a sovereign nation like that? And at six hours notice. But Hentzau knew, unhappily, that he was in no position to argue. He had little choice but to go. To refuse would be to bring instant retribution, and exposure.

Lougouev's pilot had picked him up at dawn. Whither, he knew not. He suspected Bratislava, since Lougouev had been doing business there with the Slovaks, developing a revolutionary type of combo-ration for their military. But the helicopter had taken him in a quite different direction: south-west.

As they crossed the Adriatic coast of Albania, he had tried once again to elicit from the monosyllabic pilot the exact position of their final destination. At which point the pilot had at last replied with one word Hentzau could understand: 'Yacht.' But what he now found himself approaching was certainly no yacht as he understood it. There was not a sail or a mast in sight. Just a string of burnished gold lettering along the massive white superstructure which said, simply, 'Kira, Hamilton, Bermuda.'

The sea was whipped up into a frenzy as the pilot put the machine down a hundred yards from the anchored vessel. It sank on its floats like a dog on its haunches as a launch was dispatched to fetch its distinguished occupant. The President of Globalny Foods was below decks in his gym when Hentzau boarded. He was a fit looking man, dark haired with light stubble and early forties, Hentzau guessed, dressed in shorts, a tropical shirt and flip-flops. The crew padded silently around in immaculate white uniforms and plimsolls, mixing juices.

"Welcome aboard, Minister," he purred, pausing only briefly on his cycle machine to clasp Hentzau's hand. "Sorry to hev you come all this way but, well, I thought it was good we meet together. Face to face. Because," he added, in a more serious undertone, breathing hard as he hit a hill, "we hev some serious discussions we need to hev."

Hentzau sat down, accepting a mango and carrot vitamin reviver from one of the staff, as Lougouev outlined his concerns. It was a humiliating experience for his guest: he seemed to know far more about what the Government of National Reconstruction was up to than Hentzau did. It appeared that someone from high up in that Administration had been conducting some kind of secret negotiations with a company in London called TravelCo. Lougouev knew this, because coincidentally he'd been watching the company on a quite separate matter.

"You see, Hentzau, they hev been commissioned to run

some tourist group into your territory. And do you know who has commissioned them?"

Hentzau had a feeling he was going to be told.

"Our competitor in the USA, Universal Foods. Their aims are two." Lougouev came to the wind-down plateau at the end of his programme and increased his speed to 100 rpm. His thighs span round in a blur and sweat beads broke out on his face. Hentzau had to strain to hear what he was saying. Luckily Lougouev raised his voice.

"One. A representative of Universal is secretly joined to the trip as tourist, with instructions to avoid your Government's import controls and introduce their product into your country by back door. Two. Travelling with him, and also under contract to Universal, is a football team called Arkansas Angels. Now I hev no intelligence as to what their strategy might be in this case. All I know is that they hev organised games over there."

"Our soccer teams are rather good actually," said Hentzau proudly.

"Who said anything about soccer? They are American football team."

The programme ended, and Lougouev stepped lightly off the cycle machine and flexed his muscles, before jumping down to the deck and performing a series of rapid press ups. After the last one he jumped up and inhaled loudly.

"But what is bother me," he said, slumping down into an easy chair and cracking open a bottle of beer. He proffered one to Hentzau, who declined. "What is bother me, is a visit that a functionary from your Government paid to TravelCo's offices several days ago. My associate tells me that bribes were involved." He eye-balled Hentzau menacingly. "Bank credits. Jewellery."

Hentzau wandered over to the door that led on deck. The stench of sweat was overpowering.

"But I don't understand, Yuri," he said, inhaling the salt air. "If, as you say, they are trying to circumvent government controls…"

"Hev heard of man called Boris?"

"The Minister of Economics?"

"That is the guy. He is the one who put them in place…"

"Well I know that."

"…but it appears that there is another group that wants to get around them. They are led by guy called Horst."

"Horst?" A laugh escaped before he could stop it. "Why, that's impossible! The man's just a art director."

"So maybe he is working for someone else? Who cares what fuck he is. Fact is that they are plotting to get their C-CAMs into your country, big time."

"C-CAMs?"

He was getting increasingly confused. They sounded like an intercontinental ballistic missile. It seemed to fit. The man was paranoid.

"Do not you worry yourself about the C-CAM," retorted Lougouev. Hentzau gritted his teeth once again in the face of this loathsome familiarity. "They are nothing. They are shit." He almost spat the words out. "Which is why they must be stopped."

"But I don't get it," puzzled Hentzau. "It's so out of character. Horst's more hard-white than off-white. He has no interest…"

Lougouev jumped up from his chair. "Off-white? Hard-white? What is the meaning?"

Hentzau patiently tried to explain the labyrinthine complexities of politics in the new Ruritania.

"It is plain to me," said Lougouev, lowering his voice, "that you do not know anything about what is going on in your own house. Your government is full of cliques, they are all fighting, and I am telling you, none of these yellow-whites, lilly-whites, peachy-fuck-creamy-whites is working in my advantage. It is now time for you to organise a new government more favourable to us in Moscow."

At least he was honest, thought Hentzau. He had always known that in the end, for the Russians, this was not about a commercial deal at all. Globalny was incidental. The food and the TV series were just the first salvo in a cultural war to win Ruritania back into Moscow's orbit. Who Lougouev was taking orders from, he shuddered to think, and he had no desire to find out. However, who was he to look a gift horse in the mouth? He had no idea what a C-CAM was, but clearly the Russian was opposed to them, would do anything to stop them. So he outlined his monarchy plan, and explained about Andrew and Rose's forthcoming marriage the following month. Lougouev's eyes lit up.

"Why, this is fan*tas*tic!" he roared, drawing out the word. "Fan*tas*tic! I like it! The people will like it! This will be good for business! TV-Eezy-Cook, By Appointment! Why you not get them married sooner? When can we get her coronated?"

Hentzau explained that it wasn't quite as simple as that. She couldn't simply be proclaimed. The people had to clamour for her, and then the Government had to ask her. This was the way it was done in his country, ever since the days when it was the Kingdom of Elphberg. He explained about the roses.

"We need hundreds of thousands of them, you see, Yuri. The yellow rose, we call it the Elphberg rose, is the symbol of royalty in Ruritania. It's the customary way to proclaim a new monarch. He or she is traditionally called to the throne by the people who all come out on the streets with yellow roses and proclaim the new monarch's ascendancy. All our rose beds were destroyed by the..er...communists in 1945 and we've only recently planted them again. It's a slow process, you understand, and we don't expect a full crop till at least next year. We've got agitators on standby in every town and village, but no roses. I was thinking I was going to have to use carnations. However, Yuri, if you were able…"

Yuri agreed. He'd supply as many roses as Hentzau liked, but on one condition - that the couple were married as quickly as possible, and that the agitation began immediately. For all his faults, Hentzau had to admire that about Yuri: he didn't hang about.

As soon as he was back on dry land he called his Chief of Staff and his son to arrange a summit meeting.

"And this time I want Rose along," he told Andrew. "She's got to start playing her part."

"But I've no idea where she is," complained his son. "She seems to have…disappeared."

"Then find her!" roared Hentzau. It was time to get serious.

Chapter 25

Continental with Juice

It was with a delicious feeling of wellbeing, and anticipation, that Christopher awoke the next morning in an absurdly big bed in the Hotel Tarlenheim. Bright sunshine streamed through his curtains. He leapt out and gazed dreamily out of the window. Far below in the valley a cluster of clapboard houses with steep alpine roofs huddled around a small river, while halfway up the far side he could just make out the crenellations of a castle in the early morning mist. Beyond, the snow-capped peaks of the Helsing Range soared heavenward in all their breathtaking magnificence.

Zenda! Christopher wrapped himself in his dressing gown and shuffled into the bathroom. As he stood under the shower he re-ran the previous evening in his head. She had been wonderful company. They'd laughed and talked and joked until the early hours, and when he'd finally got to bed at one o'clock it was in the firm knowledge that his problems were over. For Rosie was their tourism ambassador, which meant that from now on all he had to do, it seemed to him, was to sit back and enjoy the ride. She would do the guiding. She would answer the questions. Above all, she would ensure he got his commission from all the various tourist outlets they were scheduled to visit. If the Glockenspielhaus in Vienna was anything to go by, he'd exceed his target comfortably.

She was also intoxicating, with her fine, dark hair and teasing blue eyes.

He tried to imagine what it was he might represent to her. It was all too easy - and gratifying. How long had Ruritania been independent now? Nine months? She couldn't have had time to meet many men from the West; theirs was, after all, only the first package tour into the country. He let the steaming shower wash over him, scrubbing his chest vigorously. No doubt she would be eager to sample all the material comforts and limitless horizons that would become available with the opening up of her country. For it was inconceivable that now, given the opportunity, she wouldn't want to get out, to better herself. And he, Christopher Wainwright, could be the conduit. Why not?

But a disturbing thought struck him. What had she been doing in Vienna? And what's more, dressed up so stylishly? Was she, then, already spoken for by one of those oligarchs he had read about?

He climbed out of the shower, towelled himself down and checked his phone for messages. There were two. The first was from his little brother Max. It said, simply, *"Hope you're having a great time!"* He smiled. The second was from a number in Liverpool. *"Please transfer the funds as agreed to a/c number XXXX, sort code XXXX no later than XXX."* It no longer gave him the jolt to the stomach of the last few weeks.

He locked the door of his room and went down to breakfast. On his way he met Bob Hershey.

"Morning Chris, I'm sorry to bother you with a problem this early, I expect you'd prefer to have your breakfast first, hey?"

Damn right he would, thought Christopher. But you're

going to bother me anyway. Nevertheless he let it wash over him. He had a good feeling this morning.

"Not at all, Mr Hershey, what can I do for you?"

"My massage pillow won't work and every time I use my hair dryer the room lights go out."

"What time was this?"

Christopher had noticed his own bedroom light flicker on and off at irregular intervals while he was dressing.

"Just now."

So that explained it.

"Hey Chris!" A head poked out of a door along the corridor. It was an Angel.

"The electrics keep going."

"I know," said Christopher patiently, "I'm on it." He returned his attention to Bob Hershey and, smiling, shrugged. "That's the Balkans for you."

"But can't you do something about it?"

"Ruritania's still a developing country, Bob. We are the first tour in, remember?" He wanted to say that with hairdryers nowadays more like tanks than domestic appliances, what did he expect? "But I'll notify Rosie," he added, stepping into the elevator. It felt so great to say it.

Downstairs he walked at a leisurely pace into the dining room, mentally practising his smile and a "hi, mind if I join you?" when he caught sight of her at a far table. He felt his stomach tingle. He resisted the urge to bolt straight over, and wandered to the cereal counter instead, where he found Rosa-Lee weighing small piles of cereal on miniature scales and tapping some numbers into her phone.

"Hi Chris, this is not much of a breakfast. Watery juice, this weird cereal and no eggs."

"It's a continental breakfast, Rosa-Lee, though I'm sure you can order eggs as an extra." A soft beeping sound went off on her phone.

"You think these are like Sugar Puffs? This stuff isn't listed in my calorie app."

He picked up a packet and peered at the label. 'Roochi-Pops,' it said, but with no list of ingredients.

"I'm sure you're right, Rosa-Lee. I wouldn't know. I'd love to join you, but I've got business to go through with Rosie. See you in the lobby at 9.30?"

He sauntered over to the far end of the room.

"Hi, mind if I join you?"

She looked up and smiled. "Hi!" It was a warm smile, with a hint of shyness.

He sat down and chewed a nugget of cereal. It was not at all like a Sugar Puff. She watched him. "Sleep well?"

"Fine. And you?"

"Fine."

"What's…" "I…" they began simultaneously, and both laughed.

"I'm sorry," she said, "you first."

For the first time he noticed the freckles on her nose - it was small and perfectly formed, without a hint of make-up. "Well…OK. What I was going to say was… what's on the programme for today?"

Her eyes twinkled at him, with the hint of a tease.

"Oh, so you've forgotten already?" She cocked her head, mock offended.

He felt himself blushing. "My mind's gone blank. It happens every morning."

She smiled, brushing a stray wisp of hair away. "I know the feeling."

He wondered if she did. She looked the picture of fresh-faced efficiency.

"So first we'll visit the provincial museum, then we go to Zenda Castle. Or I mean you do. It's just as well you asked me, because I forgot to tell you. I'm afraid I won't be coming with you into the Castle."

"Oh? Why not?"

She hesitated briefly.

"A... castle guide who will show you round. I must return to the hotel."

"I see. And then they have a free afternoon, is that right?"

"Yes."

"Any suggestions?"

She shrugged. "Perhaps they'd like time for... souvenir shopping?"

He liked the sound of that. "And you'll be here tonight?"

"Of course. Would you like me to organise something for this evening? There's a folklore show in..."

"No!" He said quickly, pulling a face. "Please god, no more folklore!"

He immediately regretted it. She looked offended for real this time. "Oh, but it's fun."

"Sorry, yes, I'm sure it is, I just meant that we had our fill of folklore shows in Vienna. How about we give them a free evening?" Send the children to bed, he chuckled to himself.

"To go with their free afternoon, you mean?"

"Rosie...shopping is tiring. Besides, we've done a hell of a lot in the past few days."

She nodded. "Forgive me. You must be tired after all your travelling."

He leant forward. "Tell me something." He took a sip of his coffee and grimaced. "What's the deal on shopping anyway?"

"The deal?"

"Exactly." He smiled enigmatically.

"I'm not sure what you mean."

"I...er..thought I'd talk to them on the coach a little about what local souvenirs they might be able to buy here. Where in Zenda were you thinking of taking them?"

"Taking them?" she said, surprised. "Why, they take themselves, no?"

Christopher frowned. "Isn't there a souvenir shop somewhere?"

"There is one at the Castle." She glanced down at her itinerary sheet. "I think."

He wondered how he should broach the subject.

"Is it approved?" She looked confused. "I mean," he continued, "don't you normally take them to approved shops?"

"Do we? I don't think so."

He sighed. Evidently she was as green as he was at this business. It was refreshing for once to be the one in the know. A chair scraped back beside him.

"Oh hallo, mind if I join you?"

It was Michael, in a freshly pressed t-shirt with a pair of sunglasses slotted neatly in the collar. Prada, Christopher noticed. There was a faint floral smell about him. Why couldn't he sit somewhere else?

"Of course," smiled Rosie, not in the slightest bit perturbed.

"I just love this country of yours," he beamed between mouthfuls of overnight oats. "Everyone's so fit looking!"

"Thank you," she said appreciatively.

"So, Mike," said Christopher. "Are we all set for today? Got the maps you need? I don't think Sat-Nav works over here."

Michael glared at him, but before he could say anything, Rosie said "Don't worry, I know the way. Just follow me."

There was a sudden commotion outside. They turned to the window. The Angels were spilling out into the hotel car park and were beginning to stretch their limbs. A small crowd of bystanders had gathered to watch.

Christopher noticed Michael stop eating, and a discreet tattoo on his right arm starting to pulse.

Rosie laughed. "What on earth do you think they are doing?"

"God only knows," said Christopher.

HALF AN HOUR LATER THE GROUP WAS ASSEMBLED IN THE lobby, ready for the day's activities. A number of them crowded around Rosie, who was in animated discussion. All they were missing were the Angels. Christopher went out into the car park to round them up, but there was now no sign of them. He returned just in time to find Jackson, the coach, stepping out of an elevator. His sneakered feet squeaked noisily across the polished lobby floor.

"Morning Chris," he said, beaming. "I'd just like to inform you that my boys won't be coming to that Museum this morning. We've got a match to play."

"Oh really?"

"Yeah, arranged it when we got in last night. We'll catch up with you at the Castle."

"In that case you better meet us in the souvenir shop," said Christopher hastily, mindful of a large chunk of his clientele about to slip through his fingers. "It's the only convenient rendezvous point before we go in." He gave Jackson directions and then hurried the rest of the group out to the coach.

He failed to notice the unmarked car with tinted windows idling across the street.

Chapter 26
Footwear

"Mostly Nike," said the man in the passenger seat, squinting through a large telephoto lens. "Although...hang on, check this. Blue uppers with a white stripe and a yellow diamond on the back." Inside, an accomplice flipped through a grimy, well-thumbed catalogue.

"Probably Adidas. No Reeboks?"

"Can't see any," said the first man, auto-focussing on Michael as he started polishing one of his wing mirrors in the afternoon sunshine, checking his appearance as he did so. Then the Angels came whooping around the corner from the far side of the hotel, spilling back into the car park. They were in matching tracksuits, and set off in a quite different direction. With their buzz cuts and square jaws they looked like a squad of marines.

"Christ," exclaimed the driver, leaning across his friend to get a better look.

The lens swung round. There was a sharp intake of breath. The camera whirred.

"What do you think they are?"

Eyes narrowed. "American special forces," his partner said

gravely, with the air of a man who knows what he's talking about. "They were working out in the car-park this morning. No doubt about it."

"Oh my God!" exclaimed his colleague excitedly. "Their feet! Take a look at their footwear! Have you ever seen anything like it?"

Chapter 27

Return to Zenda

"OK everybody, listen up," said Christopher into the microphone.

Now he was settling into the tour, and mindful of the remoteness of ever meeting another tour manager in this part of the world, this morning he'd decided to discard his blazer, badge and tie, and was wearing his old leather jacket instead. Luckily he'd packed it on the off-chance. It was an old friend, and he felt in dire need of one.

"I hope you all enjoyed the museum. I think you'll agree, our wonderful guide Rosie gave us all an excellent tour?"

"Whoop whoop!" yelled Michael, into his rear view mirror.

The coach erupted into a bout of clapping.

Beside him, Rosie coloured modestly.

"Now, as she mentioned earlier, our next visit is one of the highlights of the trip, the world famous Zenda Castle, the place King Rudolf was imprisoned by Black Michael."

"My namesake!" yelled Michael again.

"Indeed," continued Christopher through gritted teeth. "And unfortunately Rosie can't be with us in the Castle, but there will be a Castle guide to show us around. But before we get there I'd like to say a word or two to you about something else." He cast a sideways glance at Rosie, but she was looking out of the window, a far away look in her eyes. "A few quick words about the other major reason - apart from the culture - that you've all come to Europe."

Twenty eager faces beamed up at him. None more so than Martha's.

"Shopping!" he boomed.

"Yes!" cried Michael. He wished to God he'd shut up and focus on driving.

"Yes, shopping, ladies and gentlemen. There'll be plenty of opportunities on this trip for shopping, and wherever possible Rosie and I will point out the best of the local products and souvenirs from each region we will be visiting. Because you must beware, ladies and gentlemen, beware the sharks, the imitations, the rip-off merchants. Leather that will turn out to be cardboard, glassware that shatters as soon as you get home, silk that is in reality rayon."

"Excuse me but not in Ruritania," protested Rosie, laughing. Christopher squeezed her arm, gently but firmly. He continued.

"I'm talking generally of course. But... you can never be too careful." He paused and looked around, to gauge the impression he was making.

"How does one know, you may ask me? Where are the reputable merchants, the people who are insured, who will take your Amex and your Mastercard? The answer is, we will tell you."

"Credit cards?" hissed Rosie. "Christopher, I don't think so, not up here."

He gave her a look, and continued, "that's what we're here for. Everywhere we go, however limited the time, we will make sure you have at least an opportunity to buy some souvenirs, reasonably priced and of good quality, from stores approved by TravelCo, for your loved ones back home."

They all looked most appreciative. "Thank you Chris."

"Appreciate it."

"Thanks a lot."

"Don't mention it. Of course they don't all take credit cards. But if that happens I can always loan you the cash until you can get to a bank."

A bout of clapping erupted. He waved them down imperiously.

"Thank you. I do my best. Now, Rosie has very kindly arranged for us to make a short stop at the Castle souvenir shop before our visit, as apparently it shuts this afternoon."

Cuckoo. A chime echoed faintly from the luggage rack, and Micheal erupted into a fit of giggles.

"IT SMELLS BEAUTIFUL ON YOU, HILDA," SAID CHRISTOPHER encouragingly, fifteen minutes later in the Castle souvenir shop, as Hilda dabbed herself liberally with rosewater. But it was wasted on her, she couldn't hear a thing. He turned to Rosa-Lee. "Don't you think so? Have you tried it?"

"It's a little strong."

"Well it would be, it's highly concentrated. It takes five kilos of roses to make just one millilitre."

She looked impressed. He surveyed the scene. It was a most depressing one. There was almost nothing to buy in the Zenda Castle Souvenir shop. And what there was, cost practically nothing. Fifteen percent of practically nothing would be almost next to nothing. Moreover, the Angels hadn't showed up.

"Ah, Michael," he said, noticing him at a clothes rack. "You too? Shouldn't you be polishing the coach or something?"

"As if! How's this for kitsch?" He held up a T-shirt. Printed on the front, under an elaborate crown, were the words 'I love Zenda'. "They'll just love this back home. I bought four of them."

"Original." Christopher fingered the material. "And so cheap."

He felt sick. His confidence of the morning had evaporated. Behind him he heard a sudden cry.

Joey Spinelli had slumped to a chair in the corner and had gone deathly pale. He hurried over. "Joey? You OK?"

"I don't believe it!" he growled, holding up a silver package. "I don't friggin' believe it!"

"What don't you believe?"

"How the fuck did this get here? Frigo Wonder Chicken Flavour!"

"En-vel-ope," mouthed Christopher to the sales manager. Rosie was nowhere to be seen. Michael had started up the coach and the last of the group were boarding. The sales manager looked bewildered.

"En-vel-ope?"

"Yes, you know, tour director's commission. *Comm-iss-ion.*" He pulled a TravelCo business card out of his wallet and showed it to the man, desperately looking around for Rosie. "TravelCo," he said. "My company. My people spend a lot of money. We can send many tours up here. Souvenir for...me?"

The man turned the card over in his hands. Just then a breathless Rosie appeared at his elbow.

"What's the hold up? Everybody's on board. We have to go."

"Ah, thank God, there you are, explain to the man, will you?"

He looked at her expectantly.

"Explain what? I'm sorry, Christopher, you're not making any sense."

"My envelope," he snapped, exasperated.

Her face cleared.

"Oh I see." She turned to the manager and said something in Ruritanian. Comprehension dawning, he disappeared into a back office, reappearing with an envelope.

Christopher held up two fingers. "Dos," he said, gesturing at Rosie. He could afford to be generous, considering it was likely to be 50% of diddly-squat.

"For me? But I don't.."

"Sssh. You've done a lot of work. You deserve it."

The man returned with a second envelope. Christopher peered inside one, then the other. They were empty.

"But they're empty!"

The manager, for a split second, appeared completely baffled. Then, suddenly, he seemed to realise what was required. He threw up his hands in excited recognition, took the envelopes back, and scuttled into his office. After a minute he returned with the envelopes sealed. They shook hands.

"Thank you," said Christopher, and he hurried with Rosie back out to the bus.

"What was that all about?" she asked.

"Small misunderstanding," he sighed, handing her an envelope. "Nothing to worry about. Thank God you're here to help me, I'm a novice at this sort of thing."

He didn't notice her puzzled look.

Christopher slumped back in his seat and tried to visualise what was inside. Maybe it would surprise him, though somehow he doubted it, the envelope was depressingly slim. He slid his finger under the flap and tore it open. Inside was a single business card, with the name of the manager in English. No sign of a banknote anywhere. Underneath he had scribbled, simply, "*With compliments. In memory of a happy visit. Please come again.*"

He slumped back. It was worse than diddly-squat. It was squat-squat. At this rate, it was game over.

Chapter 28

The Zenda Experience

"And here," Tilly said, as they crossed the drawbridge, "is where the famous Rupert of Zenda, my great great…" she hesitated, unsure of her English, despite the fact she'd practised this introduction a hundred times, "…great…no, two greats alone I think…great great…grandfather, fought a duel with the wicked Scotsman."

She looked around impatiently, as if waiting for something.

"She means that kilted fellow, honey," whispered Mary Finkelburger to her husband. "Rudy Ratzendill."

"Rudolf Ratzendill," corrected Henry Finkelburger grumpily.

"*Ssh!*"

There was a moment of awkward silence.

"Fought a duel with the Englishman…" she repeated, more loudly this time. That seemed to do the trick, for almost immediately, as if on cue, two young boys came charging out of the main gate, brandishing oversize swords. They were both in fancy dress - they could hardly be called costumes. The shorter of the two had red hair and freckles and was kitted out to look like a bad caricature of an English aristocrat, with red wig and deerstalker hat, an incongruous sporran swinging comically between his tartan-trousered legs; while the taller boy was dark and rangy, and dressed up Lord Byron style, circa 1300. Rosa-Lee screamed. Martha looked bored.

"Is this all part of the show?" she whispered.

"It's Sherlock and Watson," sniggered Michael, who'd joined the tour after parking the bus, as the boys' swords started clashing violently.

"That one must be the Duke," began Mary breathlessly to Henry, "while that other one is…"

"Thank you so much," hissed her husband.

The action began to hot up.

"Take this…and this…and this, you blaggard!" shouted the little one. His friend grinned maniacally, parrying each attack with well-practised poise. Several times he was forced up against the edge of the bridge, and each time he managed to parry his way out. Michael tried to place the video they'd been studying. It was a toss-up between *'The Prince and the Showgirl'* and *'Pirates of the Caribbean'*. On the third retreat, the taller one suddenly jumped up on the parapet. Various female passengers gasped.

"Oh dear, I hope he doesn't slip," rasped Mrs Finkelburger, biting her lip.

"Farewell, play actor!" the tall one shouted, brandishing his sword at nothing in particular. "Au revoir!"

He hesitated, glancing nervously over his shoulder down into the chasm below, as if unsure of his next move. Looking up, he caught the full force of Lilly's steely eyes burning into him. That did it. He straightened up.

"Till we meet again then!" he cried, and, closing his eyes and holding his nose, jumped off the parapet into the moat.

"Oh Geez!" Martha hastily stubbed out her cigarette and leant over to have a look. Mrs Finkelburger muttered something to her husband about safety nets. Tilly started clapping excitedly.

"Brilliant!" she cried. "Encore! Give it up for the Zenda Theatre Historical Players ladies and gentlemen!"

The short boy bowed to the tourists, while far below his companion started wading out of the mud. The Americans looked on at this bizarre spectacle blankly for a few seconds.

"OK, follow me!" screeched Tilly, cutting them short. "Next we'll see the treasure room! More acting later! Leave tipping till end of the tour please."

Chapter 29

Bigelow Comes to the Rescue

Cynthia was idly scrolling through her Instagram when the office phone started ringing.

"It's Wainwright," the receptionist called across the room. "From somewhere beginning with 'Z'."

Cynthia put her frappuccino down angrily.

"Not again! What's the matter with the boy?" She picked up the extension.

"Yes?"

Christopher shovelled a handful of coins into the Castle payphone, having failed to get a signal on his cellphone through the thick masonry. He could feel little tricklets of sweat, and he could have sworn the flies balanced on them and slid down his face.

"Cynthia? It's Christopher. Now look here. I've encountered a problem." He outlined his experience at the Castle souvenir shop. "What d'you mean, go and talk to the manager? He was the manager, for chrissakes. These people just don't have the first clue about tourism.... Cynthia, have you actually been here? No? Well let me fill you in. There is no other outfit. How the hell d'you expect me to make any money here?...What's that?...The Felixtown Rosewater Factory? Are you sure they give commission?"

He hastily dug out a pencil and scribbled down a number. As he did so he suddenly became aware of a strong smell of shampoo. He half turned. A small round man was standing right beside him, while two other men and a girl in T-shirts and baseball caps lounged a few yards away chewing gum. The smaller man was in a lightweight suit and sported a rose in his lapel. He beamed back at Christopher. He looked as if he had an urgent long distance call to make to Palermo. It was unnerving.

"OK I'll call them. Thanks. Listen, Cynthia, I've got to go, I'll call you later, OK? You're not? What about tomorrow? Ah yes, tomorrow's Sunday. Well I've got your mobile if I need it, no worries," he said brightly. "Bye." He hung up hastily before she had a chance to tell him that on no account should he bother her on her mobile.

The small beaming man stuck his hand out.

"Mr Roderick Fraser, I presume?" he said in a broad New York accent.

"Mr Roderick..." Christopher eyed him cautiously. "Yes?"

"John H. Bigelow. I've been looking forward very much to meeting you, sir. May I have a minute of your time?"

It didn't appear to Christopher as if he had much choice. He retrieved his hand from Mr. Bigelow's moist grip and was introduced to Jim the cameraman, Bill the sound man and Lucy the assistant. They set off for the half-built cafeteria.

"What can I get you, sir? Coffee, cappu, 'erb tea?"

Christopher glanced at his watch.

"Tea would be fine. Listen, Mr...."

"What about a sticky bun? Bigelow. John H. Bigelow from Los Angeles."

"Mr. Bigelow, the thing is, I have to meet my group at the end of their tour in...um..twenty minutes. Will this take long?"

The Spare and The Heir 195

"No time at all, sir. Guys? The usual?"

His companions mumbled their assent and they went to sit down while Bigelow led Christopher to the self-service line. He picked up a tray.

"Now. It was about your group I wanted to talk to you about. If you don't mind, I'd like to borrow them for the afternoon."

He helped himself to a fistful of buns and began to explain: about the Studio, the Picture and his small problem. The Picture, it turned out, was an 'action adventure thriller' with 'romantic love interest', about a female rock-star who gets kidnapped by an international terrorist outfit, and is then rescued by a team of Green Berets, but not before having 'got the hots' for one of her captors.

His problem was that some of the extras had failed to show up. They were a group of actors specially flown in from an American touring company in Berlin but unfortunately they had been delayed, for some reason nobody could satisfactorily explain to Bigelow, at immigration and were now being held at a high security reception centre just outside the Capital. His associate producer and his co-producer, Bigelow elaborated, opening a cabinet and clearing it out of donuts, were at that very moment trying to get them released, while he himself had put several calls through to the president, an old friend, to no avail as yet, and time was running out for a particular sequence they had to shoot in advance of the main crew arriving from Prague, where the bulk of the movie was being filmed. Bigelow couldn't help noticing the arrival of the American tour group at the Castle that morning and the preponderance of a large number of very large Afro-Americans. How long were they staying?

Christopher informed him they were due to leave for the Capital first thing Monday morning. In that case, Bigelow wanted to know, would they be free that afternoon? It was just second unit stuff, some establishing shots, nothing too complicated. There was unfortunately no money in it, being a low budget film an' all, but…

Christopher regretfully shook his head. It was a bit awkward. They'd been planning an afternoon excursion to the nearby Felixtown Rosewater Factory; his people were just salivating to stock up on the world-famous stuff; they'd been looking forward to it for days. Couldn't they do it on Sunday, the following day?

Bigelow leant across the counter.

"Here, you," he said, motioning to a kitchen hand. "Got any fudge brownies?" Christopher raised his eyebrows. The tray was beginning to resemble some primary school Master Chef entry. The girl replied in the negative.

"Fancy a slice of apple tart?"

Christopher shook his head and repeated his question. Regretfully not, said Bigelow, off-loading a dollop of cream onto a saucer. Sunday meant double time, and film technicians were a greedy bunch of… he stopped short, suddenly conscious of Jim the cameraman and Bill the sound man waiting for him not ten feet away.

"But what did you say that factory was? Felixtown?" Bigelow paused for a second, scratching his head. "You say you've got five days in the Capital, right?" Christopher nodded. "OK, well I know for a fact that there's this major rose water joint down there, too. Met the CEO myself, only the other day. Bound to be bigger than a provincial outlet like Felixtown. What say I arrange a little visit for you guys when you arrive?"

Christopher hesitated. He saw the glimmer of an opportunity here. He hadn't had time to call the Felixtown Rosewater Factory, but he didn't trust Cynthia. They certainly wouldn't have heard of him. But this other place sounded reassuringly expensive, and if this man could arrange something via more personal channels...

"The problem is, Mr. Bigelow…"

"Excuse me one minute," said Bigelow, turning to the cashier. "You take American Express? No? OK, cash it is." He pulled out a roll of notes and peeled one off.

That did it. The man looked like he'd been around a bit. He was a movie producer, for God's sake. Christopher decided to risk it.

"It depends on the deal."

Bigelow gazed at him an instant. "Ah...the deal." They sat down. There followed a disorderly scramble for the buns.

"So you see, Mr. Bigelow, if they can offer me an attractive percentage…" He hesitated. "Felixtown have offered me twenty," he lied.

"Twenty," echoed Bigelow, looking Christopher straight in the eye and sinking his teeth into a jam tart. "I see." He masticated noisily. "Petal?"

"Mr. Bigelow?" answered the girl called Lucy.

He handed her his mobile phone. "Get me Mr Rosewater on the line will you, there's a good girl."

Ten minutes later the deal was concluded. The President of the Ellenberg Rosewater Co-operative, in former and better times Rosewater suppliers to the Court of St. James, had been coerced into offering Christopher twenty-five percent commission, and to offer his group a tour of the factory when they arrived in the Capital in two days time. In return, Christopher had promised to make his group available to Bigelow for the afternoon. This was more like it. Things were looking up again.

After they'd polished off their tea and buns, the technicians departed and Christopher and Bigelow went to see whether the Angels had caught up with the group. They found them halfway through "*The Zenda Experience, brought to you in association with Globalny Foods Inc 'We Are What You Eat TM'*. Various young people dressed in what looked like a job lot from Munich's Hofbrauhaus (knickerbockers, braces, blonde wigs) wandered around offering small glasses of watered down roochi (*'yours to keep'*) while wax-work models of various participants in the drama came to limited life at the touch of a button. Martha was enthusing, shaking the moveable arm of Rudolf the sixth.

"Hey, isn't he just so cool?" she said. "Isn't this something? Take a selfie somebody!"

"Ever been to Disneyland, Martha?"

Martha hadn't, which explained it. A few yards away Rosa-Lee, grinning with delight, was trying her luck with a sabre against Duke Rupert, though her footwork was no match for the robotic model. After a few unsteady lunges she gave up, wheezing, although the model continued flailing away into thin air. A technician came to switch it off. Meanwhile the Angels were taking turns, amid whoops, on a mechanical bucking bronco ranged along one wall. What relation it bore to the reality of the Zenda Experience remained unclear.

"How did it go, Coach?" Christopher asked Jackson solicitously. "You missed the souvenir shop."

"Swell. 74 to 14."

Christopher laughed. "So I take it that the locals aren't naturals at American football?"

"On the contrary. They're gonna be good. Most of their touchdowns were pretty fair."

Christopher scratched his head.

"Hang on. You mean you lost?"

"Sure. The locals just love it. Reckon we got the making of a league over here." He tapped his nose. "Remember Chris...we wanna encourage them. No point in beating the shit out of them, or it'll never catch on."

Christopher watched Jackson and his happy losers drift away into the ante-room that marked the end of the exhibition. His brain hurt. But there was no time to think about it now - he had an announcement to make. When everyone had finished, he informed them gravely that he'd decided to scrap a proposed visit to the Felixtown Rosewater Factory in favour of a free afternoon.

"I'm sorry," he said, somewhat hopefully, and mainly for Bigelow's benefit.

Because the few who looked the slightest bit interested seemed more than happy with the new arrangement. "But there is an alternative I'd like to put to you. Ladies and Gentlemen... John H. Bigelow."

It was unfortunate. It was at that precise moment that Bigelow's stomach decided to belch.

Chapter 30

Panic at the Border

It was not until late in the afternoon that the helicopter returned Hentzau to Zenda. As he stepped down from the machine, what remained of his hair swirling in a vortex above him, an assistant rushed up and handed him a message.

"An emergency cabinet meeting?" he yelled above the noise. "No one informed me of this!"

The assistant explained that he'd held the shuttle to the Capital. Hentzau cursed. He'd planned to spend the night at the Castle. There was a lot to do, and he wanted a debrief with Tilly and his staff on how the American tour group visit had gone. But he knew that Blicker wouldn't call an emergency cabinet meeting on a whim.

"OK," he sighed. "Let's go." Behind them the rotor blades were already coming up to speed again as the helicopter prepared to return to Lougouev's yacht.

As he swept through the VIP channel at Immigration he noticed an unusual level of activity. Special detachments of police from the Interior Ministry were milling around with sub-machine guns, and huge queues were forming in front of passport control. Was this somehow related to the summons by

Blicker, he wondered? He pushed his way through to the office of an immigration officer he knew and asked him what was happening.

"Not entirely sure, sir," replied the officer. "Orders from the Ministry. We're to check everyone coming in, and all entries for the past week. Sounds like we're back to the good old days, sir." He grinned. As if to underline the point, the sound of raised voices came through the open door of an adjoining office, where two detectives from the Interior Ministry Police were grilling a bewildered immigration official:

"You say you gave them all stamps. How many of these men were there?"

"Am I to take it, then, that it's back to foreign imperialist scum?"

"Look, sonny, don't get smart with me…"

Hentzau said, "Are they looking for anyone in particular?"

"We've got a couple of names, sir," replied the officer. "But we think they're already in the country."

He showed him his list. It didn't mean a thing to Hentzau. Perhaps they were suspected drug dealers, he thought. Then he noticed a large box in a corner. It hit Hentzau with a sudden flash of recognition. The letters C-CAM were stencilled onto the side in big bold letters. It appeared to be plugged into a socket in the wall.

"What's this doing here?"

"That, sir? Food samples from America. Some American called to tell us to keep it plugged in until he could send someone to collect it, then when they finally arrived they left this one behind by mistake. Arrived from Vienna, sir, this morning. Local fare obviously not good enough for him." He chuckled. "What will they think of next, sir?"

But Hentzau's thoughts were elsewhere. He had only half believed Lougouev's story, but here was practical proof. It was impressive: the man's intelligence was obviously right up to date. He could score some points with this.

"Who is this American? What's his name?"

"His name, sir? Er...let me see now." The official reached over to the message pad on his desk. "The name the package is directed to is a Christopher Wainwright, but the man from the hotel said…"

The man broke off. Suddenly pale.

"Hold it, I could have sworn that that was one of the names on the list…" He flailed around for the list but Hentzau was still clutching onto it.

"Excuse me, sir," he said, hardly able to contain his excitement. "May I?" Hentzau relinquished it, opened the box and picked out a sample. He sniffed it. Behind him the official started hopping up and down.

"My God it is! It is!" He stuck his head out of the office door and yelled. People came running. When he looked back Hentzau had the sample up to his ear and was shaking it. The officer gaped for a second, then went into a blind panic, as it dawned on him:

"Away, sir, away!" he screamed.

"Ugh...What is it?" cried Hentzau, springing into the air like a cat who's the subject of some vicious child's practical joke.

"Get away, please, for God's sake, sir!" He leapt back. "It could be a bomb!"

A bomb?

Chapter 31

Some Disturbing News

"*The President of the Democratic Republic of Ruritania!*"

An old man in the wig brought his gavel down on the raised dais at one end of the cabinet room, and a faint cloud of talc rose from his head like steam. He was a holdover from the previous administration, when every official meeting with the President had been formally announced. The man was past 80 and it was his only role, and Blicker did not have the heart to make him retire.

"Good evening, colleagues," said Blicker gravely. "Please sit."

Instead of the usual shuffling of papers and last minute banter there was total silence, absolute attention, the air tense with expectation. Something was afoot. Two chairs normally occupied by Hentzau and the Minister for Culture were vacant. Hentzau's Chief of Staff was standing up at the back of the room, looking worried. Sophie Bernenstein, Rosie's friend from the PR department, was also there, next to him, taking notes.

"I'm sorry to have called you all in at such short notice," began the president. "And to have dragged you back so early from the weekend. The Culture Minister sends his apologies, he's at the Venice Biennale representing our stand there. He's having a few problems. Apparently there's been a run on yellow roses on the international market in the last twenty-four hours, which makes it very difficult for our Rialto project."

"A plot of the New York arts Mafia, no doubt," quipped somebody.

Several cabinet ministers of the Hard White tendency groaned inwardly. They were sick to death of the 'Rialto Project', Ruritania's contribution to the Venice Biennale Art Fair which involved smothering the city's Rialto Bridge in roses. They were impatient to get on to the real business of the evening - why they had been dragged out of country dachas, swimming pools and tennis courts to an unscheduled emergency cabinet meeting at the highly unsocial time of early Saturday evening. Surely not to discuss some madcap installation? They had parties to go to.

"That's as maybe," replied Blicker, "but I haven't gathered you all here to discuss that. No, the reason is, we've had some serious news, colleagues. Some very serious news indeed."

A door opened and Hentzau hurried in, expressing apologies. Blicker waited until he was seated before resuming. He glanced at Boris wearily, as if for support. It had been a very tiring thirty-six hours. But Boris's mind seemed to be elsewhere.

"There is," he began gravely, "presently, in our country, a Pretender to the former throne of Ruritania. His name is Roderick Fraser, from London, and he's apparently descended from the illegitimate child of Queen Flavia and Mr Rassendyll."

There were several sharp intakes of breath.

"You mean there really was a child?"

"The rumour was true?"

"It appears so." Blicker cleared his throat. "And what is

even more worrying is that we suspect he's here to orchestrate a monarchist coup."

There was a moment of stunned silence. Everybody except Boris stared back at him in astonishment. Unnoticed, Sophie bit her lip.

"You're joking, surely," said the Foreign Minister.

"Unfortunately I'm not. What's more, he appears to be accompanied by a highly trained team of American special forces from Little Rock, Arkansas, disguised as a football team."

More than one mouth dropped open.

"The Americans? What on earth are they doing mixed up in it? Do you have proof?"

"We have had several…indications, yes," said Blicker carefully, tapping a Camel out of its packet. "We've naturally been monitoring them closely since they arrived, and they would seem to be heavily armed. We can't risk moving in just yet. There could be a serious international incident."

"I've had no information about this," said the Defence Minister, defensively. Blicker lit up, ignoring him.

"Yesterday, for instance," he continued, through a cloud of smoke, "they had a practice game against a scratch Zenda side and lost, then this morning…"

"What did you say the name of this Pretender was?"

Blicker regarded Hentzau coolly. "Fraser. Roderick Fraser. Although we have information he may also be using the name Christopher Wainwright."

Wainwright. Hentzau's mind flashed back to the airport, and the C-CAM package.

"And you say he's travelling with an American football team, who lost to a local amateur side?"

"Amateur?" snorted Blicker. "Our guys have never even played the game before. These people are no more a football team than a tour group. You see, the entire mission seems to have entered the country in the guise of a package tour."

"Maybe they lost on purpose?" said Hentzau.

They all looked at him as if he were mad. He clenched his fists. Hell, he was giving the game away. Of course. Lougouev's analysis had been spot on. "No, you're right," he added hastily.

"And there's something else," said the President. He motioned to an assistant who handed him a sheaf of photographs. "Take a look at these."

They were passed around. The images showed the Angels in camouflage outfits and shouldering rifles. In the background loomed the bulk of Zenda Castle.

"As you can see, they're at Zenda." Blicker paused to let the full implication of what he was saying sink in. "These were taken only a few hours ago."

All heads swivelled towards the Minister for Trade.

"Hentzau?" he said casually. "Any ideas what they're doing there?"

Chapter 32

Plan B

"Are you crazy?" exclaimed Boris, pacing up and down Blicker's office a few hours later. "Why didn't you have Hentzau arrested?"

"Because we have no firm evidence. Just because they were on his property doesn't necessarily mean he invited them there. Second, if we arrest him without charging him, it will only strengthen his position. I mean, he'll make us look like dictators, for God's sake, which is exactly what he wants. And third, let Hentzau incriminate himself. Let him hitch his wagon to this Fraser imposter and then when the people see what he's really like, an armed puppet of the West, they'll reject him."

"You've said it!" cried Boris. "That's it! That, in a nutshell, is your problem."

"What's my problem, my dear Boris?" said Blicker wearily, raising his eyebrows and exhaling clouds of strawberry vapour. He was trying out a vaping stick as an alternative.

"Christ, Johann, what's with the stick? It smells revolting."

Blicker ignored him. "So, you were saying?"

Boris regarded him with amusement.

"Well, for a start, you have far too much faith in the people."

The President took a series of short vigorous puffs.

"Listen," he said, bristling, clouds billowing, "I was elected by the people for the good of the people. If I don't have faith in the people…"

"Forget it. Democracy is fine once every four or five years. They elect you because they think you can do a job, right? Then you get on with it. The people can't possibly have all the information and background briefings that we do, so they can't possibly make a rational reasoned judgement about what's good for them. Just look at Brexit. Sure, if you fuck up seriously, you become unpopular, and then you don't get elected again. They don't want to be asked. Believe me."

"So…what? You'd prefer some kind of elected dictatorship? Is that it?"

"Don't be so simplistic, Johann. For example, the organic agriculture programme. Right now they all want fast food, correct? Convenience food, they want what the West wants. If we give them a choice, they naturally choose the best one for themselves, i.e. the cheapest or the tastiest, but the worst one for the economy and the country. They choose hamburgers and ketchup, imports go up, no one eats organic, and we're forced to go back to high yields and chemical fertiliser to grow the export cash crops in order to earn the dollars and euros to pay for the junk food in the first place. If you take a macro-economic view, it's obvious madness. Besides, we have to force people to eat better. They won't do it by themselves. Or take cars…"

He paused for breath, stroking his ponytail.

"People think that going electric will solve everything. But do you know how much carbon goes into manufacturing a car? Everyone still wants to own one. Screw the environment, piss on the rest of us, fuck public transport…"

"What's all this got to do with Hentzau?" asked Blicker acidly. "Or the monarchy, come to that?"

"Hentzau is dangerous. Not just to us, but to the whole country. We have a responsibility to act on behalf of the people. If we pussy-foot around now, gathering evidence to convince everybody, he'll slip through our fingers. He should be eliminated."

"That sounds a bit extreme."

"Perhaps not literally, but put in a position where he can't do any harm." He paused for thought. "Mind you, I'm a bit surprised he's in league with the Americans. I always thought he was more likely to leverage his Russian connections." He walked to the window and peered down at the gates below, where two soldiers in Horst's ridiculous uniforms were performing an elaborate ritual and handing over guard duty. "As for the monarchy, sure, it was a good idea at the time, but if it means anything other than a tourist attraction and a diversion for the people, if it involves real power for a third party - and that is what this Fraser man looks like he's after - then we'd better forget it. The gold in the Bank of England isn't worth diddlyshit unless we have total control over it."

"Ah, well I've got all that worked out. When he makes his move we'll protest to the United Nations." Boris developed one of his facial tics. "Well? Do you have a better suggestion?"

"He's just a guy with a few beefy bodyguards. Take him out." He jabbed a finger at Blicker. "Attack, remember, is the best means of defence."

"Take him out?!...Boris, Boris, Boris…" Blicker was shocked. "This isn't Robocop, we can't just kill people! There'd be an almighty stink. We'd become just like them then. Our whole moral authority for governing would go. Can't you see that?" He looked at Boris intently and leant back in his seat. "No, we should try subtler means. I want you to go to London."

"London? Why London?"

"We must try and discredit him. He's bound to have got somebody pregnant. We'll give the tabloids a field day, and then he'll become a laughing stock." He chuckled, exhaling busily. "It's gossip we want, Boris. Not guns."

As he said it a loud bang reverberated from somewhere in the city. Blicker leapt up to join Boris at the window. About a mile to the west, from the direction of Hentzau's compound, a small orange fireball was rising into the night sky.

"Oh yeah?" said Boris.

Chapter 33

Scorpio

"Looks like they had a great time."

Christopher pointed out of the window of the hotel restaurant. Four jeeps had arrived in the forecourt and the Angels were piling out of them in high spirits.

Rosie followed his gaze. "So what is this film about?"

Christopher shrugged. "Who knows - usual Hollywood recipe. Action adventure, woman in jeopardy, tough man to the rescue."

He leant back, spooning the last of the creamy dessert into his mouth, and studied her surreptitiously. Things seemed to be going well between them. Mind you, it was so hard to tell. They probably had a whole different dating etiquette, on reflection, one that he couldn't hope to fathom in such a short time. She had made body contact with him on three occasions; she had told her all about her adopted family, upcountry farmers, and how she'd always wanted to be a physicist, but how her parents - she'd been adopted when she was five, her mother and father having been killed in a car accident - had told here that they could not afford to subsidise her studying abroad.

At this point he'd felt his heart skip a beat. Couldn't afford to study? He told her of his own little brother, Max, a child prodigy tennis player who their single mother couldn't afford to send to tennis academy. Even the scholarship he'd been offered had financial strings attached. He sympathised, he really did. He knew how heart-breaking it could be.

Although he had not intended it as a way to her heart, he saw her visibly melt before him. As he spoke, he couldn't help noticing her slender fingers as they slid up and down the stem of her wine glass, a sure sign, as far as he could remember from a drunken conversation he'd once had, that your love object was subconsciously already in bed with you. Her left foot was also pointed at his for most of the meal. He tried desperately to recall that book on body language. It meant something, didn't it?

"What star sign are you?" he ventured. Yes, it was a cliche. But then they wouldn't be cliches if they didn't work.

"Star sign?" She seemed puzzled. "What's that?"

"It's your...astrological sign, the position of the stars when you were born. Like an oracle...you know, it kind of foretells your fate. It's also used to work out whether people get on well." He leant forward. "For example I was born in April, so I'm an Aries, which means I am fiery, passionate, head-strong…" he laughed uncertainly "…and I also get on well with people born in August, who are Leos, and people born in December, who are Sagittarius. So when were you born?" He raised his eyebrows. "Or shall I guess?"

She arched her eyebrows at him. "Do you really believe this rubbish, Christopher?"

He tittered uncomfortably. "Well…"

"It's ridiculous, you in the West are so...what's the word?... *superstitious*." She swept a strand of hair out of her eyes. Christopher felt like reaching across and doing it for her, but restrained himself. "The world is a physical...a chemical place. We are atoms and molecules, we're born, we live, we die. Then...nothing. Our bodies feed the soil, the worms, the flowers, they live and die just the same. It's a circular thing. You think the stars make a difference?"

"Well, OK," he said, sipping his coffee defensively. "Maybe...but there are some things we cannot explain." He swallowed. "And anyway, I never take these things too seriously."

"No, sure, good for you, never take things too seriously," she said, with an irony that was, for once, lost on Christopher.

He put down the cup. "But aren't you interested in the future?"

"The future..." She sighed. "But why? There is no future, only choices in the present. These make the future. Who can tell me what choices I will make, except myself?"

The conversation seemed to be taking a complicated turn. Christopher had read this about Central Europeans: they were deep. They didn't seem to understand the concept of small talk, had to analyse everything, turn a conversation into a discussion, and a discussion into a Socratic enquiry. Beneath her loose white cotton shirt - a man's, Christopher noticed, and charmingly rumpled - he every now and then caught a glimpse of her cleavage - soft, firm and olive skinned. Did she like him, or didn't she like him? Until a few moments ago he had been convinced he was onto something, but now...

He timed a beat, looking involuntarily at her hair. "Rosie... you're very pretty," he said, and '*Aaagh!*' he thought, cringing inside at how it came out. "I don't think I've ever met anyone like you."

She blushed. "Pretty?" She turned away. "Please, Christopher, don't. You mustn't talk like that."

"Talk like what? Why ever not?"

She sighed. "Because." Her blue eyes suddenly moistened. They darted left and right, unnerved.

"I'm sorry. I didn't mean to upset you. It's just...I like you, that's all."

"So you told me once before."

They were silent. She looked away. To change the subject, he said brightly:

"Know any good restaurants in the Capital?" But he was left with a vague feeling that he'd somehow missed a turning. She pushed her plate away and got up.

"You don't even know me!" she cried, her eyes flashing, suddenly angry. "How can you say you like me? Desire me, more like. Like all men. Why not be honest, for once? That you want to get me into bed?"

He couldn't help it. His jaw dropped.

"Well…" he stammered, "I would be…"

"Is it not more simple to ask me?"

"Ask you?" Christopher managed, thickly. "That's hardly romantic, is it?"

"What do you know about romance?" Her eyes moistened. "You met me two days ago, the trip is just a week, already you want to sleep with me."

"You must be a Scorpio," he muttered, feeling utterly humiliated.

"Goodnight," she said, slinging her bag around her shoulder.

He caught her arm. "Rosie, wait.."

She shook him off and strode away towards the lobby. He watched her go, thought about following her, but hesitated until it was too late. He sat alone, thinking, for almost a minute, sipping his coffee in silence.

"Hi. May I join you?"

He looked up. It was Martha. There was a strong whiff of strawberries about her.

"By all means," he replied despondently, without an ounce of enthusiasm. But one thing you could say for American women. At least you knew where you stood.

Chapter 34
A Wrong Turn

When Christopher finally managed to give his excuses and drag himself away from Martha it was already late. She asked him if he wanted a drink in the bar but although he declined politely, she still appeared to want to stick with him, and they walked together towards the lift. On the way they bumped into Michael. For once Christopher felt pleased to see him.

"Oh hello," Michael said. "We missed you at the fun and games this afternoon."

"Had a good time?"

"If shimmying up and down ropes in camouflage webbing is your idea of fun," Michael shrugged. "But hey, I always wanted to be in the movies. They'll have kittens back home when they see me on the big screen."

Passing through the lobby they noticed a small group of onlookers standing in the darkness outside.

"What do you think they're doing there?" said Martha, suddenly clutching his arm and squeezing it hard. "Are we celebrities?"

"Ooh I do hope so!" tittered Michael, preening himself as

he passed a mirror in reception. "Perhaps it's to do with the movie?"

The three of them took the lift up together. Christopher wondered which floor Martha was on, and for a moment considered making an excuse to go to Michael's room with him to go over the next day's itinerary. But he decided to chance it. They reached his floor.

"This is me," he said brightly. "Night!"

Michael didn't move, just said 'night' in return.

Martha said, "Me too."

He cursed himself and they stepped out together. Would she turn left or right?

"I'm this way," she smiled slyly.

"And I'm this way," said Christopher, relieved.

She looked like she was on the point of saying something. Christopher yawned theatrically.

"Long day tomorrow. Goodnight Martha." He fumbled for his room key and turned away.

"Sleep tight," he heard behind him.

When he got to his room he noticed a folded scrap of paper slipped under the door.

"I'm sorry for my stupid behaviour. Come and say goodnight if I'm still awake. Room 217. R."

Glowing inside, he made straight for the bathroom to freshen up. Two minutes later he was knocking on her door.

There was a rustle on the other side. Was she checking that it was him through the keyhole? The door opened with a click. The first thing to come into view was a leg. A long leg, revealed where the bottom of the dressing gown had fallen away. The door opened a notch further and he dragged up his eyes. It was like expecting sugar and tasting salt. Her hair tumbled about her shoulders, her glossy lips smiling at him wetly.

"Well hello," purred Martha.

Fuck, fuck, fuck.

He cleared his throat noisily. Wafts of what smelt like incense billowed from behind her. He was about to explain that he had the wrong room, but thought better of it.

"I...er...I'm really sorry to bother you, but I just forgot to say, we have a 9 o'clock start tomorrow morning."

It was lame, but it would have to do.

"Of course. How nice." She held the door for him. "Please. Enter."

"I'd rather not."

He fiddled with the hem of his jacket. Her eyes were amused, looking at him like he was a little boy who needed educating.

"Anyway," he eyed her desperately "...goodnight." He took a step back into the corridor. "See you tomorrow!" he added cheerily, and sauntered off back in the direction of his room.

He swiped his room card, cursing, and checked the note again. 217, surely. Then he realised the seven, written in the continental style, could also be a one. He counted to sixty, opened his door a crack and peered out. The corridor was empty. He eased out again.

This time he stopped at 211. He knocked. Nothing. He knocked again. Silence. He put his ear to the door and to his surprise it clicked open under his weight. He tensed. There appeared to be no movement, the room was in darkness.

"Rosie?" he whispered. "You awake?"

From the direction of the bed came the soft murmur of someone sleeping. He crept in. She was asleep alright, her head turned towards the window, hair splayed out across the pillow. A ray of light from the street outside illuminated her face through a crack in the curtains, her head turned up slightly so her nose squashed against the blankets. The collar of a night-shirt was bunched around her neck.

He had a sudden, crazy desire to kiss it. To lift those sheets, climb into the warmth, enfold her in his arms. He stood stock still, watching her, daring not to move. She looked so tranquil. But he had sense enough not to stay, he had gone too far already, and he crept back towards the door, careful not to wake her. It was then that he noticed an envelope on the floor by the door. He picked it up. *'Rose Elphberg, room 211'.* For a moment he wondered what was in it and was tempted to open it, but the flap was glued shut. He laid it down on a table by the door and tip-toed silently away, careful to shut her it gently behind him.

Chapter 35

Bring on the Roses

It was not until the last of the policemen had left, sometime after midnight, that Hentzau's Chief of Staff arrived. He and his boss wandered out onto the terrace together to survey the still smouldering wreckage. A gaping hole in the paving stones revealed where the full force of the blast had punched its way up from the basement.

"It's unbelievable," said Hentzau. "Incredible. Where did I go wrong? It's not as if she's deprived." He shot his deputy an anxious look. "Is it?"

"Certainly not, sir, you've given her everything," replied the other.

"And What's with the chemicals?"

"Well, you know what she's like, sir."

"Apparently she's been storing it in the basement for months, and has been messing about doing experiments in secret." Hentzau sighed. "I thought it was all to do with the chemistry set I gave her a few years ago. Turns out she was doing much more dangerous stuff. If my idiot driver hadn't gone down there for a smoke…"

"Is he OK?"

"He'll survive."

"Where is she now, sir?"

"As soon as she admitted the truth I sent her back to Zenda. If the police find out it was a thirteen year old girl whose hobby is making nitrate bombs…"

He peered disconsolately at a tangled mess of wires and twisted metal hanging out of a basement wall, then returned to his study.

"I badly need a drink," he said, running a hand through his hair. "Can I get you a whisky?"

"It's a bit late for me, sir, I really ought to be…"

"Just one," he said, pouring a double scotch. "Here. Get this down you."

He proffered the glass to his Chief of Staff.

"Thank you."

"There is one benefit in all this though," he continued, as he measured one out for himself. He wanted to talk, despite the lateness of the hour. "It might get us off the hook."

"Oh?"

"Yes, the police are already talking about it. Linking it with this Fraser fellow."

His deputy looked up. "They can't really believe that? He's miles away. They're trailing him in Zenda now."

"I know, it's amazing, but they appear to be linking them. It wasn't as if I pushed it on them, either, I was extremely subtle about it. But they're paranoid. From now on anything out of the ordinary they're going to think is the work of this…madman. And apparently Blicker saw it himself, from his castle study. He went haywire, by all accounts."

The Chief of Staff yawned. "I hope you don't mind me saying, sir - the man's a buffoon." He knocked back the scotch, grimaced, and sat down. "But it still doesn't answer the question of why this Fraser is armed. We know he's tied up with Universal Foods and we know they're here on a commercial mission. But even US corporations don't go round trying to ram their products down people's throats with the help of armed mercenaries. I saw the photo of them in uniform carrying guns. Let me tell you, sir, they were the real deal."

Hentzau laughed. "Yes, well, I do admit it looked bloody awkward. But we seem to have solved that little problem. According to Lougouev, and as you heard, confirmed by Blicker, their cover is as a tour group, part of which is made up of an American football team. The match they had in Zenda, the one they lost? They lost deliberately. The plan is to hook us into a sport we think we can win, then use it like a Trojan horse to swamp us with advertising."

"But armed footballers?" scoffed his deputy. "Special forces quarterbacks?"

Hentzau swilled the whisky around in his glass. "Ah, well, my darling daughter has a theory about that."

His deputy chuckled. "Your daughter has a theory about everything."

"Did you ever meet that producer from Hollywood, at Blicker's art show the other day, the man who is making a film up at Zenda? John Bigelow?"

The other shook his head.

"I thought he wasn't coming until next week, but I'd forgotten that he was going to do some preliminary filming at Zenda for a day or two before his whole circus arrives. He was up there at the same time as Fraser's crew, and according to Tilly, he was looking for extras in the morning before she left. Specifically, young male soldier types."

"In Zenda?"

"Exactly." Hentzau rolled his eyes. "Hollywood." He paused to refill his glass. "But of course, as luck would have it, this so-called tour group of Fraser's was stuffed with young men called Leroy and Hank, so Tilly reckons he managed to persuade them to help him out."

"But what about the guns? And the uniforms? Where did they come from?"

"Props. I imagine he brought them with him. We've been trying to contact him all morning. The landlines are down, and you know what the mobile signal is like."

"That's strange, sir," said his Chief of Staff. He paused. "Have you told the president?"

"Blicker? You must be joking. Can't you see? It's extremely convenient to have someone else attempting a coup. Especially someone apparently armed. Particularly when he's got no popular support. It takes the focus off us. It makes our own, peaceful, homegrown Rose a much more attractive proposition." He smiled. "In fact I think we should do everything we can to help him."

His deputy couldn't help thinking that at that moment the family resemblance between Hentzau and his daughter seemed stronger than ever.

"Has anyone found Rose yet?"

Hentzau's face clouded over. "No, damn it. She was only back from Vienna two days before she disappeared off the face of the earth."

"What does she do for a living?"

"You think the girl works? She's currently resting, as the euphemism goes. But resting where? The only lead I have is the rumour of a sighting in Zenda. One of my men thinks he saw her."

"But that's where Fraser is, sir. D'you think…"

"Now don't you go all paranoid on me, Chief." Hentzau started to worry a fingernail with his teeth. "We'll soon know. They're all under instructions to follow up any potential sighting with a bunch of yellow carnations. Her aversion to her destiny is well known. If she runs for cover we'll know it's her."

"Excellent idea, sir."

"Mind you, I'm still hoping she'll come in of her own accord. If we have to force her it could get messy. No. Much better that she realises that it's the people who want her, not me. That she can't escape her duty. That the game's up."

Hentzau's Chief of Staff ambled over to the window, peering into the darkness. "When did you say Lougouev's roses are arriving?"

A row of long low boxes lining the drive were just discernible in the moonlight. On the lawn the remains of a couple of dozen more were scattered about the grass, blasted far and wide by the force of the explosion. It looked like the aftermath of a particularly bloody massacre: hundreds of carnation stems strewn over the grass, in the trees, on the garden shed roof, eerie in the black still of the night.

"Soon, I hope, because we'll become a laughing stock with these carnations." Hentzau straightened up. "Anyway, I've come to a decision. I'm going to bring this wedding forward to next week."

The deputy's face took on an expression of panic. "Next week, sir? But we haven't even begun the preparations yet, it'll take…"

"We can do it."

"And the foreign dignitaries?"

"Forget them. They're nothing but hangers on. I want them married, and then we can forget about her."

"But what if we can't find her…"

"I'll issue a press release: wedding brought forward." He glanced at his watch. "Come on, if we hurry we'll make the morning editions." He chuckled. "That'll flush the girl out."

Chapter 36

An Incredible Story

The next morning Christopher was up late. It was Sunday, they had the day off, and it was not until after nine that he went down for breakfast. He heard the noise as he was waiting for the elevator. Very faint, a kind of whimpering from somewhere down the corridor. Curious, he went to investigate.

At first he thought it was coming from Martha's room. The ghost of a smile flashed across his face. But no, it was coming from Rosie's room down the corridor. He put his ear to the wood. There was no doubt about it. She was crying. He knocked.

"Rosie, it's me, Christopher. Are you OK?"

The sobbing abruptly stopped. Squinting through the keyhole he could just make out a figure in a dressing gown, slumped on the bed, head in hands. He tried the door handle. Unlocked, he stepped in and she looked up in surprise, wiping her eyes.

"Oh...it's you."

"Apologies," he stammered. "I heard you crying and the door was open and…"

"It's fine." She smiled up at him weakly. A newspaper was

spread out on the bed beside her, along with the message he'd picked up the night before. On a table by the window, two huge sprays of yellow carnations were propped up in a vase.

His heart sank. Clearly someone else was wooing her.

"What's with the flowers?"

"You want some?" she sniffed. "Help yourself."

He hovered for a moment, uncertain whether he should stay, then sat down. "Want to tell me about it?"

Rosie rose abruptly from the bed and disappeared into the bathroom, leaving the door open. "You don't want to know," she called. "I really don't want to bore you."

"Try me," he said, fingering a carnation. There was the sound of running water. She returned and stood before him, smiling bravely.

"These must have cost a packet," he said. "It says here they come from Colombia."

"There used to be fields and fields of roses in Ruritania. Most were bulldozed when the communists moved in. Now they have to import them all." She gestured at the flowers as if by way of explanation. "They're supposed to be roses, you see, but everything is faked nowadays."

He smelled them. "They look pretty real to me."

"Yellow is the colour of the Royal house of Elphberg. The yellow rose is our symbol. Nowadays," she tossed her head dismissively, "people think anything will do."

She slumped down on the bed, dabbing the corners of her eyes. He watched her, mystified.

"Rosie," he said finally. "If you don't feel like talking I quite understand. I just wanted to make sure you were OK." He glanced at his watch. "Breakfast will be over in a minute…"

She touched his hand quickly. "Don't go."

He held it, surprised. "Is it…a personal thing? Something to do with your family?"

"My family?" she cried. "They're no use. They don't care what's best for me, only for…" She trailed away.

"Let me guess. It's a man."

"A man," she echoed dully. "One man, two men, many men."

Her bottom lip trembled. He wondered how he should begin. He had a feeling she wanted to let it out, whatever it was.

"I'm listening," he said gently.

All of a sudden she burst into tears again, and collapsed onto his shoulder.

"I'm so sorry," she wailed, "forgive me." She heaved, sobbing, as he put his arm around her. The feel of her hair against his cheek was intoxicating. "It's so hard…I have no one to talk with…you are…you see…oh God…I am about to…" she let out an anguished cry "…about to be married…" A renewed bout of sobbing erupted.

Christopher was aware of a sudden, involuntary stab of disappointment. He pulled away from her.

"Married? When?"

"Next week."

"Wow. That, I was not expecting." He took his arm away from her shoulder and they sat side by side in silence, and she straightened up, wiping the tears away from her eyes with the back of her hand. She laughed.

"Oh God, I'm sorry. You must think I'm really flakey."

"Don't be," he said flatly, trying to be concerned but somehow no longer feeling it. "You're nervous about it, I suppose. Everybody has last minute doubts. It's only natural."

Inside he kicked himself mentally. What a jerk he'd been. What a fool he looked to her.

"No, that's not it." She laughed again. "Not at all. This is pathetic, isn't it? Yes, I'm marrying next week. A guy called

Andrew Hentzau. He is the son of an important government minister."

So that's the end of that one, he thought bitterly. No chance, mate.

"Hence the flowers." He fingered a stem despondently.

"No. The flowers are for something else. You see…" She hesitated, peering up at him from under a tangle of hair, and sighed. "I'm also heir to the throne - I am a distant cousin of the Elphbergs, which is the reason this…man, this government minister, wants his son to marry me."

His jaw dropped. It took a while for it to sink in. Had he heard that right?

"You're joking."

She jumped up angrily. "Why would I joke?" she cried.

"Heir to what throne?" Christopher looked shocked.

"Ours. Ruritania. Who's do you think?"

"Fuck, you mean…the actual throne?"

"If the people want it, then I will be Queen, and the Republic of Ruritania will be no more." She picked out a carnation, as if about to rearrange it and then unexpectedly flung it across the room. He flinched, water droplets spraying everywhere.

"So what's the heir to the throne doing being a tourism ambassador?" She must be having him on, he thought. Perhaps she was deluded. Was all this some self-concocted drama?

"Yes! You see, that's just it!" she cried. "That's what makes me so mad! They all think I should be something special, something different! I am just an ordinary girl! I like rollerblading and baking cupcakes."

Christopher stared at her. Yes, she was either bonkers or, well, the alternative was equally unbelievable.

Finally he said, "I see. So what you mean is, you're worried this guy just wants you because of what you are? A princess?" He couldn't help laughing.

She flushed angrily. "What are you laughing for? In fact I'm not a princess technically, because they abolished all that stuff years ago. But now some idiots in this country want to bring all that back again."

With an effort, he straightened his face. "You're right, I shouldn't laugh. But surely that would be wonderful, wouldn't it? For you I mean? If you're really a princess, and heir to the throne, then…"

"Oh Christopher, you don't understand!"

"Do you love him very much?"

"No! I hate him! He's a creep."

Christopher shook his head. It was getting more and more baffling.

"Sorry for being slow here, Rosie, but I'm not sure I get it. If you don't love him, then why the fuck marry him?"

"Why?" she cried. "Don't you think I haven't asked myself that question a thousand times? It's called duty. Duty for my parents, duty for my country. They will lose everything if I don't marry him."

"But hang on, if you have a father, surely he's the heir?"

"I told you, I'm adopted." She gestured around desperately. "And now this," she said, picking up a bunch of carnations. "They want me to be Queen. God knows how they knew I was here, they must have spotted me in the street. You see, Christopher, roses are the traditional way in my country for calling for a new King or Queen. We call it the Agitation."

Christopher could very well see how it could become agitating. Then another thought struck him.

"Aha, but these are carnations, so it's invalid."

She laughed bitterly. "If only it were so simple! It's the symbolism that counts. Just wait, roses will start arriving soon."

"I see."

"In their thousands," she continued. "And the problem is, it seems they are depending on me." She picked up the message. "I've just got word from a friend in the Government that there is a Pretender to our throne, one who is trying to take it by force. He is here in Zenda, and they are worried for my safety. Until this, I thought that maybe there is a way out. But now…oh…oh.." She burst into tears again. "D'you think I want to be Queen?"

"In that case…"

"One day, yes, OK, perhaps, maybe it will become my duty, but now? So soon? I'm still young. They want to cut that off. Because of this they want to bring the wedding forward, they tell me I must be married next week. To that…ugh," she shuddered violently. "Next week! I've been engaged to him for three years, why the sudden hurry now?"

She began pacing up and down the room, casting a sideways glance at herself in a full length mirror. "They've already given me a new image. I had to have skiing lessons, tennis lessons, even a new stupid hairstyle." She bunched it up and grimaced at herself in the mirror. "I loath hairdressers! I hate tennis! It's all lies! I like chess." She turned and glared at him, as he was partly responsible for her plight. "D'you know, I wanted to read physics in Heidelberg, at the university, but they wouldn't let me? How crap is that?"

"Physics?" Christopher was impressed.

"But oh no, no way, an intellectual heir is no use at all, they want someone who looks good in a photo shoot, who goes to…" she spat the word out as if it were contaminated, "night clubs!"

Her cheeks burned with indignation.

"Well, that doesn't sound quite right. I've yet to meet a princess in a nightclub." He chuckled. "Plenty of queens though."

"And you know something?" She sat down again beside

him angrily. "The creep I'm going to marry, he's slept with every rich girl in the Capital, and now he's going to marry me. I'll be a national joke."

They were silent for a moment.

"Well," he said finally, "there's only one thing for it. You've got to get out of it."

"Smile for the camera, they say, smile for the people, keep smiling. Always smile, smile, smile." She smiled grotesquely at him, her eyes large, round and liquid, as if she was about to burst into tears again.

"Hey," he said, putting his arm around her.

"And if I refuse," she cried, a tear dropping onto his hand, "if I don't go ahead with it, what will happen to my parents? They are depending on Mr. Hentzau for everything they have!"

As she nestled into his shoulder, trying to stem her tears, he caught sight of the two of them in the bathroom mirror through the open door. Life was certainly weird, he thought. Here he was, in some foreign hotel bedroom, alone with someone who was not only one of the most beautiful women he'd ever met but also the heir, it seemed, to some foreign throne. It was too ridiculous, and yet...could it be true? Or was she, after all, just an attention seeker, hopelessly unstable? Perhaps that was it, he mused - her behaviour at dinner had certainly been a little odd. Maybe she was madly in love with him, but didn't quite know how to show it, had a destructive streak in her that alternated between wild fantasy to catch his attention, and downright viciousness.

He studied her in the mirror. No, tell him it wasn't true. Her face, her personality, everything about her seemed too innocent. Even he, with his inexhaustible talent for seeing everything in the best possible light, even to the extent of self-deception: even he couldn't square this one. The story she told was simply too incredible to make up.

And here she was, pouring her heart out to him. He raised an eyebrow at his reflection, just to check he wasn't dreaming. So where did he go from here? Nowhere, was the answer. She was a princess, and she was engaged to be married. Besides, he reminded himself, who was he?

Christopher Wainwright, former telesales rep.

Chapter 37

Background Checks

"A telesales rep? Where was that?"

"Look, I've no idea, all I'm trying to tell you is that he wasn't exactly a babe magnet, know what I mean?" snapped Mandy, as Special Agent B, alias Mr Black, handed her a second double espresso, with hot milk on the side.

They were in a sleek black and chrome coffee bar in Soho, London, and Black glanced anxiously at the piece of designer junk that was supposed to tell you the time. The commission he'd received from President Blicker's office to get some background on Mr Christopher Wainwright was certainly a world away from the work he'd done under the old regime. A lot more confusing, for a start.

"But he was a nice enough guy. Like I said, we were dating for about two years."

"And you say you never considered marriage? Children, nothing like that?"

She squinted at him over the rim of her coffee cup.

"Nope. As I already explained, we were young. Just out of school. We had living to do."

"Living?"

"Sowing our oats," she replied, deadpan. Black hesitated: it was, he felt, as good a cue as he was going to get.

"Will there be anything else?" she asked.

"Yes, one more thing. Was there…" He hesitated again.

"Yes?"

"Anything…let's say…" Mandy looked expectant. "Kinky?"

"Kinky?" Mandy went slack-mouthed.

"Well, I don't know, maybe…leather? Did he like to tie you up, tie you down? A rubber fetish? Nazi paraphernalia?"

Black trailed off. She was looking at him with a dangerous expression.

"Well, of all the fucked up questions! Look," she said, getting up hastily and lunging for her bag, "I don't know who you are or where you're from but…that's not cool! Not cool at all. This interview is over!"

∽

"You say he was nothing out of the ordinary?"

Elsewhere, Special Agent A was having no better luck. He'd tracked down Christopher's former professor at Leeds University. Christopher sounded extremely boring.

"A model student, you say?" he ventured, already sensing failure. Professor Sandberg wiped the residue of the cheese and ham submarine sandwich on his trousers, and glanced at the canteen clock. "Look, er, Mr…"

"White," prompted Special Agent A.

"Quite," said the Professor, eyeing him suspiciously. "Mr White. Tell me again where you're from?"

"I am…er…a researcher for Ruritanian TV. We have a programme called 'This Was Your Life'. We are…"

"*Was* your life?" Sandberg said, alarmed. "Has anything happened to Christopher?"

"No, no, he's very much alive," he said hastily. "Very much living."

The Professor looked dubious. "Ruritania, you say?"

"Yes."

The Professor let that one pass. "So it's a kind of...what?...celebration of his life and achievements so far, am I right?"

"Right, exactly, that's it."

"And what achievements might those be, may I ask?" queried the Professor.

"Well...possibly some, possibly nothing, we are investigating." White shifted uneasily. There was one thing about this new job of his - he'd had to learn fast. Working under Blicker's new administration meant turning your hand to anything. "But perhaps...who knows?" He chortled. The Professor made a move that looked like a prelude to going.

"Er...one last thing, Professor Sandman…"

"Sandberg."

"Sandberg, Professor Sandberg, I am sorry, yes. One last thing. Was he ever caught…" He wavered.

The Professor's eyes were fixed beadily on his visitor.

"Cheating?" offered White.

The Professor scraped his chair back.

"I thought so," he said curtly. "You people are so transparent."

"Transparent? What is this word?"

"Please. Spare me the phoney accent. And you might have chosen something a little more likely than Ruritania, don't insult my intelligence any more than you have to. I expect Christopher is running for Parliament, is that it?"

"Well no, actually, he's running for…"

"Good for him, is what I say, he's a bright lad." He glowered at the visitor. "And if you low-life tabloid hacks think you can come here and get dirt from me, with your total lack of ethics and your prurient voyeurism..."

The Professor's voice had turned to a snarl. Two students glanced across from a neighbouring table.

"...your grotesque sentimentalism and your cheap and nasty scratch-card games..." He began to splutter, his face reddening rapidly. It looked like he was about to have a seizure.

The two students hurried over. "Professor, you OK? Have you taken your pills?"

Professor Sandberg certainly didn't look OK. He hacked, violently. White looked on in alarm, unsure of what to do. Should he get him a glass of water? Or make a swift exit?

"Your..." cough, splutter "...tasteless page three..." cough... "and your disgraceful door-stepping and phone hacking..."

A student started pounding him on the back. He turned angrily to White.

"You're from the press, aren't you?" he hissed, "So go, scram! Can't you see he's an old man?"

∽

ONLY SPECIAL AGENT C, WHO WAS CALLING HERSELF MS Brown, was getting anywhere. She had gone to visit one of Wainwright's former landladies.

"Such a lovely boy," reminisced Mrs Wyver, as they sat down to a cup of tea in her lounge. "What's this all about, anyway?"

"Oh...er...his official biography, research and so on."

"Really?" Mrs Wyver was impressed. "I knew the boy would go far. He had such a way with the banjo. But strange he hasn't sent me anything. What label's he on?'

"I beg pardon?"

"Is it Virgin or one of those foreign ones?"

Labels? Brown panicked. The slightest hesitation might give her away.

"One of those foreign ones," she replied with confidence. "Now, Mrs Wyver, is there anything you forget? Was he…er…how I put it?"

She wasn't sure, precisely, what she was supposed to be looking for. The President had been so vague.

"Was he a…as you say…party animal?"

"A party animal? Oh my yes! He was certainly that!"

"I suppose he had plenty of girlfriends?"

"Of course," said Mrs Wyver, removing her thick black rimmed glasses and warming to her theme, "the girls, they all liked him. Went wild about him, in fact, I can't tell you how many of them I had down here with me, sobbing on my shoulder. Most of the time it was hopeless, I'm afraid. He did have one or two relationships, but he really wasn't that committed, if you see what I mean. He was ever such an incurable romantic. Goodness gracious, impossible. He was always looking for Miss Perfect, and, my dear, such high standards. He could never be satisfied." She sighed theatrically. "He used to get terribly confused, poor boy." She paused. "Miss?"

Brown jumped. She had been miles away.

"Oh…"

Mrs Wyver remounted her glasses and gave her a look.

"I suggested more than once that he should go for therapy."

"Therapy? You mean he went to psychoanalysis?"

Brown was suddenly excited. This sounded far more promising. For she didn't know the West well enough to realise that therapy was as common as dentistry, and that like dentists they merely existed to drill holes and fill cavities where none existed before.

"Oh no dear, he was dead against that kind of thing. Stubborn as a mule."

She leant forward and winked. "But I'll tell you what one of his problems was: too much weed."

"Oh yes?"

"Yes. He used to grow rows and rows of the stuff, plants up to here," she indicated her shoulders. "It's something to do with the south facing windows. He was on the top floor, you know. Plenty of sun. They grew like billio."

Billio was a new word for Special Agent A. "So he was a horticulturist?"

Mrs. Wyver chuckled. "That's one way of putting it, love."

Ms Brown jotted a note down in her book. It was time she was getting along. She tried one last time. Maybe there was something in this therapy line after all.

"Tell me. Did he…did he ever talk to these plants of his?"

Chapter 38

Roddy Rex

"That's that then," said Blicker morosely down the phone. It was late the same night. Midnight oil was burning at the People's Palace. In a chair across from the President, Horst fidgeted with his designs for the new Royal State Coach, fighting waves of nausea amidst the clouds of acrid cigarette smoke. It was hopeless trying to have a meeting with Blicker these days, he decided. The man was constantly distracted. He always wanted to take every call that came through, even when you scheduled a meeting after hours when you thought they'd be free of interruptions. Nothing important seemed to get fixed. Like what kind of crown they were going to have on the top of the coach. This was crucial. His assistant took the traditional line, reverting to the old Elphberg crown, but Horst favoured designing something completely new. Something avant-garde. Their's, he believed, should be a modern monarchy for a modern world, and nowhere could this be set out more plainly than what the State Coach carried on its roof, and, by extension, the King on his head.

For the field was wide open. Horst could really go to town on this one, and the very idea made him tingle with excitement. Nothing new had been designed for years, all the European Royals were still wearing headgear designed in the dark ages. Oh, well, yes, there was that ghastly abomination someone had come up with for Charles's investiture as the Prince of Wales, before he was King, but that was thankfully merely a coronet, and what an embarrassment it was too. It was like something you won at a coconut shy.

Then there was the question of the name. This was vital. He didn't think the President quite realised: there were stamps to be designed, new curtains for the Royal Opera House and the Theatre Royal. Not to mention a whole new coinage. It all took time. Horst just couldn't understand what the hold up was. The least Blicker could do was make a decision. Was it to be Roderick Fraser, Roderick Rex, or even Roderick Fraser Rex? Horst had been forced to prepare a whole series of cipher designs. Personally he favoured RR - the graphic possibilities with that one were endless. Not to mention the associations. But it was just typical of this business: no one could decide anything, and then, suddenly, they all wanted it done by yesterday.

His train of thought was interrupted.

"Are you sure?" Blicker was saying down the line, anxiously. "Absolutely one hundred percent sure?"

Someone said something far away.

"OK, I'll see you all back here tomorrow." He slammed the phone down. Horst started. What was going on? The Chief looked stressed.

"Johann…" said Horst gently. "You OK? I was thinking, about this crown…"

Blicker stared at him blankly.

"I don't like it," he said finally. "I don't like it at all."

"What do you mean you don't like it, Mr. President?" gulped Horst. "What exactly don't you…"

"He's a very likeable fellow by all accounts."

Horst was lost. "I'm sorry?"

"This Wainwright...Christopher fellow."

"Who?"

"Or Roderick Fraser or whatever he's supposed to be called."

"Well, that's just it, Johann, that's what I've been trying to tell you! What is he called?" He paused. WC? Oh my God, he hoped not.

"He's a thoroughly decent fellow."

"Glad to hear it, I..."

"Glad to hear it? It's a bloody disaster! The people will love him!"

A beat.

"Er...Johann...with respect." Horst eyed the President suspiciously. "I thought that was the…" he cleared his throat "...whole idea? I thought you wanted this guy on the throne?"

Blicker suddenly seemed to focus.

"Look...er...Horst...something came up. I forgot to tell you. Hold off on the crown for the time being, eh? There's a good chap."

Horst sat back with a thud. On, off, on, off. He wished to God the silly old fool would make up his mind.

Chapter 39

The Agitation Begins

A considerably larger crowd had gathered outside the Hotel Tarlenheim the following morning by the time the group drifted down for breakfast. There were fathers with young children on their shoulders, women with shopping bags, people on their way to work who'd just stopped by. A constant stream came and went, but with every minute that passed the crowd, for the most part patient and communicating in undertones, grew bigger. The police had thrown a barricade up, but already people were pressing up against it.

"Hey Chris," said an Angel cheerily.

Christopher was pouring himself some thick black sludge from the coffee machine, bleary-eyed.

"Morning Leroy," he croaked.

It had been a long night. The day before he'd suggested to Rosie getting out of Zenda to get her mind off things, and they'd ended up going for a hike in the hills. He should have slept soundly after that - but he'd instead tossed and turned all night. Because at least it had clarified one thing in his mind - that she was completely sincere and was telling the truth. She really was a princess - of sorts - and apparently about to be queen of this godforsaken country.

Which meant, he realised, it was game over for him. Just his luck, he thought, he finally finds a girl he feel something for and bang, she's unavailable, even though she appears to like him. Looked at rationally, he supposed it was just as well. She was a distraction. He had a deadline to meet.

"Hey, mornin'! You seen the dudes outside? You think I should go an' sign for them?"

Now this was an angle that Christopher hadn't considered. He had indeed wondered what on earth they were doing there, but he'd not for one minute suspected they might be there on account of the Angels. Then he remembered their defeat. It didn't quite add up.

"Sure. Why not?" Anything to give him a quiet breakfast. "I'll send the others along when they come down."

"Uh...better not, Chris. Don't want to freak 'em out."

With that Leroy bounded out of the breakfast room.

Next down was Mary Finkelburger.

"Good morning, Christopher."

"Morning Mrs Finkelburger, and how are you today?" After half a cup his croak was easing.

"Those poor people outside," she said, "it's a scandal. I just went out and gave them all candy. You should have seen the grateful looks on their faces. One of them gave me this gorgeous rose."

Christopher stared at it.

She sat down beside him and, producing a small bottle from her handbag, poured herself a glass of filter water.

"Why aren't the United Nations involved, that's what I want to know?"

Christopher decided not to express an opinion as to why the United Nations were not involved. Both he, and they, had better things to do. And so breakfast passed off relatively peacefully, a few quiet minutes before the furore of unpaid telephone bills, mislaid keys and suitcases which, for reasons unknown to their owners, suddenly refused to shut, that always accompanied a group transfer from one city to another. At ten to eight the hotel porters came stalking into the bar, where Christopher was busy checking off the relevant paperwork before departure.

"Bags to the bus?" they asked.

He nodded, and they started ferrying suitcases down in the elevator and out to the coach. There was a sudden commotion at the reception desk.

"Two cokes," one of the Angels, Hank, was saying. "Two cokes, one beer, period. No way did we consume four vodkas."

"Problem?" queried Christopher.

"This man says we had four vodkas. Me and Joe don't drink vodka."

"Hey, fellas," Coach Jackson butted in, "pay the man, OK? How much is it?"

"Nearly fifty bucks!"

"It's all written down here," said the receptionist, gesturing to Christopher. "It clearly shows four vodkas."

The tangled forest of squiggles on the mini-bar chit was illegible. Christopher turned to Hank.

"Are you sure no one else drank them? I mean someone who came up for a party or something?"

"Party?" said Joe, the second Angel. "No way, man, no way. Two cokes, one beer, that's all we pay for."

"You heard the man," said Christopher to the receptionist. "Two cokes, one beer. There must be some mistake."

But the receptionist wouldn't budge. Jackson had drifted away, while Hank and Joe looked at him expectantly.

"OK you two, onto the bus. I'll sort this out."

They gratefully sloped out into the sunshine and onto the bus, acknowledging the cheering crowds as they went. Rosie appeared. She was dressed in a navy blue linen jacket, with a scarf and wrap-around dark glasses. She beckoned to Christopher.

"What's with the disguise?" he smiled.

She pointed at the forecourt. "Haven't you seen them?"

So it was true. They were for her.

"Have you decided what you're going to do yet?"

She didn't answer, and started to shepherd the passengers onto the bus. Christopher returned to the receptionist. "OK then, come on, so what's the damage?"

"Four hundred ruros."

"Four hundred? That's forty US!'

The man spread his hands apologetically. Christopher glanced at the bus.

"OK, give me a minute," he said. As he approached the door into the street he nearly collided with Martha. She had been racing down the stairs and was breathless.

"Hey, I'm sorry Chris, you waiting on me?"

A black leather tasselled jacket was slung over her shoulders and she was wearing bright pink lipstick. "You will not believe this. I overslept. I woke up and looked at the clock and it says twenty after and I'm like…" She giggled.

"Don't worry, you're perfectly timed. Shall we?" he said, holding open the door for her. She had not gone two steps before she stopped dead.

"Way to go!" she exclaimed, eyes widening. "What are all these people doing?"

She stepped hesitantly out into the sunlight, closely followed by Christopher. A huge roar went up.

She started in terror, "What the fuck!"

Christopher grabbed her arm, and together they stormed through a hail of roses, carnations and miscellaneous other hurled objects, towards the bus.

Chapter 40
Red Level 4

Wherr-whorr-wherr-whorr.
The farmer cocked an ear. Why the presidential entourage insisted on always travelling at milking time was beyond him. All this commotion upset his animals. He sighed, waiting for them to pass.

First came an army jeep with a machine gun mounted on the window frame. Next came a truck full of soldiers. Then a limo. This was followed by another. And then a second truckload of soldiers, an armoured personnel carrier, and finally two motorcyclists. The farmer stared after them for a full minute as they disappeared down the road, shaking the dust from his beard and patting Elsa reassuringly. Finally he scratched his head. Perhaps there had been a change of government. Again. Nothing would surprise him. You were always the last to know in these country regions. Elsa nuzzled him, and he snapped out of his reverie. That's right Elsa my girl, he muttered. Milk just keeps coming whoever is in power, eh?

Twenty minutes later Blicker was pacing up and down in the book-lined study of Boris's country dacha. He looked strained. It hadn't helped having had to inch their way through the protesting environmentalists who seemed to be permanently camped at the end of Boris's drive.

"So you got nothing on the man?" said Boris.

"Clean as a whistle. Even composts his own food waste."

"Impressive."

Blicker jangled the contents of his trouser pocket abstractedly. "The only lead we got was some fellow claiming to have some old photographs."

"Oh? Of what?"

"Who knows? Probably nothing. I sent someone over to investigate." He massaged his temples. "I wish to God the man would make a move. This red level four security is a pain in the arse, all these soldiers following me around everywhere. It can't be kept up forever."

Boris peered out of the window. "Two truck loads, you say?"

"I left them at the main gate. It'll get back to the Security Minister no doubt. But if he had his way he'd have them following me into the bloody toilet."

"The man's paranoid," scoffed Boris.

Blicker sat down and lit a cigarette, leaning back heavily. "But there's no denying," he went on, "that we're in a very awkward position. Very awkward indeed."

"Well," tut-tutted Boris, "if you'd followed my advice…"

"If we'd followed your advice there'd be civil war by now. But let's stick to the present. This man seems to have massive popular support. Things are already getting out of hand around the country. Have you seen the news bulletins?"

"One or two."

"What I don't understand is how it's spread so fast. We've tried to suppress as much as we can, but it doesn't seem to make much difference, according to the intelligence reports. It's the White Revolution all over again."

Blicker drew a long reflective drag of his cigarette. Then he reached down for his briefcase and pulled something out.

"I've got something to show you," he said.

He handed Boris a memory stick, which Boris – rather reluctantly it seemed to Blicker – plugged into a computer on his desk. On it was a video file. The pictures had obviously been taken surreptitiously, as the images were jerky.

"It was taken this morning," continued the President. "The Tarlenheim Hotel in Zenda where Fraser and his people are holed up. How they knew he was there we've no idea, but take a look at the crowds, it's like National Marble Week."

The film showed hundreds of rose wielding well-wishers jostling for a view. Then three of the Angels came into frame, signing autographs.

"Can you believe it?" said Blicker through gritted teeth. "The arrogance of it." Meanwhile various other members of the group were starting to drift out of the hotel in the background to board the bus. Boris laughed.

"Doesn't look much like a crack military formation to me."

"Well that's just what you're meant to think," snapped Blicker. "That's just their cover. Now," he said, leaning forward intently, "just take a look at this."

The camera had zoomed into two people who were emerging from the front door sheltering under a huge raincoat. Blicker leant across and clicked the pause button.

"There," he said. "Recognise anybody?"

"You mean the man under the raincoat? In the leather jacket?"

"The woman under the raincoat."

Boris studied the hazy picture.

"I don't think so."

"It's Rose," said Blicker. "Elphberg."

"They look cosy."

"*Cosy?!*" cried Blicker, jabbing 'play' again. The images continued. "The point is, they're working together. Is it me, or does it look like she's trying to disguise herself? And just look at the reaction they're getting. It's unbelievable. One thing's for certain. That bastard Hentzau's mixed up in this somehow, just as we suspected…"

Boris stroked his chin.

"… and I'm going to nail him if it takes…"

"Hang on," interrupted Boris. "Who's that?" A second woman was emerging with the man and the crowd was going wild. "Another heir? You sure you haven't missed a cousin?"

Blicker hit pause a second time. Despite being in half shadow, Martha's tight leopard-skin trousers were clearly identifiable. Her bright pink lips wrought havoc with the video colour balance.

He squinted at her. "Fuck. I hope not."

Chapter 41

An Unpaid Minibar Bill

Back at the Hotel Tarlenheim the crowds had dispersed and the group had departed. Only a few policemen were left, clearing up armfuls of discarded flowers. Amidst all the carnations were already mixed the first sprays of yellow roses. Inside, one of the policemen was taking a statement from the hotel receptionist. It didn't take long. When it was finished the policeman went out into the street and spoke into his radio.

The man who took his radio message was the duty controller at Zenda police station. He jotted down the details and walked into the office of his boss, the Captain.

The Captain was already in congress with a senior officer from the Interior Ministry Police. He listened to the report and leaned back in his executive chair, the sort that could tilt in four different directions simultaneously. He cast a questioning glance at the policeman. The latter started to protest, laughing at first. But when the Captain remained obdurate the other became angry. He picked up the phone and dialled a number.

A receptionist at the Interior Ministry Police headquarters took the call, and put it through to the duty officer. She said a

The Spare and The Heir 251

curt word or two to her man in Zenda and put the phone down abruptly. She went straight to the radio room.

In Zenda the Interior Ministry Police officer cursed, opened his briefcase, got out a small rectangular black box, plugged it into the phone socket, fitted a radio handset, and tried the call again. It was now encrypted, for security. As an afterthought he motioned to the junior policeman, who was still standing by, awaiting orders, to get out. The man looked questioningly at his Captain, who nodded, and exited.

In the Capital the Interior Ministry duty officer picked up the call again, this time through the scrambler, and got irritated. Those provincial police really were something, she thought. Did they want to screw everything up? She hung up and scurried down the corridor to the office of her boss, the Commander. He was in the middle of his mid-morning coffee break. She explained the situation.

He shook his head in disbelief. Then he scratched it, trying to decide on a course of action, his hand hovering above the three lines on the telephone console in front of him. Finally he came down on the side of caution, stabbed the top one, and picked up the receiver.

He was immediately through to the president's office. The receptionist put him through to the president's assistant, who became flustered. No, the President was not available. He was away for a couple of hours, and she honestly couldn't say where, it was an RL4 security situation. The Commander got angry and bullied her, so reluctantly she transferred him to OPS, the Office of Presidential Security.

The man who took the call at OPS tried to connect the Commander with his boss, the General, but the transfer button refused to work. So he said something nervously into the mouthpiece, put the receiver down, got up, looked around him hastily, cleared away a few dirty mugs and a well thumbed garden furniture catalogue and hurried down the corridor to the General's office.

He knocked. There was a scuffle. He knocked again. Finally the door opened to reveal the General with a towel around his shoulders and shaving soap all the way up one side of his face. His subordinate visibly quaked as he explained the situation. The General looked him up and down furiously and then strode out into the corridor, not bothering to wipe the foam from his cheek. Various people got out of his way, startled, and scuttled back into offices.

The General picked up the subordinate's phone and spoke to the Commander. Yes? What did he want? It was really terribly inconvenient. The President was away for a few hours. Of course he was contactable, but was it important? He did realise, didn't he, that it was an RL4 security situation?

Apparently it *was* important. The General, reluctantly, told the Commander to hold the line, and he'd get him transferred to the Colonel in charge of SAD(p) - Special Armed Detachment (president).

Putting the phone down he stalked into the radio room, where a startled radio operator did as he was told and connected the line in question with the military satellite link up. Then he dialled another number. Back in his subordinate's office the phone went dead and the subordinate began to remove the traces of Old Spice shaving foam from the surrounds of the earpiece, a disgusted look on his face.

At the gates to Boris's dacha the C.O. of SAD(p) was chatting to a female eco-warrior outside a teepee. The sergeant had just brewed up tea. She was in the middle of an explanation about how the menfolk were all away on a male bonding weekend, with a glint in her eye, when a corporal came dashing up. The Colonel was wanted on the blower. Excusing himself, the Colonel walked purposefully towards the jeep, rather pleased with the impression he was creating. He picked up the receiver and was instantly in communication, via satellite, with the Interior Ministry Police Commander in the Capital, whose duty officer was still standing nervously beside his desk.

He listened, cursed, listened again, remonstrated, then handed the receiver to his Corporal and cursed again. He barked an order and the Corporal leapt into the driver's seat, switched on the ignition and they were soon bouncing their way along the wooded track towards Boris's dacha.

Inside Boris's study he and Blicker were still arguing about their next step. Boris wanted to give it another forty-eight hours, to see how things developed. But the President was adamant: events were running away from them. It was crucial they regained the initiative, and the best way to do this seemed to Blicker to be to do a deal with Fraser. That way they could, first, cut out Hentzau and second, be seen to be reasonable. If negotiation failed then they would be quite entitled to protest vigorously to the United Nations, and resort to force. But the one thing not to do was to act arbitrarily and precipitate a crisis. They would make contact with Fraser forthwith and offer him a deal that he couldn't refuse.

"I see what you mean," said Boris, staring out at the driveway.

Blicker looked up.

"One of your security detail has just arrived."

The jeep had just screeched to a halt in a cloud of dust. The Colonel was halfway up the steps to the dacha and children were already clambering over the vehicle and fiddling with the ammunition belt to the impotent consternation of the corporal. Soon there was a knock on the door and the Colonel was ushered in. He saluted.

"Sorry to bother you, sir, an urgent message from the Capital has come in on the secure comms channel, sir."

"Yes?" said Blicker testily. What now?

"Zenda police are about to move in on the Fraser group, sir. They want to set up a roadblock. Interior Ministry Police insist they clear it with you first, sir, in view of the R.O.E."

"R.O.E?"

"Rules of Engagement, sir."

"*What?*" exploded the President. "Zenda police want to move in? What on earth for? It's an Interior Ministry Police matter. If they move in there'll be carnage."

The Colonel remained impassive.

"I'm sorry sir, I know no more. I'm just the messenger. Something to do with an unpaid mini-bar bill, sir."

There was a moment of silence. Boris was the first to break it. He looked incredulous.

"An unpaid mini-bar bill? Who the fuck's in charge down there?"

But Blicker was worried. He was biting his lip.

"No. Wait," he said. "Perhaps they're trying to provoke us, maybe it's a ruse…"

Boris shot a glance at his president. The man had, it seemed, to use that well-worn Ruritanian expression, finally lost his marbles.

Chapter 42

Kidnap!

They left Zenda that morning in high spirits. No sooner had the coach pulled out from the hotel than a small procession of cars began to build up behind it, flags streaming, hooters hooting, people waving, like a troop of chattering monkeys. A police car joined them at one point, as if escorting them, but after a short distance peeled off to deal with more urgent concerns.

Christopher, however, could see that Rosie was on edge. If she really was to be married in a week, he couldn't understand how she could remain on the trip one minute longer. But all she would say was 'we'll see'. Soon the strange procession died out and they were alone on the highway, and she stared bleakly out of the window at the passing landscape, preoccupied in her thoughts and saying little.

"What's up with Rosie?" whispered Michael to Christopher. "She's seems a little down."

It was obvious to everyone that something was wrong. And it seemed to him that for every mile they approached the Capital, the closer she felt the trap closing in around her.

After two hours on the road they began looking around for

a coffee stop. The next town was a small place called Striberg, and Rosie directed the driver to the railway station. There was bound to be a cafe open there, she said.

"OK, everybody, listen up," said Christopher in his, by now, familiar refrain. "Twenty five minutes coffee and bathroom stop. Everybody back here please by..." he glanced at his watch "...twenty to."

They clambered off the coach and dispersed in all directions.

"Shall we grab a coffee?" Christopher asked Rosie, as they helped the last of the passengers off.

"Give me a minute. I have to make some calls. I'll meet you in the station bar." Christopher watched her hurry off in search of privacy.

He found the bar and ordered a beer, watching the train indicators clatter into action as each new arrival or departure was announced. Out on the platforms he could see the Angels hollering about, in a boisterous mood, while at the far end of one he caught a glimpse of Henry Finkelburger darting up and down to photograph a siding full of gleaming new freight cars. Five minutes passed. Ten minutes. Still no sign of Rosie. Perhaps she'd had problems getting a signal. He ordered a second beer, and was dismayed to see Michael, Spinelli and Mrs Finkelburger approaching.

"Hey."

"Mind if we join you?"

He pointed at the neighbouring bar stools.

"You seen the Johns? Dis-gustin'!"

"Joey, this is still like a developing country, remember? They have different priorities."

"He's right," said Mrs Finkelburger, remaining standing. She didn't look like she was comfortable risking a bar stool. "And shit ain't one of them. I don't know how these people put up with it. Nothing works. Rubbish all over the floor. Service is lousy."

Christopher tried to ignore her. It was getting tedious.

"And look at the prices," she went on, picking up a grubby 'English version' menu from the bar, and launching into a kind of running cost comparison on the price of the food back in Idaho, with the aid of her iPhone's shopping app: Vegetable soup, 85c; at *Soup 'Til You Poop* on Main Street; assorted cold meats $2.50 at S*helley's Deli*; salad (if you could call it that in Ruritania, and Mary Finkelburger was not at all sure that you could) $1.35 at *Harry's Salad Bar* in the new Mall.

"This is Europe," explained Christopher patiently, taking the beer that the barman brought him, and handing over some change. "Your dollar just isn't worth what it once was over here."

"Well it damn well should be," said Mrs Finkelburger angrily. "Europe has no respect."

"I beg to differ, Mrs Finkelburger, but have you stopped to think why? Your recent President has bequeathed a trillion dollar debt. You should be taking it up with him, not us." He smiled at her icily. "You can always stay at home, you know. Sightsee in the shopping mall."

She was too preoccupied in her own indignation to notice his barb.

"And look at this," she went on, jabbing a finger at the menu. "A hotdog for six dollars. I can get that for 69 cents back home." She looked at Christopher accusingly. "*Frankfurter Heaven*, Lascelles and Fifth."

"So there you have it, Mrs Finkelburger," he snapped, finally losing patience and jumping up from his bar stool. "One of the many differences between Shitsberg, Idaho and Striberg, Europe."

He stalked away with his beer. That was one licence plate you would certainly never see: *'Idaho. Land of Irony'*.

Fifteen minutes later Michael had opened up the coach and the group was beginning to drift back in ones and twos, but Rosie was still nowhere to be seen. Then Henry Finkelburger came hurrying across the forecourt, his camera swinging by his side.

"Hey, we gotta problem."

Christopher stepped off the bus, alarmed.

"It's our guide. Rosie. I think someone's trying to kidnap her."

"Are you serious?"

"Follow me. We need to be quick."

They ran back through the booking hall and across two platforms. At the entrance to the underpass that crossed to the third, Mr Finkelburger stopped.

"Over there," he said breathlessly, pointing. In the gap between two trains, amidst the swirling steam, was the figure of a young woman. In the distance she was hard to make out, but the outline was familiar, with the dark blue jacket and jeans. She was being bundled unceremoniously along the platform by three men, and they appeared to be arguing.

"Rosie?" he yelled. It was no use, they were out of range. Christopher bounded down the steps of the underpass. Crowds of people had begun to alight from a train that had just pulled in and were making for the exit, and he battled against this tide, pushing past the hurrying figures, his heart pounding. Could it have been her? He took the steps three at a time as the underpass emerged onto the platform. At the top he halted, searching frantically. They had disappeared. Henry Finkelburger was still on the opposite platform, watching him.

"You see her?" he yelled across.

Finkelburger raised his arms and hurried off towards the end of the platform to get a better view, searching the carriages for a sign of her. Christopher turned back and suddenly, far up towards the engine, he caught sight of three people clambering up the steps of the end carriage. One of them was carrying Rosie's distinctive shoulder bag. Simultaneously he saw two of the Angels emerge from the toilets across the tracks. He raced back down the underpass.

"Hey what's up, man, you bustin'?"

Christopher skidded to a halt, breathless. "She's being kidnapped! Mugged! Over there!" He pointed towards the train. "We've got to help her! Three men…"

"Whoa there, slow down. Waddayamean she's been kidnapped? Who's been kidnapped?"

"Rosie! Some men have just forced her onto that train! She's in desperate trouble, we've got to help her…"

Hank looked at Leroy. Joe and two others had just emerged behind them. "Fuckin' hole in the ground," growled Joe.

"You sure about this?" pressed Hank.

"Of course I'm fucking sure about it!" yelled Christopher. They looked startled.

He glanced nervously towards the train. "Look, I know it sounds crazy, but I saw them take her, just now, I'm sure it was her!" He tugged at Hank. "Please, you've got to help!"

Hank, Joe and Leroy exchanged glances.

"Hell, why not?" shrugged Hank.

"I don't understand," said Joe. "What's going on?"

"We'll soon find out," said Leroy. "*Angels…!*" he hollered, at the top of his voice.

Christopher started violently. By the time he'd got over his astonishment, Hank and Leroy had begun to trot down the underpass. The rest of the startled pack hesitated a fraction of a second then, puzzled, followed the others. Whilst inside the bathrooms the remainder of the Angels, at various stages of relieving themselves, wondered what the hell was going on. Granted, *'Anyplace, Anytime'* was their motto, the watchword of their local band of Arkansas Guardian Angels, but they never imagined it covered anything other than off-duty moments in the Little Rock Cineplex or Miller's Mall. But in the station crapper of a place called Striberg, somewhere in Eastern Europe? It seemed unlikely. But it was Leroy's voice alright, and it was bellowing their call-to-arms once again:

"*Angels...!*"

Someone must be in trouble. They emerged stumbling in various states of undress and, as if on instinct, bounded away across the platforms in search of their rallying cry.

Chapter 43

The Duke of Boots

Ruritania's Minister of Culture took a last mouthful of seared tuna and washed it down with the dregs of the Sancerre. The place was frantic, waiters semaphoring each other with napkins and the Maitre d' flitting around like a demented dragonfly.

He checked his watch: time to go. The place where he'd been told to meet was just around the corner. He paid the bill, fetched his coat, and stepped out into the warm London night. He had been on his way back to the Venice Biennale when the request had come through from Blicker to run an extra errand. About what, he had no idea, just that he was to pick up some photos.

Well, what the hell, it made little difference, he thought. The Biennale was a wash-out. Once more they'd been trounced by the New York Arts Mafia, for if there was one thing that he had achieved in London, it was the discovery that the unprecedented world-wide run on yellow roses of the past few days had been orchestrated out of the United States. The price had sky-rocketed at the flower market in Aalsmeer. It was all very well for people to say 'so cover the Rialto Bridge in roses / carnations / orchids' - but that wasn't the point, was it? The integrity of the piece demanded yellow. The Rialto in red? Who did they think he was? Jeff Koons?

The place he'd been told to meet, the Duke of Boots, was heaving. Crowds of people spilled out onto the pavement, while from deep within pulsed loud techno music. The interior, unusually for a London pub, was dimly lit. The Minister could just make out the up-lighters of a bar at the far end, next to a small stage. He pushed his way towards it and ordered a Bloody Mary from a man in a leather waistcoat. He climbed up onto a bar stool and surveyed the scene. There was scarcely a woman in sight.

"I haven't seen you here before?"

He turned.

"I beg your pardon?"

"I said - you're new here."

"I'm from out of town," he said, cagily.

"American?"

He felt a twinge of pride that this man should mistake him for an American.

"Ruritanian."

"You what?"

It was tiresome. You always had to explain it. He didn't feel in the mood. "A small country, far away."

Suddenly he felt a hand on his knee. "Nice jeans."

He reacted instinctively and brushed it away.

The man recoiled, like he'd been waved at by an arachnid.

"Keep your hair on, mate, there's no need to get shirty."

"Problems, Gary?" said an older man in denim cutaways, ambling over.

"This gentleman walked into the wrong pub," said Gary huffily.

Misha was keen to avoid trouble. He looked from one to the other sheepishly.

The Spare and The Heir 263

"I'm sorry guys, I had no idea this was a gay bar. I'm meant to be meeting a man called Simon."

There was a short pause.

"Simon?" The two of them exchanged uneasy glances. "And you are?" said the older man.

He explained what he had come about and, after a brief discussion, he was led into a back room behind the stage, where a drag queen act was just limbering up.

Simon was a small man with a bullet-bald head. He wore a tight white T-shirt, under which his rippling muscles were clearly outlined, and a pair of shorts. One hand was secured to a chair with a handcuff. With the other he waved Misha to a battered leather sofa. In the corner a young woman was setting up a lighting rig, and ignored them.

He inspected him closely. "Are you here about the promotion?"

"No. I'm here from Ruritania."

"You what?"

"About a Christopher Wainwright."

Simon's face cleared. "Aha, yes, you're the bloke who was interested in …"

"Photographs," interjected the Minister of Culture, keen to get this over with. He felt uncomfortable. "Apparently you have some from when he was a student."

"Raoul?" yelled Simon. "You got those pics?"

A second man in drag ambled in. He handed the Minister a large brown manila envelope.

"Take a look at those. If you're interested you can get back to us."

He slid the contents out of the envelope. There were two black and white prints. Both were full frontals of a naked man: one wearing what looked like a Roman helmet with a breastplate, the other holding a spear and a shield with a toga draped casually over one shoulder. He was standing against a backdrop of a large blow up image of a Coca Cola bottle. Something about the brutality of colonialism, perhaps, or the relentless march of naked multinationalism? As an installation, it wasn't bad.

"Good God. This is fascinating."

"He's the fellow you want, I think? Christopher Wainwright, aged 17, published in the first magazine I ever produced."

"You publish magazines?" said the Minister of Culture eagerly.

"Indeed I do, though they are all online now." He looked impatient. "Anything else you need? We're in the middle of a shoot."

"This Wainwright, is he an art student?" he asked. "Who's his agent?"

"No idea. What makes you think he has an agent? That was taken a while ago. He was probably just doing it for holiday money."

"Well whatever, it looks interesting," he said enthusiastically. "We are most grateful…"

"Don't be too grateful. There's a price. The negatives are yours for a grand. They include a number of variations on the same theme."

"A thousand dollars? I think we can stretch to that. It's reasonable for something of this quality."

"Pounds. Drop me an email," he said, tossing him a card, "and we'll send you the files." He held out his free hand to be shaken. "Goodbye now. I hope you don't mind if I don't get up."

Chapter 44

The Rescue

Rosie was angry. Her initial shock over, she was quiet now, no longer struggling, trying to catch her breath and take stock of the situation. But she couldn't help feeling a tremor of fright. It was a potent reminder of what the man was capable of.

Either side of her sat two men, one of whom had a hand firmly planted on her arm. A third stood guard outside in the corridor, sucking nervously on a cigarette.

"So," she said, finally. "Am I to take it that I'm a prisoner?"

The one who seemed to be in charge didn't answer.

"It's for your protection," ventured the other.

"Protection?" she scoffed. "From whom may I ask? You've no right! And get your hands off me!" She tried to shake free but the man's grip merely tightened.

"Listen, Miss...er...Elphberg. No harm will come to you. We are just doing our job, OK? You will be free to go when we get to our destination."

"Which is where?"

"We're not at liberty to say at this...er...precise moment in time."

"It's outrageous!" As she said it she attempted to lift herself bodily out of her seat with all the force she could muster. To her surprise she managed to free herself. There was a scramble as she leapt, cat-like, onto the opposite seat. They hesitated.

"Don't worry," she sneered, "I'm not going to escape."

The train was a slow one. As in many developing countries it was simple enough to upgrade the rolling stock, a high impact improvement that qualified for foreign aid budgets, but quite another matter upgrading the track. Consequently, after an hour, they were still lumbering through the flat plains that skirted the province of Striberg. She tried to get some sleep, but was soon woken by a commotion in the corridor.

"Coffee!" called a voice. "Coffee tea! Coffee! Coffee tea!"

The one in charge got up to see what was going on. Sliding open the door, he glanced out. A large black man in a blue Rurorail boiler suit was wheeling a steaming metal coffee trolley down the corridor. The man posted to guard the exit was trying to stop him.

"No. *No!*" he was saying. "Piss off. We don't need coffee here."

But the visitor, who's language skills appeared rudimentary, was determined to ignore him. The guard tried again:

"No coffee, geddit? La Qahwa!" he added in Arabic, for the benefit of what he supposed was a Sudanese guest worker.

But the steel trolley was immovable in the narrow corridor and eventually the guard was forced to give way.

"OK," he snapped angrily. "Straight through then, but no stopping."

The leader watched this charade with mounting irritation. Then, almost simultaneously, another appeared at the other end of the car.

"Coffee, please! Buns, rock cakes, soda drinks!" The guard in the corridor hurried by to block the new arrival and what promised to be a tricky pile-up mid corridor.

Meanwhile his boss retreated back into the compartment, firmly shutting the door behind him and drawing the blinds. He glanced at Rosie. She appeared to have gone back to sleep.

"What's up?" asked his colleague.

"Coffee trolleys. Bloody guest workers!"

He closed his eyes, and tried to resume his snooze. Instead the commotion from outside in the corridor got louder, despite the door being closed. The intruders now appeared to be arguing about right of way.

"*Get outta ma way!*" one was shouting.

"*Get your own lazy arse out of the way,*" reacted the other. "*You useless piece of shit!*"

He opened a lazy eye. They were speaking English, not Arabic.

The door flew open.

"Coffee tea soda drink?!" shouted one.

"Buns cakes pastries?!" yelled the other.

He leapt up.

"What the fuck? Get out! Get them out of here Spatsky!" Spatsky, the guard, stood helplessly in the corridor, one of the trolleys now forming a barrier between him and the compartment.

"Sorry boss," he stammered. "It's these damn trolleys. And these guys don't seem…"

"Don't seem? It's your job to make them see!" fumed the leader. He turned to his colleague, muttered "idiot…", and tried to pull the door shut, but without success. He was on the point of employing a head butt to get the leering face to withdraw when Rosie hastily put her hand on his arm.

"Coffee please," she blurted out, over his shoulder, "black no sugar." She said it loudly to hide her nervousness and got up abruptly. For it was Hank and Leroy that she recognised in the blue boiler suits.

"Now look here, Miss Elphberg…" began her captor, turning round and releasing his grip on the door.

"Look here yourself, whoever you are," snapped Rosie, glaring up at him. "Will you deny me food and drink as well? Mr. Hentzau will have something to say about that."

"Hentzau?"

Her heart felt like it was sewn onto the roof of her mouth. If it wasn't on Hentzau's orders that she'd been dragged away, then on who's was it? The possibility was too horrible to contemplate.

"And a rock cake," she continued blithely.

"*OK, rock cake coming right up!*" echoed Leroy from somewhere behind Hank. Rosie winced. Surely one of her captors would realise? Besides, what on earth were they doing? Presumably they had witnessed her abduction and had come to rescue her. But she didn't need their help. Were they mad? These weren't some ordinary muggers they were dealing with.

Her heart continued to pound. Whatever else, she told herself, she must try to remain cool. The leader hesitated momentarily.

"OK one coffee, one rock, that's it," he commanded. "Then out!"

As Hank poured a steaming cup of coffee the train whistled. He handed it to the man to pass on to Rosie, eyeing him carefully. Behind him, Leroy rummaged around in his trolley for a rock cake. The whistle sounded again, longer this time.

As it did so the second of her captors tensed: he had a sudden blinding premonition that something was wrong. They were on a curve. He glanced out of the window quickly. Sure enough, they were about to enter a tunnel. And it suddenly dawned on him: these were no Sudanese guest workers…

He whipped around.

"*Boss…*"

The Spare and The Heir

The other looked up, alarmed. He was clutching the steaming cup of coffee, trying not to spill it. There was a split second of realisation, but whatever speed of reaction he might normally possess was dented by an instinctive reluctance to spill the coffee. By the time he had overcome it, it was too late. With one final blast of the whistle the train entered the tunnel with an almighty roar. Several things happened simultaneously.

Out in the corridor Leroy abandoned his search for a rock cake and, straightening up, yanked the steam lever on the tea urn. A scalding jet of tiny water particles under high pressure shot out horizontally, directly into the face of Spatsky standing beside it. His scream was drowned out by the tunnel. Inside the compartment, now in darkness, Hank fell on the leader, tipping the coffee up into his face, while Rosie leapt up onto her seat. Leroy bounded in, and in the darkness there was the sound of several grunting bodies falling heavily against the sides of the compartment.

"Take that, dude!" yelled an American voice.

"Let's get her out of here!" hollered another.

"Away from the window!" screamed a third, and as Rosie jumped away the whole expanse of sealed glass seemed to disintegrate. Suddenly the noise of the train racing through the tunnel increased to a deafening scream, bringing with it a tsunami of freezing air. Several more figures seemed to enter, from where, and whether friendly or not, Rosie couldn't tell, until the whole of the small space seemed to be filled with the sounds of violent struggle. Just as they reached daylight again, the train screeched to a halt with a high-pitched squealing of brakes. Rosie was catapulted forward against something hard and metallic. She was barely conscious of being picked up, bundled out of the smashed window, and carried down an embankment into some woods beyond.

Chapter 45

Shocked!

The images were emailed through to the President's office in something of a hurry. It was the president's assistant and Rosie's friend, Sophie Tarlenheim, who printed them out, and she didn't know what to make of them at first, because they came as an attachment with no message. She examined them for clues, a puzzled look on her face. Someone dressed in a centurion's outfit, with a spear, and a breastplate, another with a shield and shoes with weird little wings attached to the side of them. It was hard to make out. Was it some kind of invitation to a fancy dress party?

Then she double took. Oh my God, surely not? She inspected them more closely, and reeled back in horror. It was. It was disgusting! Had spamming descended to this level? No, that was not possible, they'd come through from the Minister of Culture's personal email account. Had it been hacked? Plus it was huge. Then a thought occurred to her. Perhaps they were meant for Horst? What if they'd come through to the wrong email address by mistake? Had the Minister for Culture mistakenly emailed them to the President rather than to the government art director? This could be highly embarrassing…

She harboured a soft spot for Horst, and made a rapid executive decision. She would say nothing about them, seal them in an envelope and drop them off in Horst's office anonymously. She hid them under her file and went in search of a large envelope, feeling relieved that she had averted disaster but determined, notwithstanding, to wash her twenty-three year old hands forthwith.

Chapter 46

Who Will Rid Me of this Meddlesome Tour Leader?

"All I can say, Hentzau, is that you do not know shit about your own daughter-in-law."

"*Future* daughter-in-law, Yuri. The wedding's not until next week."

Hentzau was talking by telephone to the President of Globalny Foods.

"I am vell aware of that fact. I hope my credit lasts that long. My wife is buying up half the outfits in the city. Now listen to me good. My people found her in Striberg, pretending to be the tour guide. How is she connected with them, is what I would like to know?"

"I don't know. I had no idea.."

"Vell you had better get an idea. If I find she is together with Universal I will not be happy, you understand, and we will cancel the coronation. Handle this please."

"Of course," said Hentzau hurriedly. "But wait a minute. You say you found her in Striberg? So where is she now?"

"On her way to you. My people are under instructions to bring her in."

"But Yuri…"

"Listen, you wanted the roses, I got the roses. You wanted her found, I am bringing her in. But a deal is a deal, remember. I am helping you big time. I am expecting results. Call me tomorrow."

The line went dead.

"Problems, Papa?" said Tilly, sidling up behind him, uncharacteristically contrite after the exploding chemicals fiasco of the day before. "Is there anything I can do to help?"

"Oh hello," said Hentzau, fiddling with his cuffs distractedly.

She put her arms round him. "Has papa-kins forgiven me yet?" she pouted.

He looked distracted.

"Papa?"

"What is it?"

"What's a foreign element?"

He raised an eyebrow.

"I saw the news this morning," she continued. "About yesterday. And it was going on about 'foreign elements'. I'm not a foreign element am I, Papa?"

He couldn't help laughing, in spite of his own worries. "Oh that. No, darling, you're not a foreign element. It's kind of news-speak for enemies from abroad. We had to make up something, didn't we? Can't have the daughter of a government minister trying to assassinate her own father, now, can we?"

"But it was an accident, don't you believe me?" she cried.

He sauntered over to an antique oval mirror on the wall.

"It's called news manipulation." He smoothed his hair down. "A very useful skill, young lady."

His housekeeper knocked on the door.

"Your chief of staff is here to see you, sir."

"Very well, Melissa, send him in." He turned to Tilly, suddenly brisk.

"Now, haven't you got anything useful to do? Have you finished with the workmen? Where are the rest of your team?"

"They're helping rebuild the cellar. But they're … not talking to me anymore."

"Well run along then. I've got business to discuss."

She knew better than to push her father when he was in one of these moods. Especially after yesterday. She made for the door. Before she was able to reach it, it opened with a flourish and her father's chief of staff marched in. He flung her a withering look. She stuck out her tongue at him in reply, and before he could react she was out of the door.

He muttered an oath under his breath.

Hentzau looked up.

"Disturbing news, sir," he said, pulling up a chair. "I've just been up at the Palace. Something's going on. I think they're preparing to meet with the Fraser character."

"To meet with him? What, you mean they're capitulating?"

"Looks very much like it. Red carpet, the lot."

Hentzau considered for a moment.

"And I just had Yuri Lougouev on the phone. He's found Rose Elphberg. You'll never guess where she's been all this time."

"Where?"

"It's incredible, but it appears she's been in contact with Fraser."

It took a while for his colleague to digest this startling piece of news. "My God, sir! What are you saying? That she too is involved with Universal?"

"I have no idea."

"Fraser's got to be stopped," he said quietly.

But not quietly enough. Because outside the door Tilly had her ear glued to the wood panelling.

"It's all very well you saying that," she heard her father say. "But how? Let's not get diverted. We've got the girl back, that's the main thing. Now we've got to get her married off. As quickly as possible. How soon can we arrange it?"

"Sir! It's next week."

"I think we should bring it forward again. If they are planning to capitulate to Universal…" He trailed off. "Can we get it organised in three days?"

His Chief of Staff looked shocked. "Sir, *three days*…"

"Let's do it. Hell, all it takes is a priest and two rings."

"And two people."

"Yes, well, now we've got her, the sooner we get it over with, the sooner we can concentrate on the Restoration, and after that…well, even if they do try and cut a deal with Universal, even if this Fraser fellow is given the red carpet treatment at the Palace, so what? The game will be over once she's in. We'll be in a position to reverse things."

"And if she's tied up with them?"

Hentzau paused, running his hands through his hair. "Let's hope to Christ she's not. We must pray that Yuri got it wrong."

"I still think it would be better to get him out of the way, sir."

Hentzau laughed. "Who will rid me of this meddlesome tour leader?" he said in dramatic tones. He snorted. "And do what with him? Put him where? Chief, use your head."

Outside the door, Tilly straightened up and stood motionless, deep in thought. Then she seemed to reach some sort of decision and, turning, skipped up the stairs.

Chapter 47
A Telegram from Mother

Activity at the Palace had reached fever pitch. In the Cabinet Room, workmen were dismantling the long antique table piece by piece, while others were unpacking four high backed gold painted chairs upholstered in red velvet from large wooden crates. Two of Blicker's 'Blue Circle' works lay propped up against one wall, whilst back in their place were going two of the original royal portraits.

Two corridors away Horst Bangermann was running around like he was possessed. The walls of his studio were littered with a mass of hastily sketched drawings and colour washes, pinned up one on top of another and often at odd angles, impressions of uniforms, carpet designs, stagecoaches and crowns; while lined up beneath them were two large scale photographic references from Prisoner of Zenda movie history, stamped Metro Goldwyn Mayer: one in black and white of Ronald Colman, dated 1937, one in colour of Stewart Granger, 1952. Both were dressed in Hollywood's version of the Royal Robes of King Rudolph of Elphberg.

"On, off, on, off," he was muttering to himself, mantra-fashion, twirling his ginger whiskers agitatedly. "It's ridiculous.

How do they expect anyone to do anything decent at four minute's notice?"

He'd been going on like this all morning. It certainly didn't help, his assistant Georgi thought to herself. She felt like telling the old queen to shut up. Instead she said:

"What do you want me to do about the trumpeters' uniforms?"

The twirling came to an abrupt halt.

"Oh my God, I'd completely forgotten. Trumpeters. Lordy." He started to rummage around in a pile of loose drawings. "Didn't I do a sketch for those? *Merde*, where are they?" he muttered under his breath. "How can I be expected to work in this mess! How many are there?"

"Four, I think."

"Four? We'll never get them done in time. They want them for tomorrow don't they? And I've got the carpet to see to, those chairs must be placed, that new guard that needs fitting, I'll need to get these sketches presentable, I've…"

"Calm down. Can't we fit them in something else? What about those butler outfits we never used?"

"Butlers?" exploded Horst. "In black, are you mad? These are State Trumpeters, not angels of death. We need gold, we need brocade, we need long brown boots. With spurs." He considered for a moment, his brain racing. Then, from somewhere outside in the palace courtyard, a band struck up.

"God, how can I think?" yelled Horst, tearing at what remained of his hair. He paced over to the window and looked out. Far below the army band was practising the new national anthem for the arrival of the VIP the next day. They sounded like they could do with some tuning.

"Someone ought to tell that Blicker you know," he muttered venomously.

"Tell him? Tell him what?"

"Tell him how dreadful that tune of his sounds. *'Roses Over*

Ruritania'. I've never heard anything so awful. At least with his paintings you don't actually have to look at them. But that...noise..."

Georgi giggled, for the first time that morning. Horst turned round.

"And I wish to God he'd let me sort out his hair. Incidentally, we haven't got this man's measurements yet, have we?"

"Fraser? No. I've asked the president's office three times but I get the feeling it's not a high priority with those guys."

"Well piss on them then," scoffed Horst. "Excuse my French. I'm not going to messed around any longer. We haven't even got a photograph of him. We've got a job to do. We'll get them ourselves. Where's he staying?"

"I've no idea. I could find out."

"Do that." Horst smirked. "I can think of other ways of getting his inside leg…" There was a knock on the door. "Now what? All the waiter's tunics to be let out by two inches? Come in!"

But it was only a palace messenger. He handed Horst a large brown envelope and exited. Horst examined it.

"Perhaps they're the measurements," said Georgi hopefully.

"Chance would be a fine thing," replied Horst, tearing the envelope open. He drew out two scanned images and stared at them, slack-mouthed. "Well? Anything interesting?"

Horst had gone suddenly silent. And pale.

"What's the matter? Bad news?"

As nonchalantly as he could he slid the sheets back in the envelope.

"Oh nothing," he said, steadying himself. "Just a telegram from mother."

Chapter 48

A Long Journey

"Oh Christopher." He looked up at her askance. "You shouldn't have done that!"

They were slumped, exhausted, at a cafe table in a small village square somewhere not far from Striberg. The Angels were lolling around on the grass, kicking a football around with a scratch side of local kids.

"But Rosie," said Christopher gently, "you'd been taken against your will. What were we supposed to do? Sit back and do nothing?"

She shook her head. "You don't understand. It's different in my country."

"Different?" He tugged at the sleeve of his leather jacket despondently. "You can say that again."

"OK, so my father-in-law…"

"*Future* father-in-law," remonstrated Christopher. "You're not married yet, and if I have anything to do with it…"

"Please! Stop!" She laid a hand on his arm, searching his eyes. Her own were clear, and direct. "You mean well, I know that. I appreciate it, I really do. But there's nothing you, or I, can do. That man has power." She sighed. "Though I admit he can be heavy-handed."

"Heavy handed!" echoed Christopher, tearing his eyes away. It felt almost painful to look at her beauty, a beauty that was destined to go to waste.

"I'd already made a decision to face the music when we got to the Capital. But it just shows to what lengths he's prepared to go, can't you see that?" She squeezed his arm for emphasis. "He has my parents. He can decide what sort of life we will lead. And you saw the reception we got in Zenda? The people want me as Queen. What will they say if I break off my engagement? It's meant to be a fairy-tale. A wedding made in heaven. They will be disillusioned. Can you imagine how badly it would damage the monarchy, before it's even begun? Can you?"

"A good thing too, I should think. I mean, you don't really believe all that rubbish do you, Rosie?"

"Rubbish?" she said, pulling away from him.

"That monarchy bollocks."

She raised her head, fingering stray strands of her hair. "Well don't you? You're English."

"Half American actually. My mother was from Baltimore. So there's a bit of sanity there, thank God."

"Christopher, it's about destiny. Duty." She gazed out over the dusty hills, with their steep, narrow terraced fields. "Besides, perhaps I can make things better."

"Ha! Destiny. You sound like a Buddhist. At least don't deny yourself free will. Doesn't your personal happiness count for something?"

"There are more important things than happiness."

"I have to tell you, that's a most un-modern attitude." He paused, deep in thought. "But listen Rosie, maybe I can help you. Help your parents. You can get out. Come to London. Because this monarchy thing, do you really think you can make a difference? It's a democracy here, correct? There will always be a political leader. If we are honest – and please, let's be honest with each other – Kings, Queens, they're just for tourists."

She contemplated him for a while in silence, then said, wearily, "You don't get it. I'm an Elphberg. If you realised what that meant you would be ashamed you asked me to do such a thing. Why should we go anywhere? This is our home. As for free will…" She trailed off. "You forget, there is responsibility, too."

"Exactly, responsibility to yourself."

"You also do not understand, perhaps, the role of monarchy." She frowned. "It's about…how do you say it?... a form of political magic, except it's not political, that's the whole point. And in Ruritania, if the people support it, then it can have the power to create good things. Yes, I know, people say what's the use of magic? What's the use of ritual? They want everything to be rational. But really, the truth is, they don't understand our need for magic."

He laughed. "That sounds seriously odd, coming from someone who wanted to be a physicist."

"Perhaps even you, in England, with all the troubles your monarchy has had, no longer understand these things. But it is deep in our history, in the history of our ancestors, it's a bond with them, and it holds a power for us that it can never hold for a foreigner. It's a continuity, a sense of nationhood. Apart, that is, from all the other benefits.'

"Name one."

"Well…a head of state without power, for a start. There's no argument, no one votes for him – or her. No one appoints the monarch. The monarch is above politics, he just is, for all time." She paused. "And whoever actually runs the country – your Prime Minister – well he can be got rid of without any upset at all. They cannot usurp power as there is a greater power above them. A power that is institutional rather than personal. Your great Queen Elizabeth was a totem. A magic totem."

"Well yes, I will give you Liz. She was a saint. But what happens if you get a dud?"

"Same thing. There's no argument. And because they have no power, what damage can they do? You have to remember, Christopher, that it's the monarchy that's the magic. Not the monarch."

"And do you think it's fair that they have all that money?"

Here she paused. "I agree that it's not really fair. I suppose that's the price we have to pay. But they pay a price too, remember. Their destiny is also a burden." She sighed. "Like mine."

He reflected on what she had just said. It all sounded overly romantic to him. In Britain it had become a soap opera, so what was to prevent it turning into the same thing over here? That Walter Bagehot bloke was right - let daylight in, and the whole edifice collapses. As for the political benefits, he wasn't convinced. The whole concept, truth be told, was anti-democratic. Anachronistic.

He told her about the Mayflower, the Boston Tea Party, and the Statue of Liberty; about how his mother had been a Daughter of the American Revolution.

"That's good," she agreed, "so you have romance in your mother's history too. Americans have their ancestors, we have ours."

"Look, two days ago you were telling me you didn't want to be Queen!" he cried, getting increasingly exasperated. Was she in denial, or just incredibly stubborn? He'd thought the kidnap would have changed her mind, but he felt her slipping through his fingers once more.

"Nothing would make you more unhappy. So what has made you change your mind?" He snorted. "Three men on a train? Have you forgotten what you said, that you would never be able to ride the metro again?"

"Nothing has changed my mind," she snapped. "I still don't *want* to be Queen. But what choice do I have?"

"Well at least allow me to come with you to your village, to your parents house, to make sure you are safe."

She didn't want him to come. But he was adamant. So they reached a compromise. She would travel with him as far as the Capital, and the following morning he could take her home.

∽

THE JOURNEY BACK WAS UNEVENTFUL. WHILE THE ANGELS went back to Striberg, to lead the coach on later, Christopher and Rosie made straight to the Capital, just in case further danger might be awaiting them back in Striberg. But communications across this part of the country were difficult. The local train they finally caught rattled and creaked at little more than twenty-five miles an hour, stopping at every two-horse backwoods hamlet. It seemed it wasn't even necessary for the stops to have a platform to get on at. Several times the train pulled into places with just a goods shed and at one point came to a grinding halt in the middle of a corn field, from where about a dozen grimy labourers emerged with chickens under their arms to clamber aboard. The carriages were very soon filled up with livestock of all descriptions, and Christopher found himself wedged between Rosie on one side and a large wicker basket containing two squealing piglets on the other. Which made conversation almost impossible.

"Is it always like this?" shouted Christopher above the din.

Rosie laughed, smoothing the folds of her dark linen jacket on the rack above her. She flicked her hair back behind her shoulders, and sat down.

"It wasn't always so bad," she said. "Only since the Rose

Revolution. Before that all the people used the buses, but now, often, the train is the only way."

"How come? Don't they have roads up here?"

The piglets fell suddenly silent, as if eager to know the reason why they were being subjected to this juddering indignity.

"Petrol's expensive. The price is more than three times what it used to be. And the government has this crazy environmental policy. It might be good for the environment, but it's surely bad for the people."

He yawned.

"You must be exhausted," she said, solicitously.

"Emotionally traumatised, more like."

"I'll give you an example," she continued. "They want to make everybody convert to electric cars. They put high taxes on petrol, and they tell people to use trains. But do they know anything about the country over there in The Capital? About the country people, the working people? Of course they don't. It's very good for the city, OK, sure, less cars, less smoke, better life, good transport system. Tourists come, they say what a nice clean country, what a clever enlightened government, why don't we do the same thing in London, Paris, New York. But who ever sees the country? Out here in the mountains where the tourists never go, the people are poor. Dirt poor. Petrol is too expensive, but no way can they afford electric cars. And if they can't afford it, you can bet the government can't. So everybody takes the train - the old train, because they're not yet able to afford the new one, like the special express from Striberg to the Capital for the rich businessmen. But who cares about the people in the countryside? It's a scandal."

She glanced at the piglets, who were beginning to get the message, becoming restless again.

"The same is true in all areas of life," she went on. "The people are poor, and they get poorer. We have this crazy

The Spare and The Heir 285

economics minister who says do this, do that, we'll make ourselves a green country, the envy of the whole world. Fine for the middle classes, no problem, but for the poor? I don't think so. It's hard enough for them to afford the latest trainers for their kids, kids who watch TV all day. You know what? They're made in Taiwan. Cost twice as much as our own. Then on the other side we've got this other minister who says we should grow things, make things to sell to the west. But then what do we grow for ourselves? We can't eat sunflowers, we can't eat roses! These people always argue about dogma, never about reality." She gazed into the distance, a far-away look in her eyes: "Maybe, if I am Queen, things will be different. That's one good thing at least."

The piglets scrabbled, a chicken clucked and somewhere a few rows away a breast-fed baby started to wail, as if underlining the nature of the reality which she was trying to address. She looked across at Christopher. He was fast asleep.

∽

WHEN HE AWOKE TWO HOURS LATER, HE FOUND HER LAID across him. Her head was in his lap, her dark hair bunched up, her long legs curled up on the seat. The carriage was almost empty now, the farmers and their livestock gone. He watched her. Innocent, vulnerable, her breathing light, her chest rising and falling evenly as if she didn't have a care in the world. He touched her gently. She stirred, and nuzzled her head into him, turning slightly. He stared out of the window at the washed out colours of the hills fading in the afternoon light.

She'd evidently been awake, for when he stopped she sat up and rubbed her eyes.

"Where are we?" she said.

"How should I know!"

She laughed, messing her hair lazily, and looked up and

down the carriage. "Where is everyone?" He shrugged. "Oh well, can't be far now." She flashed him a coy smile. They stared at each other. Where before he would have felt awkward, now he felt warm. Warmed by her, his proximity to her, tinged with a heavy melancholy. He'd finally found a girl he wanted to spend time with, and she was unavailable. Outside, telegraph poles sliced dreamily by, as if in slow motion, floating in the air.

The carriage was empty, they were alone in the late afternoon, the shadows lengthening, thickening on the hills where greens turned slowly to blacks, blues to mauves. There was nothing to lose, he thought to himself. This moment in time was all he was going to get. He leant over and kissed her. She looked at him in surprise, but didn't push him away.

"Am I taking you home?" he said.

"I've been thinking. I don't think that's a very good idea."

He kissed her again, this time on the lips, and he felt hers curl under him and then open hesitantly. She remained absolutely still, her hands resting easily on her thighs, as he felt for her, his fingers tracing the line of her neck. She smelt warm and scented. They kissed slowly for a full minute, exploring each other, then she nipped him gently and pulled away.

"I can't," she whispered hoarsely.

"I'm sorry," he said thickly, "I couldn't help it."

She gazed at him steadily. "Christopher, I know. Me too. But it's impossible. You know that."

"Why should it be?" he said, pulling away from her, suddenly animated. "Why should you get married to someone you don't love, live a life you don't want, a future you don't seek. It's so fucking unfair!"

She had turned to face the window as he said this, and now returned to him and touched his cheek, a sad look in her eyes. "I know....call it...how do you say, bad timing." Her hand fell onto her lap. "Let's just think about the present, these hours, this special moment. We've had a few good days haven't we?" She lowered her eyes. "Let's remember that."

"And tonight?"

She returned to him. "Tonight?"

He didn't answer, but leant over to kiss her.

"No," she said, "you know we can't do that. Would that, after all, be fair?"

"Fair on who? On him?"

"No, you idiot," she said softly, "on me," turning away so that he couldn't see the tear in her eye.

Chapter 49

Next Steps

"So how are you going to play this?" queried Boris, staring at his laptop.

Blicker was pacing up and down his study, his corduroy jacket flapping, furiously pulling on a Camel.

"We know what hotel they're booked into. We'll put a message through asking him to come to meet us at the palace. We'll make it sound innocuous, give him, and us, a way out if he declines. Just a simple reception as the 'tour leader' of the group. I don't think we should acknowledge him as anything important until we see what cards he has to lay on the table. What d'you say?"

Boris idly scrolled the screen. He was itching to get to the surf report, since the weather chart showed a hurricane heading Cuba's way.

"Boris!" said Blicker sharply. "You with me?"

"Oh yes, boss, sorry, good idea."

"Always give your enemy an off ramp, Boris," Blicker went on, jabbing his cigarette at him for emphasis, "never back him into a corner. Otherwise, mark my words, he'll fight."

"I thought that's what enemies were for." Boris leant back

in his chair and yawned. "By the way, did those photos you mentioned ever show up? If we can confront him with something…"

"No damn it, they didn't. And our minister of culture seems to have gone AWOL in London."

Boris laughed.

"Clever old minister."

Chapter 50

A Special Invitation

It had been a long day. His feet ached, and he'd just taken an aspirin to dispel the first rumblings of a headache, so it was with a sense of long-delayed relief that Christopher finally lowered himself into the scalding bath in his room at the Strelsau Intercontinental Hotel.

He was gripped by an immense feeling of loss. He had tried everything: begged to come with her; offered to take up her case; reasoned with her to see if she couldn't find another way. But it was no use. He ran the enormous chrome tap some more and poured in a second capful of Intercontinental Hotels bubble bath. Lying back in the soapy froth, he sighed. The trip still had five days to go, but it felt almost over already.

Over, that is, after breakfast the following day. At least she'd promised him that. And who knows, perhaps she would come to see him tonight? She'd left the glimmer of a possibility open.

But somehow he doubted it.

His phone vibrated. He jumped. It was another missed call from the 0151 number. His heart sank. He'd almost forgotten. They were chasing the money. But for how much longer?

Then he heard the gruff voice of Jackson calling through the door:

"Hi, Chris, you there?"

"Come on in Coach, the door's not locked." He heard it open and close. "I'm in the bath. Help yourself to a drink if you want. Shan't be long."

He suddenly remembered he'd asked Jackson up to go over the arrangements for the next day's football match. The Angels had organised to play a friendly in the Capital and none of the paperwork from the Sports Federation that was supposed to be waiting for them had arrived, so Christopher had said he'd contact them to find out what was going on. Unfortunately he'd done nothing about it. It wasn't that he hadn't had time. He'd simply forgotten. He'd had other things on his mind. It was too late now, it would have to wait until the morning. He decided to forestall the question with an answer.

"I...er...I called the Federation," he lied, through the door.

"Oh yeah? What did they say?"

"The man we need to talk to, wasn't there. But I left a message, told them you were here and looking forward to the match on Saturday, and someone will get back to us. Hopefully before the morning."

"Hey, good work," said Jackson. "Let's hope they get back to us tonight. I gotta tell my boys something."

"Well, I wouldn't count on it," replied Christopher cautiously. "They sounded pretty disorganised down there."

"Goddamit," growled Jackson. "Why can't they get their act together? We've flown three thousand miles, we gotta practise tomorrow, we haven't even got a pitch to use. Shit."

The phone rang.

"Coach, can you get that?"

Jackson answered it. "Hey!" he boomed. There was a silence. Then: "Say again? I didn't quite catch that?...The president's office? Which president?" Suddenly the bathroom door opened and Jackson's face appeared, the receiver up to one ear. Christopher shot bolt upright.

"OK, one minute, Miss," he continued, "I'll get him." He covered the mouthpiece with a large bejewelled hand.

"Hey, get this," he whispered, a puzzled expression on his face. "The president of this goddam place has his office on the line, wants to speak to the tour leader." He gaped. "That's you, ain't it?"

"The *president?* You sure?"

"That's what the lady says."

Christopher relieved him of the handset, gingerly.

"Or could it be me they're after?" whispered Jackson.

"Yes? Can I help? It's the tour manager speaking."

He listened while the woman on the other end of the line extended to him, Roderick Fraser, an invitation to a palace reception to be held the following afternoon.

There must be some mistake. "You...er...sure you have the right person?"

The woman assured him she had. He was the Tour Leader, was he not? She put a peculiar emphasis on the word 'Leader'.

Jackson was gesticulating to him but Christopher waved him away. He suddenly realised he was naked, as the last of the soapsuds evaporated from his midriff with a hissing sound.

"But...er...how do I know that you're calling from the president's office?"

The woman explained they'd be sending round an official invitation, and a chauffeur-driven car the following day. He could ring the palace himself, if necessary, just to confirm it. Then an idea suddenly struck him. Doubtless the president was inviting him to some large reception, like a garden party, on the strength of their being the first foreign tour into Ruritania. It made sense, good public relations and all that. He climbed out of the bath excitedly, motioning for Jackson to throw him a towel.

"Will I actually be able to meet the president? In person?"

The woman assured him he would. Here was his chance. To bring up the subject of Rosie. They agreed a time and the woman hung up.

"Well?" said Jackson, wide-eyed. Christopher stood mesmerised by the door, pondering this stroke of luck.

"It's incredible. The president has just invited me to tea."

"Why?"

"No idea. Presumably because he wants to find out what we, the first foreign tour into their country, think of the place. How they can improve it." He paused. "How very enlightened of them. They're sending a car at four tomorrow afternoon."

"Can we come?"

Christopher laughed. "Oh God, I'm sorry Jackson. I forgot to ask them that."

"So how about you check it out. Just me and one of the boys. This is an opportunity you know, a real opportunity. If we can interest the dude in football…"

Christopher agreed to see what he could do.

Chapter 51

The Countdown

At exactly this moment, events were moving at pace elsewhere.

"*Got it!*" whispered number four, otherwise known to his mother as Hans. Hastily he reconnected the line and turned to Tilly. They were in a machine room deep in the bowels of the Strelsau Intercontinental, somewhere adjacent to the underground car-park.

"You sure?" queried Tilly anxiously. She couldn't afford to mess this one up.

"Course I'm sure. That was the call that was put through to room 302. There were voices. When I disconnected this one..." He pointed to a mass of pink, blue, yellow and green wires "...the line went dead."

She looked unconvinced.

"That was the right room, wasn't it? This Fraser person's room?"

"Yes, yes," she said, distractedly. "What were they talking about?"

"How should I know? You didn't ask me to listen."

That wasn't quite true. One of them had been a Mr

Jackson, coach of the visiting football team. He had no idea what Tilly was intending, but when it was all over he was determined to go up there and get the man's autograph.

"OK well done, number two," said Tilly. She looked at her watch. "We've got three hours till zero hour. Might as well go and get a coke. Now you sure you can find your way back here alone?"

"What, all by myself?" blinked Hans. "I thought you said you were coming with me?"

"Well how can I, stupid, when I'm up there?" she snapped, pointing to the ceiling. "It's a doddle. All you have to do is cut the wire. We'll synchronise watches, so you can't go wrong."

Hans looked bolshy.

"It'll cost you…" he muttered. A sharp pain shot up his body from his groin as Tilly brought her knee up hard between his legs.

"Ouch!"

"Now listen here, you little squirt…"

Chapter 52

A Bad Dream, or...

Christopher had just finished shaving when he thought he heard something. A kind of scuffling, and then a rattle, followed by silence. He glanced past his face in the mirror. Then it came again. Perplexed, he put the razor down, wiped the remains of the foam off his face, and went next door to investigate. Something was definitely going on in his wardrobe. A hanger rattled to the floor, a door creaked.

He approached, cautiously, listening intently but whatever it was had stopped. He yanked at the door. There was a scuffle, and a pair of legs disappeared through a hidden connector into the room next door. His dry cleaning swung violently.

What the fuck?

He leapt in and stumbled into an adjoining wardrobe. As he did so the door to this new wardrobe was hurriedly jammed shut by the fleeing intruder. Suddenly it was pitch black, and Christopher found himself flailing around in a swirl of silk, cotton and polythene bags. He cursed, scrabbled for the door handle, and heaved it sideways. The handle came away in his hand and he swore again. Shoving forward with all his might he emerged just in time to see the door into the corridor slam shut. A key turned in the lock.

"Hey...!"

The room seemed to be empty. Then he noticed the length of canvas measuring tape dangling from the bed. One of his pairs of trousers lay discarded, and another was jammed in the wardrobe, the belt loop caught on a hook and half ripped. He got up, and went over to examine the measuring tape. The man had obviously dropped it in his hurry to escape. What did it mean? Burglars who go around measuring up stuff before they decide to nick it? Theft to order? Probably they had a scam going with the laundry. What a weird bloody country.

He returned to his room just in time to hear the knock on the door. His bowels did a pirouette. But it was Spinelli. He took a deep breath. This was doing his nerves in. What the hell did he want?

"Yes?" he said suspiciously.

But the man looked unruffled. He was dressed in a pair of freshly creased white trousers, a black leather jacket, and what looked like a pair of black patent leather dancing pumps. His hair was greased back and he reeked of alcohol. He looked like he belonged in Chicago, circa 1926. In no state to measure up anything, except perhaps a coffin.

"You wanna come out on the town, pal?"

"What, at this hour?" said Christopher, making a show of looking at his watch. He realised too late that he was no longer wearing it.

"Sure. Why not." Wink. "It's still early where I'm going."

Christopher hesitated for a fraction of a second, mindful of Donald's instructions to bend over backwards for this guy. But no more than a fraction. He didn't owe Donald anything.

"Thank you for the offer, Joey, but...er...no thanks."

"Sure I cannot tempt you, Chris?"

"Sure," Christopher said. He imitated a snoring noise.

"Bedtime for tour manager."

Spinelli shrugged. "OK buddy, no problem. You be good now."

Christopher watched him march down the corridor, checking his reflection in a large plate glass window as he went. Christopher closed the door and switched on the TV. He'd had enough for one day. A kidnap attempt, the unrequited love of a Princess, an invitation from the President, and now the attempted burglary of his dry cleaning.

A male announcer with a rich American accent was informing the viewer over a background jingle which fine hotels in the Balkans took CNN. It was a jingle all too familiar to international hotel hermits everywhere, a tune which went hand in hand with jet lag, late night room service and ice cold air-conditioning. Christopher switched channels. A message came up: '*Warning. After three minutes viewing you will be charged for this movie*'. This gave way to two panting and groaning Scandinavian couples - or they might have been Dutch - doing things to each other that he did not think possible. He watched with mounting fascination as one of them approached what sounded like an orgasm. After about two and a half minutes, by his reckoning, the action was fast and furious, but still not resolved, so it was with some reluctance that he switched channels. There, the same message came up, but the action was considerably tamer. After a safe interval of about thirty seconds he switched back, only to find the Scandinavians embarked on some new routine. He felt his interest flagging. There was a third knock on the door.

Third time lucky, he realised with a renewed surge of excitement. This had to be her. Darling Rosie, please let it be you. Composing with care a casual smile of welcome, he opened it.

"Hi," she said, huskily.

"Oh...hello," he replied, his heart sinking.

Martha smiled. There was something odd about her, but he couldn't quite put his finger on it. Her lips were strangely moist-looking and there was a faint whiff of strawberries.

"Well?" she said, finally. "Aren't you going to ask me in?"

"Er...um..." he stammered, involuntarily making a play for his watch again. But his reactions had improved this time, and he managed to divert the impulse to his underarm, rubbing an imaginary bruise. But as he did so he pulled a small but significant part of his towelling bathrobe across his body, and suddenly became aware of something still stirring within it. He dared not look down, and, turning hastily, darted back into his room.

"Come in," he mumbled awkwardly. "Entree."

Too late he realised his new mistake. Bruno, Borg, Britt and Birgitta were once more approaching a noisy resolution, this time accompanied by a flashing message which read: *"1000 ruros have been added to your hotel bill. Have a nice time"*. He flicked it off and fled into the bathroom.

"That is," she continued, looking around her with a sly expression, "if you don't have company?"

"No, no," he said, puce-faced and out of sight, "I...er...I'm all on my own. Won't be a moment." He took a couple of deep breaths in an effort to regain his composure.

"You okay in there?" she said.

He stopped abruptly, conscious of the noise he was making. "Fine, fine. So," he stammered, wishing this woman would just leave him alone, and mentally kicking himself for not having turned her away at the door. What the fuck had he been thinking about?

"What's, er, how are you?"

There was silence. Perhaps she hadn't heard him. He scarfed down a glass of water and, tightly securing the bow in the cord of his bathrobe, stepped out of the bathroom gingerly.

At first he didn't see her. Then he heard her, behind him.

"Take me," she whispered. He started violently.

"I'm sorry?"

He turned. But he needn't have bothered. She stood in front of him with her coat open, milk white. He swallowed.

"*Fuck* me," she said, more menacingly this time, and with one smooth continuous movement she stepped towards him and untied the good work of a few moments before. His bathrobe fell open.

"Mmm," she said approvingly, grabbing him around the waist, a hungry look in her eyes. In vain he tried to maintain his balance, and they fell back on the bed together. She pinned his arms to the mattress and started to bite his neck. The whiff of strawberries became suddenly overwhelming.

"Listen, Martha..." he gasped. Her hair brushed his face while her tongue darted down his torso, and he couldn't help a grunt. Suddenly, she let go of his arms and with one swift arc of her head switched her attention to the source of his embarrassment, gobbling it eagerly, flicking her long thick hair to one side. He sat bolt upright, but she was surprisingly strong, and had his legs in a vice-like grip. He fell back on the bed with a thud.

"Oh my God, Martha, what the fuck are you doing..." he groaned.

"Exactly that," she purred, slamming his arms away as he struggled to right himself. Then she bit him. He shot up, yelping in pain.

"Aaagh! Be careful!" he yelled, fending her off. She stared up at him with a good imitation of drug-crazed eyes. They tumbled to the floor.

"That's right," she moaned, "take me. Fuck me, fuck me, *fuck me...*"

He stared at her, desperate to avoid sinking beneath the waves of her lust. Dear God, he thought, what the fuck?

The Spare and The Heir

∼

MEANWHILE, BACK IN THE BOWELS OF THE HOTEL, TILLY AND her Zenda Pioneers were synchronising watches. Sixty minutes to zero hour. *Number two?* Check. *Number three?* Check. *Number ten?* Check. Numbers four through nine had quit her gang after the chemicals in the cellar fiasco – mostly because their parents had forbidden them to have play dates with her - but she had decided to retain her old numbering system for a while, just in case they decided to come back in the fold. It had been a hard job, though, explaining the logic of that to number ten. They were all set. They did the Zenda Pioneer three fingered salute and dispersed.

∼

FLAT ON THE FLOOR, CHRISTOPHER GULPED HARD, LIKE A FISH fighting for air, his neck sticky with the vestiges of her strawberry lip-gloss and numb from the clashing of dental work. He was vaguely mindful of Donald's parting words: "Just remember one thing - your clients' happiness is your only concern." He had to find a way to let her down. Gently. Then he heard it.

"What was that?" he whispered urgently, struggling to sit upright.

"Christopher, where are you going ..." she went, clinging to him desperately.

He heard it again, more distinctly this time. A light tap on his door. He stared at it in horror, upright now, Martha slumped on his lap, as the handle slowly turned. Oh my God, he thought, please, dear Lord...

She stood in the doorway. She saw the upturned pair of high-heels. Dreamlike, her eyes wandered to the bed. They locked onto Christopher's for a second, then hastily pulled away.

"I'm sorry," she said simply, and before he could reply she had closed the door behind her.

"*Rosie?*" he cried, clawing on the bed to haul himself up. Easier said than done, she was still fastened to one of his legs.

"*Rosie!*" he shouted a second time, finally wrenching free. Martha slumped back on the floor: stunned, frustrated and boiling with humiliated fury. With one bound he had reached the door, what remained of his dressing gown trailing behind him. He clutched the cord around his waist and exploded into the corridor. She was nowhere to be seen.

He began trotting urgently towards the elevators. He got there just as one pair of doors were sliding shut, and their neighbour sliding open. He froze. An elderly gentleman stepped out, cried out in alarm, and stepped back in again. He retreated, aware for the first time of a cool breeze at about waist height. Looking down, he realised why. He fled back to his room in disarray. He felt sick.

He entered gingerly, but Martha was nowhere to be seen. He checked the bathroom. She'd gone. He slumped on his bed, the faint waft of strawberry clinging to the sheets the sole remaining evidence of what had gone on just a few moments before. And wept.

Surprisingly, it wasn't long before he fell asleep, exhausted. Though Rosie was in his thoughts as he drifted off, she wouldn't come to him in his dreams. She had deserted him. He wanted so desperately to explain. It was the Angry One who haunted him.

"Grrr," she growled, "lick pussycat."

In his dream there was a wild hammering from the floor above. The whole hotel seemed to go a-hammering, giant saucepans swinging crazily down from the ceiling and crashing against the walls. In his dream he tried to calm her.

"What d'you mean *Ssssh*?" she said angrily. "You Brits are all the same. This is sex, not a goddam game of cricket! Let's do it."

In his nightmare they did it, she like some great diabolic vortex, sucking him in. Her hands shot up to the headboard and he kneaded her breasts, white quivering mounds of flesh that suddenly turned into dough, great long strands of it breaking away and getting stuck in his fingers.

"Eugh!"

She clasped, she frothed, she juddered and tightened. Terrifying. The litany repeated itself.

"Do it! Do it! Do it!" she moaned.

"Come on! Come on! Come on!" she groaned.

"Yes! Yes! Yes!" she screamed.

More hammering, the clashing of cymbals. Martha sank her nails into his arse.

"Deeper! Deeper! Deeper! Aagh...aagh...aagh…"

There was a crash, and a brilliant white flash. The whole room seemed to light up, for a second everything was paralysed. He tried to move, but somehow the messages from his brain never reached where they were supposed to. Had they bonded together, he wondered dreamily, in some strange tantric voodoo?

Slowly she started to fade. But the light didn't. It got brighter. He regained consciousness. Or at least he thought he did. He blinked. A little girl with pigtails stood over him, the light of the room was on. Smoke billowed from the carpet.

"Get up!" she snarled, with an unnecessary amount of aggression it seemed to him, clamping handcuffs to both wrists. National practical joke day? University rag week? She seemed a bit young for an undergrad. He desperately tried to focus, to concentrate, to wake up.

He must still be dreaming.

Chapter 53

The Palace Reception

"There...er...there's no answer from his room, sir," said the hotel receptionist to the waiting chauffeur.

Jackson hovered uncertainly at his elbow. He'd been trying to find Christopher all day. To discover whether he'd made that call. His suit was pressed, his shoes were shined, his solid gold jewellery stood out on his fingers like costume props. But Christopher was nowhere to be seen.

"Where the hell is he? He wasn't down this morning, either, the new guide was looking for him. What time's this reception?"

The chauffeur shifted from one foot to the other.

"Right away, sir."

"I imagine the boss-man's on a tight schedule, right?"

The chauffeur looked blank.

"Look, never mind, I tell you what, wait here. Give me five," he said, pointing at his watch.

Jackson scurried up to his room, bounding up the steps two at a time. It appeared Christopher had checked in under a different name. At first, he had thought the chauffeur had got the name wrong, he didn't know anyone called Roderick

Fraser. But when he'd checked with the receptionist, it transpired there was no Christopher Wainwright booked into the hotel. Just a tour manager called Roderick Fraser, in Christopher's room. He supposed it must have been a last minute switch, and they hadn't had time to change the paperwork, though he thought that it was odd that Christopher hadn't mentioned it.

He stopped first at Christopher's room. No reply, and the door was locked. It didn't do to pass up an opportunity like this, thought Jackson. If Christopher wasn't able to make it, then why not him in his place? He stopped in mid-corridor to think about this for a moment. But no, dammit, he was black. They'd be expecting a white dude. Then he had an idea. He knocked at the door of Christopher's neighbour.

It opened and Michael peered out, in his bath-robe.
"Yes?"
"Michael? Man, I need your help. Now."

~

WHEN JACKSON, MICHAEL AND SIX OF THE ANGELS FINALLY appeared, the chauffeur was on the point of leaving.

Michael looked dubious. "Sightseeing in a limo?"

Taken by surprise, the chauffeur ran around the car to try to bar the way, jabbering in Ruritanian. But too late: the Angels were piling into the back seat, pulling Michael with them. The chauffeur began to gesticulate, wildly. It appeared he wanted them out. Jackson lowered the window.

"You speak English?"

"Yes sir," said the chauffeur, hopping about. "But I am only under instructions…"

"You come to pick up the Roderick Fraser, right?" He pointed at Michael. "Well that's him."

Michael stared at him. Where had he heard that name

before? Then it suddenly dawned on him. Of course! It was Cynthia's spare passport visa ruse, to give them flexibility when there was a last minute change of tour manager. He'd heard of other tour managers using the scam, it was an open secret in the TravelCo office.

However, he had a sudden panic. When Jackson had collared him out of his bath and asked him whether he minded pretending to be Christopher for a few hours to take a private sightseeing tour he'd thought sure, no sweat. But it was one thing to be Christopher, it was quite another to impersonate someone impersonating a dead person. He could be an accomplice to a crime, for heaven's sake.

"Hang on…" he said.

Jackson jabbed him in the ribs. The chauffeur mopped his brow.

"But these other people…"

"His friends," explained Jackson.

The chauffeur hesitated for a moment, then scuttled round to the driver's seat, rubbing the back of his head, to make a call.

~

A MILE AWAY IN THE PALACE, BLICKER WAS STRAIGHTENING HIS tie in the Cabinet Room. The place was now kitted out with dusty old portraits of past royals - dreary as hell, in Blicker's opinion - and a red carpet stretched from the door to a small semi-circle of chairs at one end. He was flanked by Boris, two cabinet ministers, his Cabinet Secretary, and Sophie with a clipboard. Outside in the courtyard a band was playing, and a small crowd stood patiently outside the gates.

"I thought we said this was going to be a low key affair," muttered Boris, fiddling with the bow-tie Blicker had given him an hour earlier. "I mean look at those trumpeters. What the hell are they wearing? They look like something out of a Broadway musical."

Blicker couldn't help chuckling. They did indeed look like something out of a Balkan production of the Lion King, all gold lame and velvet. Luckily they were high up in the gallery and barely noticeable.

God knows where Horst had dredged them up from, he thought. That was the thing about his art director - he insisted on making a meal out of everything. Nobody had ever mentioned trumpeters. He glanced at his watch impatiently: besides, where *was* Horst? Fraser could arrive at any minute.

"The first thing I want to ask him," said Boris, "is whether he's an admirer of King Charles."

"King who?" asked one of the ministers.

"Charles. Of England. Because we want someone with a social conscience, someone who believes in organic farming, in…"

"Talking to trees?" queried the Cabinet Secretary, with a smirk. Boris scowled.

"Now, now, gentlemen, this isn't an interview," said Blicker. "All we want to ascertain are his intentions. We are not offering him the throne at this stage, whatever he says. Let me do the talking."

"Do we bow or something? What's the form?"

"Certainly not. Just behave as if he's a perfectly ordinary human being."

The minister tittered. "You know what I do on these occasions?"

There was a short silence.

"No, but do tell us," said Blicker acidly, with a touch of impatience.

"I imagine them sitting on the toilet." Next to him Sophie burst out in a fit of giggles, but stopped abruptly when she saw that no one found it, or chose to find it, particularly funny. Only Boris smiled.

"That's the best idea I've heard all day."

An official hurried up and whispered something in Blicker's ear. He frowned. "Are they armed?" The official shook his head. Blicker pondered for a second.

Finally he nodded his asset - apparently Fraser was coming accompanied - and turned to the others.

"There's been a short delay," he said gruffly. He strode off towards a side exit, fishing a crumpled packet out of his pocket as he went.

Twenty minutes later they were back in position. Outside, the band played a rather more polished rendition of *'Roses Over Ruritania'*, while inside the trumpeters took over with a forty-five second fanfare. It was oddly discordant. They'd been caught short on trumpet fanfares, so they'd had to get some sheet music specially couriered over from Prague. Listening to it, Boris wondered idly whether it had been composed by that great honorary Czech and god of the Czech underground, the late Frank Zappa.

A large group of people entered the room, led on by a uniformed footman. All bar one were huge, and towered over everyone else in the room. Blicker started. He might have said yes to a bodyguard or two but this was ridiculous. Moreover they all seemed to be dressed in sweatpants. What was this, some kind of a joke?

"So which one d'you suppose is Fraser?" whispered Boris to his neighbour, stifling a laugh.

Slowly the entourage processed along the red carpet.

∼

MICHEAL LOOKED ABOUT HIM IN WONDER. FAR ABOVE, HE SPIED four trumpeters in gold costumes doing some kind of a routine, while four gorgeously-attired guards saluted to one side. My God, what the hell had he got himself into, he thought to himself? This was no private sightseeing tour, as Jackson had intimated, something that Christopher had arranged and was now unable to take advantage of. Jackson had been smirking the whole trip, so he'd been expecting something. But not this. It was one thing driving up to the palace to have a look, it was quite another driving right the way in; sweeping through the gates amid a mob of flag waving locals and an army band. Going to meet the President? Was he kidding? He wasn't even dressed right. And now this. And impersonating a dead person.

A man in a suit was coming towards him. Should he bow? He executed a kind of half nod that he imagined might be fashionable in court circles until he remembered, too late, that this was a republic.

"Welcome," said the man, smiling uneasily. "I'm Johann Borovski Blicker. You must be Roderick Fraser."

What a dark horse Christopher was. What should he do? Come clean? He gulped. "Well I'm...er...pleased to meet you, sir, I'm…"

"My good friend Roderick," boomed Jackson, striding up beside him and planting a firm hand on his shoulder. "Yes. And may I introduce myself, Mr. President, sir! The name's Jackson! Coach Jackson!" He laughed heartily and stopped, aware that the President wasn't laughing with him. Indeed he was looking at him rather oddly. "Over here to interest your people in a real world-class game," he added.

"Indeed?" said Blicker coolly. "Nice to meet you, then." He returned to Michael and smiled: "Now, let's get down to business, shall we?"

Michael swallowed hard. "Business?"

"Precisely," he said, leading Michael over towards the semi-circle of armchairs. He motioned to Sophie, who had come up beside him, and she peeled off.

"Nice...er...nice paintings you've got here," said Michael, eyeing the Royal portraits on the walls in an effort to make small talk as they silently trod the length of deep red pile carpet to the far end of the room.

"Oh good," said Blicker through gritted teeth. "I'm glad you like them. We thought you would."

Huh? Michael was on the point of analysing this last piece of intelligence for any further clue to what the hell was going on when he noticed, terrifyingly, that Jackson and the Angels were no longer with him. He stopped abruptly and turned round.

"Er...where are they going?"

Jackson and his crew were being led off, protesting, into a side room.

"Don't worry," said Blicker, taking him by the arm and propelling him forward. "We have arranged some little refreshments for them. Although I have to admit," he laughed, "we weren't expecting quite so many." They reached the rest of the welcoming committee.

"Now then, let me introduce my, ah, my team. This is Boris Kurtz, my Minister of Economics..."

"How you doing?" said Boris.

Michael suddenly felt paralysed by fear. His hand shot out automatically. "...and my Minister for Foreign Affairs..."

"How do you do, sir."

Sir? thought Michael. His heart was racing. This was no longer funny. Ten minutes ago he'd been in the bath with his plastic stress duck.

"And my Cabinet Secretary. Do sit down."

Michael did so. Heavily. There was a short silence. Blicker flicked his tie and smoothed out a crease. "I thought I might first ask you, your...er...Mr. Fraser, what exactly your intentions are in coming to Ruritania?"

A thought flashed into Michael's head. Perhaps

Christopher had been picked out as some kind of model tourist to Ruritania, a country where tourism was still in its infancy, one who had been invited by the Government to give his opinions on his visit so far. Perhaps that was it. But odd that Christopher had mentioned nothing about it, and even odder that he wasn't here when he was supposed to be. God, what if he walked in now?

"I'm just visiting," answered Michael. Blicker and his ministers remained expressionless. "On tour."

"Yes well we know that's the...er... story, your...er... Mr. Fraser, but what we want to know is, what precisely are your real intentions? Your attitude to the people of Ruritania for example?"

Michael shuddered. He could get banged up in jail for things of this sort. You were guilty until proved innocent in foreign places like this. What if they found out he was an imposter? Perhaps they would think he was a spy. No one would ever hear from him again. The blood drained from his cheeks.

"Er...the people...er...they're very nice, people, very pleasant indeed." He paused. "Sir." An idea struck him. "Especially our guide, Rosie, now she really was a most helpful lady, really most helpful, I really cannot commend her enough. Elphberg I think her name was."

He paused, eager to do what he could to give her a good recommendation. "Perhaps you should write that down?"

There was another short silence. Blicker flung a sideways glance at Boris. "Helpful, you say? Helpful to you, you mean?"

"Oh, extremely," said Michael. "Couldn't have been sweeter. If there's any award or anything..."

He trailed off.

"So am I to take it," said Blicker, "that you don't support her, er, claim?"

Michael effected a rapid mental calculation. There was

obviously some vital piece of info he was missing here. Whatever claim it was that Rosie was making, he felt it was his duty to support her. And he felt sure that Christopher would have done the same. Yes, that was it. She had been replaced by a new guide only that morning. Perhaps this 'claim' was for unfair dismissal.

"Oh absolutely," he said confidently. "I mean, yes."

"Yes you do support her claim," interrupted Grigor sharply, "or yes you do not support her claim?"

Michael tittered.

"I…er…I support her claim, yes."

"I see."

Boris started to stroke his goatee furiously.

"So if you support her claim, why are you here?" he said.

"Why am I here?" croaked Michael, bewildered.

"Precisely."

"Well, I…er…I was sort of…invited…" he stammered. "Wasn't I?"

"By whom?"

"By you…er…Mr. President, least that's what…" He cast around frantically for any sign of Jackson.

The foreign minister leant forward: "So what you're really saying, Mr. Fraser, is that you support her claim but you're open to offers? Is that it, sir?"

Michael blinked, fingering his earring. "Offers? What kind of offers?"

~

BLICKER BEGAN CRACKING HIS FINGER JOINTS. WHAT THE HELL was the man playing at? He was being extremely cagey, not giving away anything. He turned to his finance minister.

"Boris?"

"Thank you, Mr. President," said Boris, pleased at last to

get his teeth into this ear-ringed imbecile. For that is what he was rapidly turning out to be.

"Now then, Mr. Fraser, could you give us your views on how you see Ruritania developing over the next, say, five years?"

"Pardon me?"

"Let me offer an analogy. Are you in favour of fast, packaged, convenience foods, and all the rest of that…er…consumer culture that the West has to offer, or are you…do you…"

"Talk to flowers," blurted out the Cabinet Secretary for the second time that afternoon.

"Mr. President..!" protested Boris, turning to Blicker.

The President held up his hand and shot a look at his minister. He returned to Michael.

"You see, Mr. Fraser, we have many shades of opinion in our government, many shades indeed. We work by diversity, discussion and consensus here, and we find that that is the best way forward for the good of the people generally. Now since the…er…area we are talking about is…ah…essentially non-political, I think that we can allow you to ignore the second part of my Minister's question and concentrate on the more general question of how you view the situation in Ruritania…um… generally."

∽

GOD, THOUGHT MICHAEL, HE NEVER REALISED HOW HIGH-powered Christopher really was. Because it suddenly dawned on him. This was a job interview. Either that or a contract. Of course, why hadn't he seen it before? Christopher would kill him if he screwed this one up. He was obviously delayed elsewhere due to circumstances beyond his control, and he could imagine what he was feeling right now. Tearing his hair out, he wouldn't wonder. He quickly cast his mind back to that conversation he'd had with Christopher in the canteen at Zenda Castle about packaged foods and the commission he'd been offered by their VIP client, Joey Spinelli. They had laughed about it then. He'd been under the impression that Christopher had treated the whole thing as a joke. But what if he hadn't? What if he'd managed to secure this, the ultimate lead? Why wasn't Spinelli here? He wished he'd paid more attention.

"Well, no, Mr. President," he began "I have no objection to...er...addressing the question of convenience foods because as you well know I am one of America's leading experts in the field of...ah...premium quality microwaveable entrees and...er....shelf ready outers. For instance our own brand of ready-to-eat convenience ready meals, the C-CAT, is currently the market leader in North America and soon, we hope, to be a major product over here." He paused for breath. They were all spellbound, and whole chunks of Boris's goatee appeared to be coming out in his hand.

"So in answer to your question, Mr. President," he continued, "about how I see the situation in Ruritania generally, the bottom line is...well, I mean, at the end of the day, it is an enormous market, is it not, and one which has great...ah...tangential possibilities. At present, I mean, that is."

What the hell was he talking about? thought five people. What new garbage was this? But no one said anything.

He blundered on.

"In fact I would go so far as to say that sales of all convenience and packaged products, and not forgetting soft drinks, could rocket, given the right...er... environment."

You could have heard a fly fart.

"En-vir-on-ment..." echoed Boris, softly, slowly and deliberately.

"Precisely."

A side door opened, and a footman approached. He bent down and mumbled something in Blicker's ear.

"OK, send him in," said Blicker wearily. The footman padded silently back to the door, opened it, and Horst appeared, followed by Sophie. He looked flustered. Everyone got up, relieved.

"My profuse apologies, Mr. President," he began "for my late arrival. We had a scare in the dye shop." He stopped, noticing Michael for the first time. Blicker stepped forward.

"May I present Mr. Roderick Fraser? Horst Bangermann, my artistic director." They eyed each other as they shook hands, Horst's ginger moustache quivering imperceptibly. "Oh, and Sophie, my PR assistant."

∾

Blicker sat down again and offered Michael a cup of tea. No point in prolonging this craziness any longer than they had to, he decided, the man was obviously totally unsuited to any position of responsibility whatsoever. He was raving mad. So he made polite small talk about the man's interests - steam engines, heraldry and the burning of witches in sixteenth century England - and prepared to wrap it up for the afternoon. But he soon realised he'd made a mistake. He had no idea Horst was such an expert on the Counter-Reformation. When they got onto the subject of the Spanish Inquisition, he'd had enough.

"No need to take notes, Sophie," he said, laughing pleasantly. "Now then, Mr. Fraser," he got up, and everybody else followed suit, "we must say, we much appreciate your coming in at such short notice like this, and if we may we will be in touch with you in your hotel if there is anything further we need to discuss with you. How long do you…ah…plan to stay, Mr. Fraser?"

Michael was feeling considerably more relaxed. All in all it had been, in the end, a very pleasurable experience. Just imagine what he could tell them back home? Tea with the President no less...

"Only until the weekend," he answered. "I have to drive the coach back to Brighton…" He halted, suddenly aware of his error. "I mean, with the driver…"

Horst nonchalantly brushed at a hair on his jacket.

"You live in Brighton, England?"

A look passed between them.

"Presumably we'll get another chance to speak at the wedding," continued Blicker. "You do know it's been brought forward, I suppose?"

Here was one last hurdle to cross. Nearly there.

"The...er...the wedding..?"

"Yes, of course you do, all this chopping and changing must be wreaking havoc with your travel plans." He smiled at him. "So nice to have met you. Let me see you to the door."

"One moment, Mr. President," said Horst quickly, inspecting Michael with a worried expression. "I wonder whether I might be allowed a few minutes with Mr. Fraser before he departs? Alone. There are one or two measurements I need to check."

"By all means, Horst, but I'm sure you'll find that that won't be necessary."

Michael noticed the President shoot his art director a funny look.

"Measurements...?" he tittered.

"For example your inside leg. I've got you down as a 32." He chortled. "If you're a 32 then I'm the Pope."

"Well…"

"Won't take a minute. We'll pop over to my studio, it's just along the passage. We'll meet you at the front entrance in what, say, ten minutes Mr. President?"

"Whatever you like, Horst, whatever you like. But I have to say…"

"Good. Come along, Mr. Fraser."

Chapter 54

Confusion

"Oh God. Sophie, he was there. In bed. With a woman." Rosie was rocking herself back and forth, two barefoot legs poking out from beneath a knee-length white T-shirt. Sophie put her arm around her.

"Well...it just goes to show. All men are shits. At least now you don't have any illusions."

Rosie dabbed at her eyes, and sniffed. "About what?"

"Love. Marriage won't be nearly so bad."

She jumped up cross-legged onto the sofa. "But that's just it! I can't! I was really beginning to fall for him."

"Don't be ridiculous. You only knew him for a few days. How can you say that?"

Sophie smiled inwardly at her friend's naivety. She'd always considered herself to be the more level-headed of the two. Nevertheless, she couldn't help but feel a slight twinge of envy. She obviously thought she'd been in love. Sophie had never even got that far.

"What did you say his name was?"

"Christopher." She sobbed. "Oh...oh...and now I can't even say goodbye!"

She sunk her head in her hands so that her long hair fell down and touched the floor.

Sophie paused. Somewhere, deep down, an alarm sounded. Where had she heard that name before?

"Why don't you call him? At least then you won't always be...wondering. Maybe he's got an explanation for his behaviour."

She tossed her head up, flicking her hair back angrily. "I can't just call him. Why hasn't he called me? I thought he cared for me." She stared into space, worried. "Why hasn't he begged for forgiveness?"

Sophie smiled encouragingly. "I tell you what. I'll go and see him."

"What's the point of that?"

"Write something. You can't leave it like this. I'll see him personally and deliver it."

Rosie seemed to consider it.

"By the way," continued Sophie, fingering the stem of a yellow rose sitting in a vase on the floor, "while you were in Zenda, did you ever hear anything of that...Pretender?"

"Mmm?"

"The Pretender I told you about. He was reported to be there with an armed group of…"

Rosie shook her head. Her mind was elsewhere.

"Odd, because in fact he turned out to be…"

"Now *ssh*," snapped Rosie. "I need to concentrate." She had picked up a pencil and was now sucking the end of it while gazing out of the window.

∞

"I don't get it," said Jackson later that evening in the bar, where a few of the group had gathered to go over the day's extraordinary events. "It doesn't add up."

He knocked back his Jack Daniels and glanced at Michael. "Do you?"

"You know I don't. Where the hell is he?"

"I mean what went on in the palace."

"Oh that." Michael sucked his teeth. "We should never have done it, you know, we should've come clean. Can you believe it, the man even started measuring me up."

Martha raised an eyebrow.

"When we got that call in his room he was as baffled as I was," said Jackson. "He had no idea what it might be about. Have you talked to Spinelli?"

"Can't find him either. The concierge said he asked for a list of restaurants then took off this morning."

"And there was that burn mark on the carpet in his room."

Martha squirmed. They hadn't actually asked her what she was doing in Christopher's room, but she was sure they suspected.

"Beats me," she said. "Like I say, someone came to the door and I mean, like, he just went after her."

"Her? You followed them?"

"As if!"

"Well did you see her?"

She sniffed. "I think it was Rosie. He seemed to think it was."

"Excuse me, sir." The concierge hovered above them. "A call for a Mr Michael, the coach driver."

Micheal cocked an eye. "It's probably my company back in London."

He returned five minutes later.

"It wasn't my company in London," he said shakily.

Five pairs of expectant eyes turned to him.

"It was someone else. Said he knew where Christopher was. Said to meet him tomorrow afternoon at two." He looked from one to the other. "At Zenda."

Chapter 55

Imprisoned

Outside, the rain bucketed down against the thick stone walls, the occasional rumble of thunder echoing in the distance.

When Christopher had calmed down sufficiently, he tried to rationalise the situation. He knew it was unlikely that he'd been kidnapped by terrorists, although not impossible. They must have given him some hallucinogenic drug, because he distinctly remembered a vision of a girl in pigtails, merged with a horrific nightmare about...he couldn't even bear to articulate her name.

More likely it was related to the business with Rosie. His helping her escape the first time had evidently thrown them badly. It was his only hope. Because if so, she would be able to get him out. She was, after all, he reassured himself, to be married in a few days to the son of the bastard who was most likely doing this to him, and would soon be well on the way to becoming Queen of the godforsaken country. They needed her.

But would she even know he was here? Even if she did, would she care, given his behaviour?

He had been in this hole for over a day now, with not a glimmer of an explanation from his monosyllabic guards as to where he was, what they were holding him for, nor for how long. Indeed he'd had virtually no communication with them at all, his food being shoved through a hole in the wall, despite repeated, shouted requests, in the course of the first few hours, for either a lawyer, or someone from the British Embassy - though you could hardly depend on the Foreign Office these days, he thought to himself dejectedly. What snippets he did catch seemed to be delivered in strange, falsetto voices by people who appeared, through the small crack in the door, to be no more than five feet tall. It was like a Game of Thrones episode - minus the dragon. It was a mystery, and one which he hadn't even begun to find an answer to.

And TravelCo? Would they notice his absence? He had to laugh, relieved to find he still retained a sense of humour. Of course not. Cynthia didn't exactly welcome his calls. As for the group, a new local guide would have turned up the following morning, as Rosie had arranged, and everything would have gone on as normal. It just showed how redundant he was. They'd turn up at the Ellenberg Rosewater Co-operative and someone else would get his fucking commission. One he'd arranged personally. A percentage larger than anyone had probably ever dreamed of. One he desperately needed.

Chapter 56

Debrief

"Well, I think it's a shame, whatever you say," said Horst, lifting up a tuft of Blicker's hair and razzing it with his scissors. Something he'd been wanting to do for months.

"Think what you like," said Blicker sniffily, staring at his reflection in the mirror. "He was clearly unsuitable. We checked out his so-called bodyguard, and d'you know, they turn out not to have anything to do with him at all? It's a farce. They're merely a football team from Little Rock, as they were supposed to be all along. They're due to fly back on Monday. Why no one had told us earlier, and what that man thought he was going to do here, I can't imagine."

He pulled away sharply.

"Careful! I've got a bald patch under there!" He felt the back of his head. "Besides, I've no doubt Huntzau bought him off with some offer or other that he couldn't refuse."

"Mmm, lucky boy," mused Horst. "His gain, our loss." He combed Blicker's hair forward from the crown. "But can't we at least make him Duke of something? After all, he comes from a legitimate line."

Blicker favoured him with a wry smile in the mirror. They were silent, each in his own thoughts, accompanied only by the snip snip snip of the scissors and a light drizzle that pattered on the window.

"So," said Horst eventually. "What's it going to be? King Andrew and Queen Rose?"

"No, no, no, not King Andrew, God forbid, no, he's just the consort." Blicker sighed. "But I suppose he'll have to get some title or other. Probably his family title, Duke of Zenda. Mind you, it all depends on a referendum."

"Which looks like a foregone conclusion, no? Mr. Hentzau wins again."

"So it would seem," said Blicker gloomily.

The rain started to come down more heavily. Their silence resumed. It was interrupted by a loud racket in the courtyard.

Blicker snorted. "And there goes my bloody car."

They learnt forward to get a better view.

"Look at it!" he said, pointing below with ill-concealed fury. "Down there! With all those bloody cans attached to the back of it!"

The sleek black Mercedes – with its RUR 1 licence plates - was making it's way towards the gates dragging several long lines of old tin cans behind it along the cobbles, and a large banner attached to the back window saying 'Just Married'. He sat back, seething: "I hope it breaks down on them!"

"You mean you lent it to Hentzau?"

"I didn't lend it...far from it."

"Well what then? I was told," said Horst sniffily, "that it was only to be used on state occasions."

"That's as it bloody well should be," retorted Blicker, "but that's not what it looks like now, does it? He's got the limo, he's got security, he's got the audience chamber for his damn reception. The bastard managed to sneak it onto the Cabinet agenda. Maintained it was an occasion of 'national importance'. You should've seen it. They were all falling over themselves to curry favour with him." He reached for a cigarette and lit up. "I couldn't exactly veto it, could I?"

"I'd...er...rather you didn't smoke, Mr. President."

Blicker shot him a look. Horst pretended not to notice, then relented.

"Oh all right, just one."

"And I'll tell you something else," continued Blicker, inhaling deeply. "I've about had enough of all this. When it's all over I'm going to resign, get back to my painting. Boris can take over. He's got more energy to fight Hentzau than I have."

Horst stopped snipping, shocked.

"Mr. President, you cannot be serious? I mean...what about the country? You're the only one who keeps it together."

"Don't kid yourself, Horst. Politics is a dirty game. I've learnt that. I started out with ideals, but...to be successful you've got to have more than just ideals. You've got to be a bigger bastard than the next person. I can do more for Ruritania on the international art scene than I can ever do as president, prime minister or whatever the hell it is they're going to call me now."

He took another drag of his cigarette and blew a smoke ring into the mirror, contemplating his half shorn head.

Behind them were stacked several dozen of Blicker's 'Blue Circle' works which had been temporarily removed from the audience chamber, itself a temporary removal from the Cabinet room. Horst glanced at them. He might be a philistine; Georgi might tease him for his taste for the nostalgic and the kitsch; but still, somehow, he couldn't quite believe it.

∼

"Excuse me, I'm looking for someone called Christopher Wainwright."

Debrief

The receptionist tapped a few numbers into his keyboard.

"I'm sorry, madam, we don't have anyone under that name staying in the hotel."

"There must be some mistake," said Sophie. "Wainwright." She spelt it out for him. "Christopher Wainwright."

"I can assure you madam…"

Had he checked out already? She was about to call Rosie when she heard a voice. "Excuse me, ma'am."

She turned. And started. The man confronting her was none other than the one she'd had to 'entertain' at the palace the day before. "Oh…"

"Ah…"

Sophie and Jackson stared at each other in confusion.

"You were looking for Christopher?" ventured Jackson cagily. She nodded.

"You wanted to follow up from yesterday?"

Sophie looked clueless. "Have I...met him?"

"Yes, ma'am," exclaimed Jackson, and stopped himself. He had a creeping suspicion they'd been rumbled. "In the palace. Roderick Fraser. He is Christopher Wainwright."

Sophie's jaw dropped.

"We met you yesterday, remember?"

It was as far as he got. She fainted.

∿

IT TOOK A LARGE GLASS OF BRANDY FOR JACKSON TO BRING HER round. He shook her. "Hey, wake-up, lady!"

Sophie nodded groggily. "I'm so sorry...forgive me."

"What's your name, honey?"

She sipped the brandy and grimaced.

"No hurry, take your time."

"Sophie," she said eventually. "Bernenstein."

"Can I ask you something, Miss Bernenstein? You work for the government, right?"

She rubbed her head, eyeing him guiltily.

"Well...er...yes, that's true, but I'm on a sort of... private errand."

"Oh?"

"A friend of mine wanted me to deliver a message to someone called Christopher Wainwright. I had no idea he was the same person that I met yesterday."

Jackson hesitated. It was a risk, but one he felt he had to take. Because he was worried. They all were, especially after that phone call, more than ever convinced that Christopher was in some sort of trouble. Whatever the reason for his disappearance, could it have had something to do with his invitation to the palace?

"He wasn't," he said simply.

She sat up with a jolt, spilling the brandy. "But you just told me.."

"Listen, ma'am, can I speak to you in a private capacity? Off the record so to speak? In complete confidentiality?" She looked alarmed. "Because I think we've gotta problem here."

Chapter 57

Get Christopher

Sophie's heart was beating fast and furious as she ran up the stairs to Rosie's apartment barely three hours later. She still had no idea how she was going to play this. What she had learnt from Jackson and Michael, about Fraser (alias Christopher)'s disappearance, and Michael's impersonation of him at the presidential audience, was certainly incredible. But how much of it was true? It just didn't make sense, especially since the Jackson man turned out to be no more than he pretended, the manager of a football team. He was unaware of the rumour that Fraser/Christopher was the Pretender to the throne, and Sophie was careful not to enlighten him. Had Blicker - and the country's entire security forces - got it so wrong? And then Christopher's disappearance: that was certainly suspicious, pointing to more than met the eye.

What should she tell Rosie? Should she try and get the wedding cancelled?

Then there was the whole matter of Christopher. He had, after all, been caught in bed with another woman. What did he really feel about Rosie? And if it was true that he was the Pretender, would they want him on the throne, or would he turn out to be just like the other one? Should she tell Blicker? Or was the whole thing a terrible mistake? Maybe the man who called himself Jackson was making it all up. But why?

Plus there was Hentzau to contend with, she realised. If she acted, he would react. Sophie was terrified of him. It was no use jumping to conclusions unless you were in full possession of the facts. There were so many imponderables and unknowns. So much was at stake, so little time to resolve it. She felt way out of her depth.

"Well?" said Rosie eagerly when Sophie had finally got her breath back and was settled on the sofa with a large vodka and tonic. "What did he say?"

Sophie put the drink down carefully, painfully aware how badly her hand was shaking. Rosie looked dishevelled. She still hadn't changed out of her T-shirt, and bottles and empty food cartons and hairbrushes were strewn about the room in disarray.

"He wasn't there."

"So where was he?"

"It seems he's disappeared."

"Gone back to England?"

"That's one explanation."

Rosie started pacing up and down, pulling at her hair distractedly. "I knew it! He can't bear to face me!" She turned abruptly. "Or has he gone with that woman?"

"I talked to her."

Rosie shuddered. "You did? What did she look like?"

"Nothing special," said Sophie unconvincingly. "She admitted she tried to seduce him, but he resisted. What you saw was him trying to get away. She told me he went racing down the corridor after you, and that was the last she, or anyone else, saw of him."

The blood drained from Rosie's face. "He came after me?"

"Yes. It was all a big mistake. The girl's really apologetic. She had no idea you and he…"

"Oh God," she wailed. "Why did you have to tell me that? He's most likely thrown himself down a lift shaft, he's probably…"

"Rosie, calm down," exclaimed Sophie nervously. She still had the worst part to come. But at least Rosie's nerves served to disguise her own uneasiness.

"The poor boy, he was probably waiting for me!"

"*Pa-lease!*" scoffed Sophie. "Spare me the phoney sympathy. He'll get over it."

Rosie slumped to her bed, tears streaming down her cheeks. "How can I ever get married now?"

Sophie hesitated. Now was the time to tell her. If she was going to. But what if...

"Rosie," she began warily. "What did you know about Christopher?"

Her friend looked up. Her dark hair had fallen over her face, and with her smudged mascara she was beginning to take on the look of a woman demented.

"About his other life?" she continued.

"Oh I get it," said Rosie bitterly, a mad gleam in her eye. "Hentzau's been talking to you."

"What d'you mean?"

"Of course he has, it's…"

"Rosie I swear, I haven't even seen him!"

"So why did you ask that question?"

"Why? It's just.." Sophie searched wildly for a way forward, without blowing everything. It was like walking a tightrope. "I heard rumours."

"Well let me tell you, I'm sure he wasn't."

Sophie caught her breath. "Wasn't what?"

"Working for Universal."

Sophie looked blank.

"Hentzau tried to persuade me yesterday that Christopher was here as the secret representative of some American food corporation called Universal. That he was here to undermine Hentzau's own business plans. That he only befriended me as a way to get to him."

Sophie took a large mouthful of her vodka and tonic, feeling the fizz hit the back of her throat. Here was a whole new scenario. It was getting increasingly complicated. What was truth and what was lies? The man apparently had his finger in every pie going. The only answer, it seemed to Sophie, was to find Christopher, Roderick or whatever he called himself. She had agreed to take the first step in that direction with Jackson that very afternoon. Only then might they be able to sort fact from fiction, fantasy from reality. Not the least of which was Rosie's own fantasy. Were they really in love? Or was it just the emotional turmoil within her playing strange tricks on the eve of a loveless marriage?

"I see."

"All fantasy," scoffed Rosie. "It's just a way to get me to forget him." A puzzled frown crossed her brow. "Although how Hentzau knew about me and Christopher, I've no idea."

∽

THE OBJECT OF ROSIE'S ANGER WAS IN AN ALTOGETHER different mood, as he tried on a variety of silk waistcoats in preparation for the wedding the following day. An expansive one. Everything seemed to be finally coming together. There had been some sticky moments, Hentzau reminded himself, they'd had to bring the wedding forward twice, but now it was at hand, he could finally relax.

The TV Regulatory Committee looked like it was going to be a formality. The soap opera trials had gone well - despite the odd hiccup with the electricity company. Lougouev would be pleased with him. The meeting was not actually until two days after the wedding, but he had done some hard lobbying of late, and it was amazing how people's attitudes had changed towards him, just over the space of a week. Yes, he had exclaimed modestly when he was quizzed about it, with just the right mix of surprise and innocent pride, this whole monarchy business was rather sudden, wasn't it? Hadn't thought much about it, as a matter of fact. He was just pleased his son was marrying such a nice young girl. Whether the young woman in question would decide to accept the throne or not he really couldn't tell, but in any case, he would laugh, she wouldn't have much time for a foolish old man like himself, now, would she? Honours lists? No, he had no idea. He wasn't aware that modern monarchies still did that sort of thing. And so on.

His stringers, too, had done a fantastic job getting the people whipped up into a monarchist frenzy. It was all over the world press, and suddenly everyone was clamouring for interviews with Rosie and Andrew.

As for Fraser, well yes, he had received reports of a meeting at the Palace two days previously, but by all accounts it hadn't gone at all well. What was discussed, or what was offered, he had no idea, because the whole thing seemed to have been kept a closely guarded secret by Blicker and his cronies. But as for Rosie, she seemed to know nothing about Fraser's being in the pay of a foreign corporation and, strange as it may seem, he tended to believe her. She looked like an innocent, the whole thing a complete coincidence. Moreover, she had behaved quite how a queen should behave. Admirably. He had been worried at first that she might kick up a fuss, but amazingly she'd buckled down.

He picked up a square, blue, leather jewellery case and opened it. Inside was a large silver star set in purple velvet, with a red, white and yellow ribbon attached. The Star of

Zenda, first class, a decoration that had belonged to his father. He held it up against his chest and squinted in the mirror. Mmm, not bad.

Andrew. He was the only slight midge in the water. He had been damnably bad-tempered about the whole thing. The boy didn't know how fortunate he was. He'd had to give him a talking to on more than one occasion. He would bloody well have to pull his socks up. The first five years were crucial, he'd have to be on his best behaviour. He did grant him one concession, however. If after five years he still felt the need, and hadn't found a way to be happy with Rosie, then he could take a mistress. But not before. Hentzau was adamant about this. He knew his son only too well, he'd have to watch him like a hawk. It was vital to let the monarchy take root. And there would have to be an heir by then, he told his son, in no uncertain terms. The look on Andrew's face…

His reverie was interrupted by his housekeeper poking her head round the door.

"Telephone call for you Mr. Hentzau, sir!"

"Who is it?" he snapped grumpily.

"Your daughter, sir."

Tilly? What was she doing phoning? She was supposed to be writing out the place cards for the banquet. He smoothed down his hair and picked up the bedroom extension.

"Tilly? What on earth are you doing? Where are you?"

"I'm in Zenda, Papa."

"Zenda!" exploded Hentzau. "What the hell are you doing there? I thought you were downstairs!"

"That's right, and I've got Roderick Fraser prisoner."

Hentzau took a step backwards.

"Hang on a minute! You've got who?"

"Roderick Fraser. I thought you'd be pleased. We…"

"Release him at once!"

"Papa, calm down, will you? It's just until after the wedding, then I thought we could deport him."

"What on earth for?" Hentzau was aghast. "Where did you find him? I mean, how?"

"It's what you wanted, isn't it?" She was starting to sound whiny.

"Let him go at once, d'you hear? You can't just go round…kidnapping people!" Hentzau paused, stunned. "I mean…what if he complains? He could sue us!" He ran his hand through his hair. "Me, he could sue me! This could ruin everything!"

"Papa, what is the matter with you? D'you want to take power or not?"

"Take power? Take power of what?"

"Mao says…"

"Fuck Mao. Now you listen to me, young lady…"

But this time he'd gone too far. The young lady had hung up. After staring into space for a couple of moments, he leapt into action and dialled his Chief of Staff on his mobile.

"It's me. Tilly's gone mad."

"Oh?" He could have sworn there was a smirk in his Chief's voice at the other end. "You don't say."

"She just called from Zenda, says she's holding Fraser prisoner in the castle."

His deputy burst out laughing. "Why, the most intelligent thing she's done for a long time."

"Chief!" remonstrated Hentzau, "What are you talking about? We have a wedding tomorrow, we can't afford this sort of complication. He's been to the palace, they've had their meeting, and nothing came of it. So what have we got to fear?"

"But it can't harm to keep him there until after tomorrow, then…"

"No! I want you to go up there and get him out. Keep him

away from the press for twenty-four hours, sweet-talk him, anything you like, but repair the damage."

"But that'll mean I'll miss the wedding!" protested his Chief of Staff.

"That can't be helped. We've got to be squeaky-clean on this one. We're trying to create a monarchy. Think of that title I promised you. I want no scandal, d'you hear?"

"And what if your daughter resists? You know what she's capable of."

Hentzau sighed. "Just get him out, Chief."

He had had no idea what his daughter was capable of. Until today.

Chapter 58

Hotting Up

Christopher sat up and listened. He could have sworn he heard the sound of a helicopter, somewhere far off in the distance. Nothing. He got up and went over to the wall, where, high above, a darkened grate seemed to be his only connection with fresh air. Still nothing.

No, wait! There it was again! The faint clump clump clump of rotor blades. It was unmistakable. Had someone, at last, arrived to get him out? He told himself not to be an idiot. It was probably a commercial transfer from some airport or other. He went back to his bed and sat on it dejectedly. The helicopter droned away into the distance.

Still, he couldn't help wondering.

∽

IN FACT HELICOPTERS WERE COMING IN TO LAND, BUT AT QUITE another airport, far away from the scene of Christopher's incarceration. Despite the last minute nature of the invitation, the first arrivals were beginning to trickle in for the wedding and reception the following evening, the

The Spare and The Heir

reception at which Andrew and Rosie, respectively heir to the Dukedom of Zenda and heir to former throne of Ruritania, would be presented to the world. Everyone likes a party, especially on official government business. And everybody loves royalty.

There were dignitaries from Prague, deputies from Warsaw, diplomats from Bucharest, and an assortment of 'friends' from around the world. Hentzau had arranged cars to meet every one of them, and chauffeurs jostled at the arrivals barrier waving a variety of impossible and mis-spelt names. There was one name board, however, which stood out both for its neatness and the attention to detail of its information. *'Globalny Foods,'* it read, *'You Are What You Eat* ™.*'* Indeed it had to be good, for the President of the corporation himself was arriving.

At 11.40 Lougouev swept through the arrivals gate flanked by three clean cut young men with shining black briefcases. They towered above him, all chiselled chins and buzz cuts. He immediately noticed the board. He strode up to it, stopped, and glared at the uniformed man who was holding it. "*You* are what you eat?" he growled.

The chauffeur looked none the wiser. He was not to know it should have been 'we.'

∽

SEVERAL HUNDRED YARDS AWAY, THREE OTHERS WERE STEPPING onto the tarmac.

"God it feels good to be home," said Black.

"You're telling me," said Brown, flicking her hair.

Blicker's three agents began walking towards the terminal building, their investigative mission to the UK over. There had been very little to dredge up on this Wainwright bloke after all. He had a clean bill of health. As they approached, they noticed a large crowd on the observation roof, and more behind the fence.

"What the hell's going on?" grumbled White. "I've never seen so many people."

They stopped and stared, and a little girl clutching a paper flag on a stick waved it vigorously in their direction. They waved back, nonplussed.

"Perhaps we're heroes," said Black. He was only half joking.

The helicopter had gone. Christopher was lying on the hard metal bed, daydreaming. If only he could somehow get word to Rosie, explain what had happened. He sighed. They said you recognised the love of your dreams the moment you set eyes on her. Well he had recognised her, damn it.

He sat up with a jolt. He could have sworn... But no, it was probably workmen dynamiting a quarry. Then there it was again. An explosion, nearer this time, followed by a lazy pop, pop, pop. He started to fantasise: what he would give for that to be automatic gunfire. Maybe they'd sent the SAS in to rescue him. Black-clad superheroes would come storming through the grating of the window any minute, stun grenades at the ready, a book deal close behind. In your dreams, he told himself bitterly.

∾

MARIA, THE NEW GUIDE, OR RATHER THE OLD GUIDE reinstated, glanced at the hotel clock angrily. Where on earth was everybody? She'd told them all to be in reception at midday for the much postponed visit to the Ellenberg Rosewater Co-operative (the Ellenberg Rosewater Co-operative? Who on earth had added that to the schedule?), and it was already five past and all she had were a couple of old ladies. Why couldn't Sophie's friend have finished the job? It was totally unprofessional. Where was the sports team she had heard about? Where, moreover, was that dozy coach driver and his stupid coach?

"Morning Maria, feeling better?" came a voice. It was Mary Finkelburger, coming down the stairs followed by her husband. "Ready to go?" she added pleasantly.

That made four.

~

Something was definitely going on.

For forty minutes, helicopters had been buzzing the castle. And it certainly sounded like automatic gunfire. Feeling slightly stupid, but nevertheless determined not to be caught short by any eventuality, Christopher began dragging his steel bed towards the door to provide as much protection as possible. Just in case.

Suddenly the action seemed to hot up. A chopper seemed to be hovering directly overhead, and the explosions were getting louder and nearer. He grabbed his leather jacket and leapt under the bed. There was the sound of voices on the outer wall, apparently sashaying down it on ropes. Oh my God! Did '*Her Britannic Majesty Requests and Requires*' mean something after all? Any second now. Please for chrissakes be careful...Dear Jesus...His heart was racing, a mixture of terror and anticipation.

Then he heard it: "*Cut..!*"

~

"There it is!"

They all peered out of the window. Up ahead was a sign: '*Zenda Bus Park. Catering trucks, keep left.*'

"Catering trucks?" exclaimed Michael.

He pulled off the main road.

The place was packed. Trailers, caravans, jeeps, trucks all jostled for space. Like a hornets nest, people with walkie-talkies strapped to their belts and wearing baseball caps sporting the legend 'Blackjack' bustling backward and forward across the parking lot.

"Christ!" said one of the Angels, peering out of the front of the coach, "now what the goddam we gonna do? It's this fuckin' menagerie again."

"Hank!" snapped Jackson sternly. "Watch your tongue. Remember, we got a lady on board."

Sophie, the lady in question, looked confused. Jackson explained about the film crew.

"I see," she said when he'd finished. "So what exactly did the man say when he called?" asked Sophie.

"Simply that he had information on Christopher's whereabouts, wants to meet us here, don't call the police."

"I know, but meet you where?"

"In the parking lot. 2pm."

They looked around hopefully. It was certainly a big parking lot. A youth hurried up to the bus, slapped a large sticky red square on the windscreen, and motioned Michael towards a space. As soon as he'd parked and switched off the engine, a girl with a California tan and a blond pony-tail skipped aboard.

"Hi folks, you're early," she said cheerily.

"We are?" said Michael, puzzled.

"Sure." She checked her clipboard. "According to the sheet you have a 3.30 call." She glanced up and down the coach, frowning. "Hey, you're not the local peasants we ordered…"

What new bullshit was this? thought Michael.

"They're football players," he said, gesturing at his passengers behind him. "The Arkansas Angels."

The girl ran a finger down her clipboard, puzzled. He had a sudden flash of inspiration.

"Your producer, John H. er…"

"Mr. Bigelow?"

"That's the one. He…er…he suggested he might be able to use them today. They were extras last week. The…er…mercenaries in the rescue scene. Second unit stuff."

She looked from one to the other dubiously. Jackson frowned. She unclipped the mouthpiece of her walkie talkie. "Hey, Bill…"

"Reading you, babe," came a crackly voice.

"I got some guys here called the Angels, who played in the second unit mercenary scene last week," she radio-ed. "Say that Mr. B. asked them to come along today. There's nothing on the call sheet. What d'ya want me to do?"

"Send 'em to lunch and then come over here and suck my dick…" came the reply from the other end. Michael raised his eyebrows. She reddened, giggling nervously. "Bill…"

There was a cackle.

"Shall I check it with Mr. B?" she pursued.

"No way. He mustn't be disturbed." There was a short pause at the other end. "OK, send 'em over. Mebbe we can use 'em in the break-out scene. Get 'em over for rehearsal. 2.30 on set."

"Thanks Bill, over and out."

She clipped the mouthpiece back onto the collar of her sweat shirt and returned to Michael.

"You're in luck. You can leave your gear here, we don't need them in costume for the rehearsal. The dining truck's ahead of you. I'll pick you up around 2.25." She turned to go, then stopped. "By the way, what's your name?"

"Michael," said Michael cheerily. "An' this is Sophie, Coach Jackson and the boys."

She waved down the aisle. "Nice to meet you folks. I'm

Katrina, third assistant director. See you later, OK?" She jumped off and disappeared into a stream of human traffic.

"For Lord sakes, Michael," said Jackson, watching her go. "Now what have you got us into?"

"You're a fine one to talk," Michael shot back haughtily.

∽

Sophie was beginning to regret she'd come. This was not at all what she had expected. What if it all went wrong? These people didn't exactly strike her as reliable.

"So let's...er...let's be rational about this," she said. "We need time to think. We're in, no? All they can do is throw us out. Meanwhile we've got to find this man. What did you say his name was?"

"Hans. I bet he didn't know about this crazy circus."

There was a yell from the back of the bus.

"Hey, look guys, it's her!"

"It's who?"

"That lady on TV! Over there, stepping outta that caravan!"

"Hey, yeah, he's right, it's what-da-ya-call-her!"

"What do you call her?"

Before Jackson could stop them four Angels had leapt out of the back door of the coach and were racing towards a platinum blond heading across the lot in a silk dressing gown. Sophie looked on aghast.

"Stop them Jackson, what on earth are they doing?"

"Hey miss! Hey miss!" they were calling. The platinum blond recoiled, raising her hands involuntarily in a gesture of self-protection. Two beefy security men hurried over as Jackson, followed by Sophie and Michael, clambered off the bus.

"Hey, you, get outta here!" yelled the men. "Who the hell are you? No autographs on set!"

The men barred the way. Meanwhile the Star recovered her poise and, with a flick of her hair, went on her way.

"For God's sake, guys, loosen up," hissed Jackson. "You wanna get us all kicked out?"

"Stuck up bitch…" mumbled one of the Angels.

"I think we'd better get out of here," whispered Sophie.

"Excuse me, sir," came a man's voice. "Are you the American football players?" They turned around. A middle-aged man with a shock of black hair stood before them, clutching the hand of a little boy in a Zenda Pioneer T-shirt.

"What of it?" said Jackson cagily, evidently not keen to attract fans of their own in this situation.

"I am Jorg Hubel," said the man in an undertone. "And this is my son Hans. Where can we talk?"

"This is Hans?" exclaimed Jackson. "The kid?"

"*Sssh*," whispered Hans, otherwise known as number two, glancing around nervously. Sophie watched Michael and Jackson exchange looks. She was beginning to get the feeling she'd been set up.

Chapter 59

The Eighth Circle of Hell

Christopher at least now knew where he was. It was Zenda, and outside were Bigelow's American film crew. He couldn't help feeling a stab of disappointment that it hadn't been Special Forces. Still, wasn't it a stroke of luck? But after shouting at the top of his voice for twenty minutes right underneath the grate, he thought otherwise. His voice was hoarse. Obviously no one could hear him. The walls were too thick, and whatever it was covering the mouth of the grate prevented any sound escaping. Dejected once more, he slumped onto his bed. Outside, he could hear the helicopter flying away into the distance. Then:

"OK fellas, you can come down now!" It was a male American voice shouting through a loudhailer. "We're wrapping for lunch!"

"Oh great…" said Christopher sarcastically out loud. "Thank you very much."

∽

"You sure about this?" Michael was hunched over a plastic disposable cup in the back of the coach while Jackson perched beside him. Father and son and Sophie were seated in front of him. Sophie said something to the boy in Ruritanian, and Hans launched into an animated explanation, munching on a donut.

"So he claims," said Sophie dubiously.

Michael sipped his coffee and thought hard.

"So in plain english," he said, "Christopher's a prisoner. A hostage."

Silence.

"Goddammit!" exclaimed Jackson. "What do they want, a ransom?" He got up. "We'd better call the police."

Sophie followed him. "I...er...I don't think that's a very good idea."

"Why the hell not?" he growled.

"Because...the problem is, Jackson, that if he is telling the truth," and however incredible it seemed, a part of her said yes, it fitted, "the man who appears to be holding your friend is an important Government minister."

Jackson glared at her. "One of your lot?"

"Exactly." She smiled apologetically. "You see, there are a lot of factions."

They glanced from one to the other. She was about to propose returning to Zenda and forgetting the whole thing, when the boy's father spoke up: "My son says he has a plan."

Oh great, thought Sophie. Well under four feet, with freckles and a large gap in his teeth, and the boy had a plan.

∽

Time was marching on. Far away, and unaware of all the activity on her behalf, Rosie was having a final fitting for her wedding gown. It wasn't the traditional white, rather a cream coloured taffeta dress with a navy blue jacket designed in New York.

The assistant who was fitting her was chatty and cheerful. But the more she chatted away, the more miserable Rosie began to feel. It wasn't the headache she said she had - that was feigned - nor even the realisation that the life she had led since childhood was about to come to an end, although that played it's part. No, it was, rather, the unconscious assumption in the girl's mind that this was the happiest day in Rosie's life, that really triggered off her misery. In some obscure way she felt she was betraying her sex. The innocent, excited banter of the young girl who was dressing her was like a dagger to her heart. It was a sham.

She had thought she could handle this. She had rationalised the situation endlessly in the months and years of her long and barren engagement, and become resigned to the loss of a romantic or even a real marriage. But however much she had intellectualised it, however cynical she had forced herself to become about marriage itself, it proved no defence now against the desperation she felt inside. It was all the Englishman's fault. If only they'd never met! And if only she'd never been allowed to hope, even for those few precious hours!

Why did it have to end so badly? Why, in her own mind, couldn't she end it? Could she - should she - really go through with it?

These were the thoughts that were turning over and over in her mind. Once again she steeled herself. What choice did she have?

∼

BY THE TIME MICHAEL, SOPHIE AND THE BOY GOT TO THE moat, the lunch break was over, and the film crew were on set again. They'd left Jackson and the boys behind, and had gone to see what the boy proposed. The scene about to be filmed was an action sequence on the drawbridge: six mercenaries were to retreat across it under fire from advancing marines. Michael couldn't help chortling.

"Oh, awesome," he hissed. "Those guys are pretending to rescue some girl while we've got a real life hostage in there. Ironic, no?"

They walked up to one end of the drawbridge where they had a good view of both sides of the moat.

"Get outta there!" yelled a voice. "You're in shot! We're just about to turn over!" Nervously they hurried after the boy until they were well covered by a patch of thick undergrowth. They halted. Hans began chattering excitedly, pointing.

"He says over there," motioned Sophie.

Michael followed her sightline. Sure enough, there was a large round plastic pipe protruding from the castle wall, just beside the drawbridge. It disappeared into the moat below. The boy started whispering urgently.

"What's he saying?" mouthed Michael.

"He says that the original pipe was constructed when King Rudolf was held captive here," said Sophie softly. "It was called Jacobs Ladder. Apparently it was built as a way for his captors to escape, if the castle should ever be stormed, and runs directly from a grating in his old cell. They would kill the King, weight his body, and slide it down the pipe into the moat. Then they themselves planned to escape the same way."

Michael glanced at the boy suspiciously.

"Look, tell him to cut the fairytale stuff, just tell us…"

"He says it's where Christopher's being held."

They peered more closely. The boy continued.

"In the King's old cell. He says he and his friends built that pipe as part of the Zenda Heritage Trail - a recreation of Zenda history from long ago. He proposes that he crawls up the pipe, force open the grating, and pull your friend down it."

"You're kidding!" exclaimed Michael.

"No, he says he's rehearsed it a number of times, because they aim to re-enact the scene for tourists next season."

"But the moat's empty, no?" said Michael. "They'll shoot out into mid-air, won't they, in full view of everybody? Not only that, but they'll also be on celluloid."

Hans whispered something and began creeping forward.

"He's going to show us the moat now."

They crept forward into the undergrowth. It was all very well for Hans, thought Michael - he was small. But by the time the men had emerged the other side, on the outer bank of the moat, they were covered in scratches.

They peered down into the empty chasm, and an amazing sight greeted them. Because in one sense it wasn't empty. What looked like blue plastic sheeting was stretched across the length of it, for as far as they could see, in an effort to simulate water, and occasionally a man further along the bank would turn a huge roller that ran under the plastic and a ripple would be created, running the length of the sheeting until it reached the next roller. The effect was theatrical on a grand scale.

"Hollywood," said Hans in English, the first intelligible word he'd uttered. Michael let out a low whistle. Either they had no budget for CGI or animation, or they planned to superimpose a fake moat in post production. Then he saw the pipe. Instead of dangling, helplessly exposed, twenty feet above the bottom of an empty moat, it disappeared under the far edge of the blue plastic, providing perfect cover for anyone emerging from the end of it.

"You understand?" said Hans in faltering English.

Michael looked dubious. "OK," he conceded, "supposing he can get him out this way. What I don't understand is what's in it for him? Ask him that."

Sophie put it to the boy.

"Apparently he wants to settle a score with someone. He

says he was involved in the kidnap, but didn't know what he was being asked to do, and now wants to make amends."

A ten year old boy involved in a kidnap attempt? mused Michael. It seemed unlikely. But it was the only hope they had. His thoughts were cut short by a sudden commotion.

"Cut! Cut! Cut!"

A small fat man was striding around on the drawbridge in a Timberland hunting jacket and wielding a loud hailer. "Jesus H. Christ!"

The crouching mercenaries straightened up and relaxed.

"There's people in the foliage!" boomed his voice, echoing the length of the massive stone walls. "Over there! Will someone please remove them?"

Suddenly all eyes were on Michael, Sophie and the boy, caught like rabbits in torchlight. They turned and fled, stumbling through sharp brambles. The indignity of it all, fumed Michael, scrabbling around in the undergrowth like this, at risk of ripping his Stella McCartney jeans. First the excruciation of the Presidential audience, and now this. The things he did for TravelCo…

∾

"Can I do your hair now, ma'am?"

Rosie mumbled something and sat down. She realised that all these years she'd been acting a role. Watching herself in the mirror, being pinned and buttoned by the girl, it was as if one part of her had left her body and was floating above, detached, recognising the reality for the very first time. There was a sense of fright. But also a curious feeling of relief that the pretence would soon be over. Or would it?

The rain streamed down the windows, beginning now to come in torrents. Where was Sophie? She was late.

CHRISTOPHER WAS EATING AN APPLE THAT HAD BEEN LEFT HIM by his captors when he heard it. "*Psst*", came a voice.

He stopped chewing and looked around. Had he heard right?

Nothing. He must be imagining things. He took another bite.

"*Psst!*"

He jumped up, clutching the fruit. Someone was definitely calling him.

"Who's there?" he whispered. He could have sworn the noise came from the grated window. He peered up, but couldn't see anything. Then he heard some groaning, and two sets of tiny fingers curled round the outside of the bars.

"Hello?" he whispered urgently.

There was an almighty crash. Suddenly the hands went, and daylight appeared. A loud scraping noise followed, then silence. Christopher stared up at the grating, now showing blue sky. Perplexed.

~

ON THE OTHER SIDE OF THE MOAT THERE WAS PANIC.

"Oh God," said Sophie, biting her lip.

"What just happened?" said Jackson.

"The pipe!" she exclaimed. "It's slipped! I knew this was a crazy idea!"

The pipe had crashed. Hans was evidently too heavy for it, and it had broken its moorings and now lay resting against the masonry five feet below the newly exposed window of Christopher's cell. They weren't the only ones who were concerned.

"Hey hold it," called the cameraman, on the drawbridge.

"Something's different. Something's changed." He came away from the eyepiece and squinted along the moat. Then he saw it. "That pipe over there by the wall," he said. "It's moved."

"What do you mean it's moved?" yelled the director from a hydraulic platform just behind the camera. "Pipes don't move! You crazy?"

"I'm tellin' you, Brent, it's moved."

"Continuity!" yelled Brent Brooks, the director.

"Yes Mr Brooks?" said the continuity girl, hurrying over.

"Gary says that pipe moved," he said, pointing. "Over there by the goddamn wall."

The girl squinted at it, then rewound her video monitor. Brent lent down impatiently. "Well?"

"He's right, Mr Brooks," she said shortly. "It's moved. About five feet vertically down."

Brent swore.

"How many shots we done this direction?"

"Six, Mr. Brooks."

"Fucking hell," he muttered.

Two carpenters were summoned to rig up the pipe again. The crew sat down on boxes and lit up cigarettes, while Brent clambered down from his platform to take a piss.

∽

INSIDE HIS CELL, CHRISTOPHER WONDERED WHAT THE HELL WAS going on. The hands he had caught a fleeting glimpse of clutching the bars of the window had been on the small side. Very small indeed. Could it have been a kid playing pranks? Maybe it was one of the children he'd heard playing outside the day before. No sooner had he relaxed again, however, than more developments began to unfold around the window area. He heard a kind of clunking noise, then a British voice:

"OK Harry, haul her up."

A face appeared at the aperture. It was the large, fleshy, well-fed face of a man, sweating profusely. He appeared to be checking the fittings around the window frame. Christopher's heart leapt. Someone must have heard him! They would get him out after all!

"Hey," Christopher whispered, urgently. "Over here…"

"Ugh…" The man started, a look of sheer fright on his face. "Fuckin' Ada!"

He swayed slightly, clinging to the bars, trying to regain his balance. He peered anxiously into the gloom of the cell. "Allo?"

Then he noticed Christopher staring up at him from six feet below. He relaxed.

"Gave. Me. A. Turn. You. Did!" he began, in a very loud clear voice. "Sorry, mate! Shan't. Be. Long. Now! Chop! Chop!"

He resumed whatever it was he was doing on the exterior of the window frame. Christopher cringed. Did the man want to blow the whole thing?

"*Sssh…*" he hissed. "They're just outside the door.."

The man stopped, surprised.

"Oi, you English?"

"Course I'm bloody English, what did you think?" retorted Christopher. "Now keep your voice down and let's get out of here."

The man looked puzzled. Finally he smiled, and put his finger to his lips. "*Sorr-ee.*" He swung out of sight.

"Lift her up, Harry," came a voice.

"Ready when you are, Tom," came a second.

"Come on…" thought Christopher, waiting expectantly beneath the window for a rope, a ladder, anything…

There was another loud scraping noise. Then, suddenly, gloom. The window was once again closed off as the massive pipe slotted back into position. Christopher stared up in disbelief.

"Hey…" he cried, as loud as he dared. But there was no answer. He didn't damn well believe it…

∿

ON THE FAR BANK THERE WAS A COLLECTIVE SIGH OF RELIEF. They only hoped Hans hadn't slid down the length of the pipe and was now having to climb his way up again for the second time.

"OK, stand-by," yelled the director, climbing his platform. "Turn over!"

"Camera running," said the cameraman.

"Sound running," echoed the sound man, "speed…"

Brent glared at the pipe.

"Action…!"

The mercenaries began their tactical retreat across the drawbridge for the second time.

∿

CHRISTOPHER LAY FULL LENGTH ON HIS BED THINKING ABOUT home. He wondered idly how long they would all mourn for if he was killed by his kidnappers. One thing was for sure. If he got out in one piece, he'd spend some time doing exactly what he wanted to do. He'd paint, play music, study acting - anything, except the dreary succession of dead-end jobs, selling this, selling that, bullshitting the other. He'd expand his mind, take acupuncture, learn Shiatsu, live life. Someone was definitely trying to tell him something. He'd heard of people on rafts about to be swept under who'd had a sudden illumination into the futility of their life. The fog of existence and hum-drum routine had been stripped away, and they'd seen the truth. For some it was too late. But for the lucky ones...

"Hello?"

Christopher shot up. This time there was a small boy's face behind the bars of the window.

"Shit, who are you?" gaped Christopher.

"One moment please..." whispered the boy. He wiggled around, searching for something. There was a loud cracking noise. He, and the pipe, disappeared for the second time. Christopher remained rooted to the spot.

∾

"*CUT!*" YELLED BRENT, WRIGGLING IN HIS CHAIR. "I DON'T fuckin' believe this! It's gone again! Davina..?!"

The first assistant director hurried over.

"This is costin' us time. If those dozy fuckers can't fix that pipe right, we're gonna lose the whole of the next scene. I want it fixed, and fixed good, you hear? Jesus..."

Once more he clambered down and scurried over to the mobile production office. The camera operator, Gary, wiped his forehead and grinned at the continuity girl. The continuity girl yawned. The sound man took off his ear-phones, sat down and lit another cigarette.

After three minutes Brent returned.

"Well?" he said. "We ready yet?"

They peered over at the pipe. It hadn't moved.

"Doesn't look like it," said Gary pessimistically. Brent fumed.

"Wake me when we're ready will you?" he growled, sprawling out on the ground. "At the rate we're goin' we'll be here 'till midnight."

∾

The Spare and The Heir

"You don't seem to understand," Christopher was saying angrily. "I'm a prisoner here. I'm being kept against my will. I'm British and I need your help."

"A prisoner?" replied the man dubiously. He was back again at the window, fixing the pipe. "You serious?"

"Of course I'm fucking serious," said Christopher through clenched teeth. "Can't you tell from my accent. I live in Stoke Newington, I can tell you the entire line up of the England men's World Cup squad…Listen, I've never been more serious in my life. Now please get me out of here."

The man continued to work frantically, hammering in a couple of nails.

"Look, what are you doing?" hissed Christopher. "Can't your stupid repairs wait?"

The man began to look uncomfortable.

"Thing is…er…mate, it's…er…it's a bit awkward right now. We're behind as it is, director's doing his nut. More than my job's worth." He hitched up his trousers. "But I tell you what…"

Christopher clenched his fists in an effort to maintain self-control.

"What?" he said acidly.

"When…er…when we've done this little set-up, I'll have a word with one of the production blokes and we'll report it to the castle authorities."

"Are you mad?" yelled Christopher. "I could be dead by then! It's the castle authorities who have banged me up for Christ's sake!"

The man hesitated for a second and scratched his head.

"It is?"

"*How much longer, Tom?*" came a voice. "*They're asking.*"

"Won't be a sec," called the man, hastily resuming his work. "Look, mate," he continued, "I feel sorry for yer, I really do, but what do you want me to do? I can't help yer now, we're in the middle of filming. How about we tell the police?" He paused. "Ready Harry, swing her in!"

"You do that," muttered Christopher. It was rapidly turning into a farce.

"See yer then," said Tom jauntily. "Best of luck mate."

With that he swung out of view, and with a scrape and a clunk Christopher was once more plunged into gloom.

~

SOPHIE BIT HER LIP ANXIOUSLY. "I HOPE HE'S ALRIGHT."

There was a rustle. Jackson scrambled up the side of the moat through a gap in the plastic.

"Well?" whispered Michael. "Where is he?"

Jackson got his breath back. He looked worried. "No sign of him," he said. "He must still be inside." He stared up at the pipe, now firmly in position for the third time. "Holy shit," he muttered, "he's been in it for half an hour." He turned to Michael. "Shouldn't we speak to the film people?"

Michael pondered. "It's up now. Let's give him one last go."

~

CHRISTOPHER FELT EMOTIONALLY DRAINED. HE WAS LYING ON his bed, trying to look on the bright side. At least he had been able to get word out. Someone now knew where he was.

Because it was probable that even Rosie didn't know that. Yes, the likelihood was he'd be released after the wedding. But he couldn't rely on that. There was one danger, however. What if the authorities were alerted, and they did try to rescue him? What if they messed up, forcing his captors to take more drastic action? He hadn't seen any guns so far, but he was in no doubt that they had them. He shuddered, and told himself not

The Spare and The Heir

to be so defeatist. If they intended releasing him tomorrow, why risk killing him today?

He shifted around to get comfortable, or as comfortable as was possible on an iron bed. Then he closed his eyes, and was soon in a deep sleep of exhaustion.

In his dream he was with Rosie. They were in some kind of forest clearing, with tall trees all around them, and they were lying side by side. Christopher felt an overbearing desire to be close to her, yet somehow he couldn't. The more he tried to hold her, the more elusive she seemed to become, as if fading away. He lay back on the grass and watched her get up, smooth her dress, and calmly walk away. He called after her but she didn't stop, merely turned round and smiled at him, and then she was gone into the darkness of the forest. He stared after her for a long time, tears coursing down his cheeks.

Someone was shaking him. He opened a bleary eye.

"Please, mister," whispered a high pitched voice urgently. "We must go." Christopher opened the other eye and started. A little boy with a grubby, blackened face and a torn shirt was standing beside his bed. He looked like the kind of street urchin that went out of circulation with Charles Dickens.

"Who the fuck are you?"

"No time," said the boy, ignoring him. "Quick!"

He started tugging at Christopher. He sat up, and immediately noticed a rope ladder dangling down from the now grate-less window. So he was finally being rescued! This was it! At last! By whom, or why, he had no idea. But there was no time to think about that now. He leapt up.

"Where? Over there?" he said anxiously, pointing at the ladder. It was a question prompted by nerves more than anything else.

"Follow," whispered Hans. They climbed the flimsy ladder. As Christopher scrambled up, it swung wildly, smashing him against the wall, but finally he reached the narrow window opening. Beyond he could see a kind of tunnel. Hans, ahead of him, had turned around so that he went in feet first, and he motioned Christopher to do the same. He struggled, he twisted, he swung, and he struggled some more. It was easy enough for a boy of Hans' stature, but for Christopher...

"OK?" came a voice from behind and below him.

"OK," said Christopher nervously.

"Let's go," said Hans, and he shot away into the darkness.

∽

ON THE DRAWBRIDGE BRENT, HIGH UP ON HIS DIRECTOR'S platform, thought he heard something. A kind of long drawn out, high-pitched whooshing sound, like someone blowing across the mouth of a giant bottle. They were in the middle of a sensitive dying marine scene, just in front of the castle portcullis. The man had a number of significant last words to recite, and there had to be absolute silence.

He shot a questioning glance at Lennie, the sound man, who was frowning.

Lennie shook his head, then drew his finger across his throat in the universal gesture for kaput, dead, finished. Brent clicked his tongue impatiently.

"Keep the camera running," he shouted, "sound's no good, we're going again. First positions please, quick as you can!"

The actors scuttled back to where they were a minute previously, when the scene began. Brent glanced anxiously at the sky: they were rapidly running out of daylight.

"OK," he hollered. "Standby. *Action....!*"

∽

Christopher, despite his elation, was nervous. Where the hell would he end up, in some kind of sewage dump? In a lake? He took a deep breath, shut his eyes, and let go.

He slid two feet and stopped. He was jammed. With great effort he wriggled and hauled his way back up to the rim. By the time he got there he was out of breath. Now what? He thought rapidly. He was obviously too bulky to slide down the pipe. He would have to get rid of something: his jacket.

He hauled his upper body back through the window opening and, reluctantly, stripped it off and tossed it on the floor of the cell. He hesitated for a moment. That leather jacket had been with him since his teens, through thick and thin. He remembered the girl he'd first kissed in it. She'd had long, black hairs which kept reappearing at awkward moments from various seams for years afterwards; the accident where he'd slid off a friend's motor bike, concussing him - the large patch on one arm a loyal reminder of how it had literally saved his skin. He bade it a hasty farewell and slipped back through the window. Pull yourself together Christopher Wainwright, he thought to himself, don't get sentimental. It's only a jacket.

He screwed up his eyes, and launched.

∽

"Do this one favour for me, Captain," whispered the prostrate Marine, theatrical blood oozing out of his chest.

"What is it, Colonel?" asked the kneeling Captain gently.

"Take this letter to Annie, and tell her...tell her…"

Whoosh...

Brent twisted violently in his chair, glaring at Lennie. Lennie shook his head.

"Christ almighty!" yelled the director, "what the hell's going on?"

"Shall we cut?" asked the cameraman.

"Once more..." hissed Brent through clenched teeth. "First positions..."

There was a crash. The pipe split from the window, and tumbled down the wall, sparks flying as the metal bracket at the end came away with it and scraped the ancient stone. The sound it made was excruciating. It bounced onto the blue plastic sheeting and slithered to a halt in the middle. Brent stared in disbelief.

"*Cut, cut, cut, cut, cut, cut, cut!*" he screamed furiously, jumping down from his crows nest. He'd had enough. Someone else could direct the sodding movie.

∽

WHEN CHRISTOPHER CAME TO, EVERYTHING WAS BATHED IN AN eerie blue light. He was in some sort of valley, strewn with boulders. He looked up. There was no sky, no stars, no moon, only a translucent kind of blackness. It wasn't day, it wasn't night. Just pure blue limbo. For one awful moment he thought he was dead. Two faces loomed over him. He couldn't quite make them out.

"You friggin' scared us, dude. Welcome back."

Welcome back? He gulped, and a sudden terror gripped him. No! Dear God, surely not? An image from Dante flashed into his head: the eight circle of Hell, the home of fraudsters and perjurers, condemned to march forever, driven by demons, along evil ditches of stone...

Chapter 60
OMG

St. Felix Cathedral was filling up. Slowly, in twos and threes, men in dark suits and polished shoes with women in outsize hats were beginning to be ushered to seats, pews and galleries. For a wedding that had only been finally fixed several days before, there was an amazing turn-out, although the company was not perhaps the most illustrious - this was the B-list, rent-a-crowd circuit after all. But the B-list never misses a party where royalty is concerned, especially royalty that promised to be as glamorous and potentially lucrative as the Ruritanian one.

Hovering at the edges were the bodyguards, and behind them came the press. Great hulking men with beards carrying cables, cameras and odd-shaped boxes, accompanied by bright young women and men in crisp suits clutching microphones. And, beyond them, restrained by ropes and ooh-ing and ah-ing at every arrival, the great unwashed: the general public. Many were still arriving, some had been in position since the early hours. The traffic cops and the town police were in jovial moods. Everyone likes a party.

Meanwhile two sniffer dogs did a last minute check, and a phalanx of sober-suited men with moustaches stationed themselves outside the door in preparation for the more important arrivals.

~

THE MOST IMPORTANT OF WHOM WAS TRYING TO PULL HERSELF together. As Rosie came down the stairs, her taffeta dress held up by her dressmaker, the staff who had lined up in the hall to wave her off burst into a spontaneous round of applause. Despite her feelings, she smiled. They weren't such a bad crowd, even though they'd kept her virtually under house arrest these last few days. Her future imprisonment as Hentzau's queen promised to be far more onerous.

She shook a few hands and kissed a few cheeks, swept up in the expectation of the moment, and stepped nervously out onto the gravel drive and into the waiting limousine. Leaving took a few minutes, but finally the bodyguards had all adjusted themselves in the Mercedes in front, her dressmaker and make-up artist had climbed in the car behind, and they were ready. Rosie began to feel nauseous. With a solid crunch of tyres they eased onto the drive, through the saluting police cordon at the gates, and out into the street.

Meanwhile, five miles away in St Felix Square, a loud cheer was going up amongst the crowd. RUR1, the presidential Mercedes, had arrived, trailing a string of empty cans, making a hell of a racket, and was parking itself just around the corner. The security men consulted anxiously. No one had told them. A din like that could easily disguise the noise of a gunshot, or a small explosion. Two of them hurried over to check the car, while three others were detailed to crowd control.

Next came a smaller saloon. Two suits dashed down to

open the doors, glancing about them professionally, and out stepped the bridegroom, looking handsome and arrogant as always, clean shaven for once, and wearing a navy blue Armani suit. He gave the crowd a condescending half-smile before climbing the steps, followed by a little girl in pigtails and a smart French frock. She was wearing an English straw hat that was several sizes too large for her. His cute little sister, someone whispered.

∽

Rosie was not the only one feeling queasy. Not far from where she was, Christopher was having to pump down whisky to quell a rising tide of nausea of his own. He was sitting in a bar across the street from the Cathedral, and had been noting the arrivals with mounting concern.

Where the hell was Sophie? If she didn't arrive soon it would surely be too late.

"She said that?" exclaimed Michael, incredulous. Christopher switched his attention back to his former coach driver. For, as of some hours ago, he considered his responsibilities regarding TravelCo firmly at an end. "That you are in fact the heir to the throne of this place?"

He'd been explaining to Michael what Sophie had told him on the way in from Zenda; of the extensive research she had done into his family tree, which proved that Roderick Fraser's great great grandparents were Rudolph Rassendyll and Queen Flavia. The fact that he was illegitimate apparently had no bearing on the matter. It was bloodline that counted in Ruritania. It was a watertight claim to the throne.

"Call me cynical. Call me stupid. But I find that pretty hard to swallow. Even if it was a hundred years ago."

"Michael, it's not me that's the heir," said Christopher with a sigh. It would be so much simpler if it was. Of course, he'd denied any knowledge of it to Sophie. Who wouldn't, he'd been in shock, for God's sweet sake. But he couldn't very well deny he was Roderick Fraser. That he was in Ruritania on a false passport. They'd lock him up again, this time officially.

"I thought you said, that she said, that you were."

He took another swill of the whisky, baring his teeth in a grimace. "That's what she thinks. But only because she thinks I'm someone called Roderick Fraser. But clearly I'm not. It's a case of mistaken identity, pure and simple."

Silence.

"Ah," said Michael, the truth dawning on him. "Of course! Roderick Fraser! I get it now!"

"You do?" Christopher looked surprised.

"Sure, I know all about that visa scam of Cynthia's," said Michael. "I must say, not come across if before on my other trips, but I know tour managers who have had to use it. I had no idea that you were having to be Roddy on this trip." He laughed. "But the heir to a throne? Why, that's incredible! Wait till I tell Cynthia!"

"Yeah, and the reason they want an alternate heir is that Rosie, the official heir, is marrying the son of the son of the bitch who locked me up, and …"

This time Michael was truly shocked.

"Wait a minute!" he said. "You mean Rosie the guide?!"

∿

At last. Peace and quiet. Boris was listening with rapt attention to the Caribbean Shipping News through his earpods, the lilting cadences of exotic place names soothing his soul like buttered toast.

His concentration was interrupted by the soft bleep of an incoming call.

"Boris," he answered wearily. It was Blicker's PR assistant,

Sophie. What the hell did she want? "No, the president's not here, he's at the reception like everyone else. What? You've got who? Fraser?"

'St Martin's Head, gale force seven, to gale force eight, rising; Captain's Creek, storm force ten…'

Reluctantly he muted it to give his full attention to this new intrusion.

"Wait a minute, I thought we'd been through all this."

He listened while Sophie explained. He sat up, startled.

"You mean that man we met, he wasn't Fraser? Then who the," he gritted his teeth and made a clicking sound, "was he?"

Here was a whole new ramification. He began to scratch his goatee vigorously. It sounded incredible, but Boris was only too willing to believe it. Thinking it through, it was the best news he'd heard in days. Because the despondency that had gripped the Blicker camp since their abortive meeting with 'Fraser' was palpable. Hentzau had won. Not only had they not been able to prove a connection between him and the Fraser camp; but the other option, turning to the Fraser camp as a last ditch alternative, had proved equally untenable. The monarchists were in the ascendant, and the only credible heir was about to be married to the son of the bastard.

Until now. He listened with rapt attention as Sophie explained that Hentzau had whisked the real Roderick Fraser away and locked him up. But he'd escaped, was at this very moment on the streets of the Capital, and could be about to wreak his revenge.

"But there'll be a bloodbath!" exclaimed Boris. "It'll split the country right in two!" He listened distractedly as Sophie happily agreed with him. "Wait on the line," he ordered hastily, grappling with the landline phone on his desk and punching in Blicker's number.

There was no answer. He suddenly remembered where

they all were. He dialled the guardhouse, muttering to himself: "This madness can't go on."

~

Something was bothering Blicker. He felt a curious sense of unease as he waited in the audience chamber along with the rest of the guests for the happy couple to arrive. He checked his watch. They'd be getting married any minute. It had all seemed so simple nine months ago. Now there were factions, cliques, agendas.

Despondently he examined a crude 19th century landscape that graced one of the walls, in a spot so recently occupied by one of his Blue Circle works. People were milling around, gossiping, laughing, main-lining canapés; they hadn't even noticed, dammit. He could stick a great big Jeff Koons inflatable up there for all they cared. Why bother? People were really such... philistines. As for those ghastly old royal portraits... He frowned crossly. A tall woman with an angular profile was talking loudly to Horst a short distance away. She had a face that was somehow familiar to Blicker, a self-important one that strained to be noticed. Horst's bald cranium shone. And that was another thing. It was all very well for Bangermann: he had no hair. But that didn't give him carte blanche to live out his fantasies on other people's.

He toyed with his glass and idly looked around the room. But he kept being drawn back to this woman. Was it her face? Her voice? Or the loud red dress she was wearing? He stared at her rudely. Then, all at once, he saw it. In a flash it was there. Red. Red squares. He would create huge bold red cubes. Nothing subtle, harmonious or rounded about them, no mysteries or veils. Oh, no. These would be large angry beasts, full of corners and inconsistencies. A revolt, a protest. You had to bellow these day if you wanted to be heard above all the vulgarity. Red. That was it. He waved away a waiter bearing a tray of champagne and hurried towards the door. As he did so he caught sight of himself in a mirror. Bloody hell. He fled into the corridor and, bending down, ruffled his hair vigorously. A fine spray of highly conditioned clippings rained down on a trolley of hors-d'oeuvres waiting to be wheeled in. The waitress looked concerned.

"Mr President, sir...is everything alright?"

Blicker merely scowled, stalking off towards his studio to make some preliminary sketches. He'd hardly turned the corner when his battle-axe of a social secretary caught up with him.

"Sir," she said breathlessly. "Excuse me sir! Call for you on the secure line from the Minister of Economics."

He turned. She was sweating profusely. What did Boris want now?

"You can take it in the library, sir," she puffed, beckoning for him to follow.

He picked up the extension and pressed the scrambler button: "Yes?" he snapped.

The battle-axe watched his expression switch from irritation to bafflement to astonishment and back again.

"You mean that wasn't Fraser that we met?" The President listened as Boris relayed the news of the Pretender's imprisonment in Zenda Castle, and his escape. He realised that he was getting thoroughly sick of this Monarchy business, he wished to dear holy God he hadn't started it now.

"So what d'you want me to do about it?" Blicker glared at his watch. "They'll be married any minute, haven't you seen the crowds?" Boris explained the situation. "Look, Boris, we've done what we can, I'm not going to go down there and argue it out with Hentzau, I've got work to do. Besides, what difference will it make? Let him find out afterwards."

He was too old for this, he realised, too jaded. He had no

energy left. He had already made up his mind to give over the fight to a younger generation and retire. Let Boris slug it out with Hentzau.

"We'll organise a referendum then. Three votes. Fraser, Rose Elphberg or President...Boris, for all I care!" A beat. "Yes, I'm aware she'll be married to Hentzau's son, but that can't be helped now, can it?"

He listened while Boris explained why it did matter, and how it could be helped. At the end of it he sighed, wearily.

"Listen, Boris, if you can stop it, off you go, good luck to you. I'll leave it in your capable hands. Now let me...What? Of course you have my authorisation." He raised his eyes skywards. "OK, yes, if they haven't showed in two hours, I'll send all the guests away."

He harrumphed loudly, handed the phone back to his startled battle-axe, and began to trudge slowly back in the direction of the reception hall. Could you believe it?

∽

Hentzau was halfway across the city in his chauffeur-driven Mercedes when his own call came through, flashing up as a private number on his mobile.

"Hentzau here!" he answered brightly, in anticipation of yet another of the dozens of congratulatory well-wishes that were winging in from all over the world. His composure quickly turned to a frown. "Yes Boris, what do you want?"

He listened with barely concealed impatience, and laughed. "No of course I can't meet you, my dear man, I've got a wedding to attend, or have you forgotten, now if you don't mind....no! not even for ten minutes, I..."

His jaw tightened. "What d'you mean I could be arrested? You leave my daughter out of this!" he exploded, so that his chauffeur momentarily lost concentration and the car careered off track towards the oncoming traffic. A blare of horns brought both Hentzau and his driver to their senses.

"Now look here, Boris…" he began darkly.

∽

"So what are you going to do?" exclaimed Michael. They hadn't moved from where they were. More dignitaries and guests had been arriving at the Cathedral. The square was now packed.

Christopher, who had changed into a pair of Michael's jeans after his escape from Zenda, pulled at the pockets to give himself a little more air, readjusting his bottom on the bar stool to get more comfortable.

"And where's Sophie?" pressed Micheal. "Surely you need to tell her that you're not Fraser."

"Are you mad? They'd bang me up again if I did that. Impersonating a dead person, travelling on a false passport, applying for a visa under a fictitious name - they'd probably even accuse me of trying to foment insurrection by impersonating a dead heir," he added gloomily.

"Well, you weren't to know he was the heir."

"They don't know that, though, do they?" Christopher paused. "Besides, think about it Michael, it's actually quite convenient to be mistaken for the true heir. For the time being, at least. Sophie explained it to me. That when this Hentzau bastard realises that he's been rumbled for kidnapping the heir, and that he - I - have escaped and mean to press my claim, then he will be forced to pull back, to call the wedding off. If Rosie's claim is no longer the strongest, then he'll no longer want to marry her to his son who, by all accounts, is just as reluctant as she is." He slid off the stool and peered through the window into the street anxiously. Sophie was cutting it mighty fine. "It's a long shot, I agree, but it's what Sophie's trying to do now. By the time they find out I'm not the heir, it'll be too late."

"So then *you* can marry her!" cried Michael, clapping his hands.

"Well, I wasn't suggesting…"

"Which means she'll still be the heir - and you'll be King!" Michael clapped his hands excitedly.

"I wouldn't go that far, I'm not really interested…"

"Why, that's brilliant!" Michael started hopping up and down. "Brill-i-ant! Just one teensy-weensy request?" He grinned. "Because I'm a sucker for titles."

But Christopher's concentration had switched elsewhere. A stereo echo of his heartbeat was thundering at either temple, and all talk of suckers, titles and his own brilliance was lost in a clash of cymbals that threatened to crush his skull.

A new car had arrived.

It drew up within inches of the Cathedral steps. A hush descended on the crowd, their clutched roses suddenly stilled. A chauffeur got out and went round to open the rear passenger door. A leg stretched out gingerly. A bunched white dress emerged and, then as the first wave of cheering began, Princess Rose herself. The crowd went wild. She looked everything a Princess should look like: her dark hair piled up on her head like a Greek goddess, a light flush on her cheeks, her bare arms pale and slender and gloved in soft white kid.

A hail of roses flailed through the air, while thousands of little red and white flags began jigging up and down madly. She didn't stop to wave. The security detail hurried her up the steps and into the cathedral.

Christopher caught his breath. He had a sudden urge to rush over and drag her away. But he knew that he mustn't. It could wreck everything. Wait for me, Sophie had said. Trust me. How hard that was. The tension was unbearable. He took a series of rapid deep breaths and steadied himself against the bar.

"You OK?" said Michael anxiously.

"Sure. It's just...she's arrived."

"Who has?" boomed Coach Jackson, striding in from the street and slapping him on the back. "Hey, how ya doing, Christopher? Feelin' better?"

Christopher smiled ruefully.

"Never felt better."

"Cheer up, young dude," he said, inspecting the bar list, "we're outta here in three days. Chrissakes, what a crush out there! What I need is a drink." He looked up. "You guys wanna freshener?"

"You'll never guess what we've discovered," said Michael excitedly.

Christopher shot him a warning look. "Don't you dare."

"What's that?" said Jackson. "It's about time I was filled in. You and that Sophie girl, in cahoots all the way from Zenda…"

Michael and Christopher remained silent, a tension in the air. Jackson shrugged. "OK, suit yourselves. Order me a Jack Daniels, would you? I need a piss."

As soon as he was out of earshot Christopher sat down again and turned to Michael.

"By the way, mate, one thing I forgot to ask you. Did you ever make it to the Ellenberg Rosewater Collective? With the group, for the factory tour? I was gutted I missed it."

"Absolutely. The group loved it. Spent a fortune."

"They did?" Christopher's eyes lit up.

"Yeah. Oh, and I almost forgot. The guy there gave me this to give to you." He delved into his bag and retrieved an envelope. "Your commission."

It was a fat one. Christopher ripped it open. 1450 Euros in notes.

"Whoa!" exclaimed Christopher. "This is awesome. Means I've made my target. My little bro will be pleased."

"Your little bro?"

Christopher hesitated. He'd not wanted to tell anyone. In case it didn't come off, in case he jinxed it. But it looked like it would now.

He smiled. "No harm in telling you I suppose. My little brother, Max, won a scholarship to a tennis academy, but we had to stump up the first £2000. Deadline to accept is next week. Our Mum didn't have it, said I would try and find it myself. Been working to save it for the past couple of months." He waved the envelope excitedly. "This should do it!"

Michael looked at him admiringly. "Wow! Wish I had a brother like you."

Christopher coloured, and opened his wallet to transfer the cash. As he did so, he noticed the torn out scrap of newspaper that Ali had given him before his interview with TravelCo. It seemed an age away.

"Oh my God, look at this!" he laughed, proffering it to Michael. "This is what got me into this mess in the first place!"

"'*Presentable, well-spoken Tour Manager wanted,*'" read Michael, peering at it. "'*Exciting new tours to Eastern Europe.*' Ha! You can say that again!"

But Christopher was no longer listening. He'd gone suddenly pale. He was staring at the next line in amazement. *Contact Ms Cynthia Fraser.*

"What is it?" said Michael. "You alright?"

How the hell had he missed it?

"Don't you see?" yelled Christopher, jumping excitedly off the bar stool. "Her name's Fraser!"

"So?" quipped Michael. "What of it?"

"The visa! Roderick Fraser! They must be related!"

"Well yeah," said Michael. "Duh! Course they are. Didn't you know? Roddy was her younger brother. Died five years ago, a climbing accident in the Himalayas, apparently. It was Cynthia's idea to to use his passport to cover for these last minute visas. She…" He suddenly trailed off, as the significance of it dawned on him. They stared at each other.

"O. M. G.," they said in unison.

Chapter 61

The Wedding

Inside the Cathedral there was consternation. Mixed, in certain quarters, with scarcely believable hope. For Rupert Hentzau had not showed up. He was not just late. He was very late. What on earth had happened to him, the priest wanted to know, anxiously consulting with the principal parties who were milling around in the sacristy, where the bride waited with her guardian for the ceremony to begin. The bridegroom, unusually, was also present, smoking a cigarette and sniffing loudly. Outside in the nave they could hear a babble of whispered conjecture, rising by the minute, while the organist went into his introductory fugue for the third time.

"Shut up!" snapped Tilly. "He's probably stuck in traffic. Be patient." She bit her lip, getting through to his voicemail for the third time.

∽

"So you see," said Boris coldly, "it appears that this man does have a valid claim to the throne, and I am here to inform you that if you go through with this wedding we will have no option but to advance his claim against Miss Elphberg's."

Hentzau stood before him with a thunderous expression. He'd had little option but to divert en route, wasting precious minutes arguing with this buffoon. Because thanks to Tilly he faced imminent arrest. Somehow they'd discovered she'd kidnapped this Fraser idiot. But what new wool were they trying to pull over his eyes?

"*We?*" he hissed.

"I remind you that I am the president's representative this afternoon."

"How can I be sure you are talking for him?" He glared at Sophie who was lurking behind Boris, as if for protection.

Boris smiled. "You can't. You'll just have to take my word for it. But remember, I can have you arrested right now on suspicion of…"

"Alright, alright." Hentzau waved a hand impatiently. He began to fiddle about for his cheque book. "So how much do you want?"

"May I remind you," said Boris, "that bribery is a serious offence. Now listen to me carefully, Hentzau. It appears this Fraser man has escaped."

Hentzau's expression changed immediately. "When? How?"

"If the wedding goes through and you continue to advance Miss Elphberg's claim, we risk serious trouble. You must call off the wedding until we have had a chance to discuss these matters with Roderick Fraser. The real Roderick Fraser. Ascertain his intentions."

"Call it off? Now look here, Boris…"

"I'm sorry Hentzau, but you are in no position to argue. Or do you want me to call it off for you?"

Hentzau's look would have withered a plastic daffodil. "Listen, my dear Boris," he began, in more conciliatory tones.

"I realise you all think this Fraser fellow is some kind of…pretender." He laughed uneasily. "But I can assure, from reliable sources, that he's nothing more dangerous than a fast food salesman."

"Sophie?"

Sophie handed Boris a file, which he opened for Hentzau's inspection. "Here's an email from our investigators in London, showing the direct lineage. See there? His great grandfather was the son of Queen Flavia and Rudolf Rassendyl. Queen Flavia was his great great grandmother. And this letter here…" he drew out a sheet of paper headed 'Bank of England' and dated only a few days previously is an acceptance of his claim to the throne for the purposes of approximately…ah…" he checked the figure in another part of the file "Forty-five million sterling." He paused. "No, that was in 1945."

Hentzau took a step back. He'd told no one, not even his daughter, not even Lougouev, about the money. Hell, how could they have found that out? As for the other thing, it was inconceivable Lougouev had got it so wrong. They must be bluffing. He said, almost to himself, "There's something wrong here."

"There certainly is. And if we're not careful, it's going to take us all with it. Take it from me, Hentzau, we've done extensive research. If this isn't proof enough for you then I'm sorry. As I say, I am not asking for your cooperation. I am demanding it. Pending a full investigation." He untied his ponytail and began to rearrange it in what Hentzau decided was a most disrespectful manner.

But what could he do? He suddenly realised he was in a cleft stick. Whatever the outcome, he could certainly kiss goodbye to the gold. Boris was right in one respect - perhaps it was wiser to postpone the wedding until they'd sorted out the lineage. If the rumour was true - God forbid, since Rosie's claim was no match for that kind of romance in the minds of the people - then his daughter had just imprisoned the direct descendant of the offspring of Queen Flavia and that bloody Englishman on the day of his son's wedding to a rival. It was too big a risk to take.

It all, suddenly, became crystal clear. The meeting in London that Lougouev had reported had not been about Universal Foods at all - but about this imposter's claim to the throne. Boris and Blicker had been scheming all along. He felt a thick clot of foam rising in his throat.

"After all," Boris went on triumphantly, noting his discomfort, "if you hadn't kidnapped him in the first place, we probably wouldn't be in this mess."

Hentzau was about to protest that it was his daughter who'd kidnapped him when he stopped himself. He had to protect her at all costs.

"You realise of course that I will deny all charges," croaked Hentzau thickly.

"Of course," replied Boris, "and if you cooperate I'm sure we can...work something out."

Hentzau glared at him. But he knew he was beat.

∽

"I THINK WE SHOULD START, LADIES AND GENTLEMAN, DON'T you?" said the priest, consulting his watch anxiously, as the organist flourished the final bars of his piece once more, and the church went suddenly quiet. "Time marches on."

"*No!*" cried two people simultaneously, from separate sides of the room. The priest looked up in surprise.

"That is, er," stammered Rosie, "I don't think it would be a good idea until Mr. Hentzau arrives. Something may have happened to him."

"I quite agree," chipped in Andrew hastily. "I couldn't agree more." It was likely to be the first, and last time, that he would see eye to eye with the woman sitting ten yards to his left. Tilly looked at her brother suspiciously. Something was wrong. She'd tried her father's mobile, she'd phoned the house. Apparently he'd left over half an hour ago.

"Well," said the priest, shifting. "I've got a funeral to do in an hour and a half. If he doesn't show up within the next few minutes I'm afraid…"

He coughed, and trailed off. Rosie began to hum quietly to herself.

Yes, your own, thought Tilly malevolently, if you don't get on with it.

∽

OUTSIDE THE CROWDS WAITED PATIENTLY. THE MINUTES TICKED by. Suddenly there was the sound of sirens. *Wherr-whorr-wherr-whorr.* The security men tensed, urgently scanning the area to see where it was coming from. Then two police outriders rounded a corner and pulled up, followed by a yellow taxi. "Blimey, they must be economising," said a member of the crowd, a farmer up from the country, to no one in particular.

The doors of the taxi flew open, and out stepped Yuri Lougouev and Hentzau's Chief of Staff. The crowd raised a renewed cheer out of sheer habit and the security men gave vent to a collective sigh of relief. They were a little concerned, however, when Lougouev skipped the normal formalities and suddenly bounded up the steps. His companion followed more slowly, scanning the crowd anxiously.

∽

INSIDE, THEY HAD HEARD THE CHEER. ROSIE LET OUT A BARELY audible cry and looked like she was going to faint. Andrew scowled.

"Told you so," whispered Tilly triumphantly, peering out into the aisle. But her expression changed when she realised it wasn't her father.

"Hev you married them?" cried Lougouev breathlessly, bursting in.

The priest looked concerned.

"Excuse me sir, this is a private…"

"I am vell aware what it is. I'm a guest," *puff*. He turned to Tilly.

"What's going on?" she whispered. "Where's my father? What are you doing here?" she added, turning to her father's deputy.

"There's no time for that," snapped the Chief of Staff. "This wedding's got to continue. Now. Something may have happened to your father. Fraser escaped." Tilly's eyes widened.

∽

Back in the bar, Christopher, Michael and Jackson heard a huge roar in the square outside. Christopher bolted to the window.

"Now what's going on?"

"Has someone else arrived?"

"Doesn't look like it."

The crowd were restive. They were obviously expecting something. A PA system sprang to life.

"*My Lords, Ladies and Gentlemen. We are gathered here today…*" Christopher suddenly realised what was happening. The marriage ceremony had begun. Sophie was too late. He turned to Michael wildly. "Michael, it's started! They're getting married!"

"Oh shit."

"What am I going to do?"

"What *can* you do?"

He went back to the window. He had to buy time. But how?

"*...to consecrate the union between...*"

He leapt up and raced out into the street.

~

THE SECURITY DETAIL WERE RELAXING ON THE STEPS OF THE Cathedral, checking the crowd for faces they knew, when they noticed a commotion to their right. Someone was struggling through the throng, trying to get to the rope, and heads were turning, muttered angry comments were rising in volume, as whoever it was barged his way past with scant regard for the people up front who'd queued all day to get where they were.

"Oi, who d'you think you are?" shouted someone.

"Ssh," answered someone else, as everyone strained to hear the rather crackly priest booming from the loudspeakers.

"*...marriage is a holy estate.*"

Still, people parted for him, startled by his sheer ferocity, fighting his way to the front as if gripped by a terrifying claustrophobia. They'd hardly had time to react when the man burst through, stumbling onto, and over, the security rope. He looked about him like a scared animal then darted up the steps towards the Cathedral.

"*What the...*" cried one of the guards, leaping up.

"You can't come up here!" snarled another.

But the man just kept coming, wildly, flailing and snorting like an angered bull, brushing aside one of the guards and making a sudden lunge towards the door. A murmur went up amongst the crowd.

"*Stop him!*"

"Halt or we fire!"

As if in unison the crowd gasped: "*Aah...!*"

"*And if any man has just cause why this man and this woman should not be joined together in matrimony, let him speak now, or forever hold his peace."*

"Yes!" yelled Christopher, charging up the last of the steps and bursting through the huge double doors, hotly pursued by two of the security detail.

"*Ooh....!*" groaned the crowd behind him, like a football crowd denied a winning goal in the final seconds of extra time.

There was a sussura of hats. A number of people in the back rows turned, startled. At the far end of the nave, on the steps of the altar, the priest looked up momentarily, bewildered, as the sudden intrusion echoed around the cavernous vaulting. He peered into the gloom, but could see nothing. He coughed, and went on: "In that case…"

Christopher managed to get halfway down the central aisle before he was manhandled to a skidding halt by two of the guards.

"Yes!" he yelled again. "I do!"

The congregation rustled in whispered consternation. Rosie and Andrew, on their knees, twisted round to see what was going on.

She gasped. "Christopher…"

"Who is this?" hissed Lougouev to Hentzau's deputy.

"Fraser!" gulped Tilly, her stomach churning.

"Who? Speak up!"

But she was already out of her seat. "Stop him, someone!"

The security guards, guns drawn, hesitated. One, they were in a church. Two, it was at least two-thirds full with press people. And three…the man had just put his hands up.

"Go away, Christopher!" whispered Rosie, bustling back towards him. "Have you lost your mind?"

"I have just cause!" boomed Christopher, shaking himself free. "Get off me, you thugs!"

Rosie moaned, putting her head in her hands and sinking

to her knees on the cold stone floor. Two people leapt out of their seats to go to her.

"Get a doctor, someone!"

"The bride needs help!"

"Who is this jerk?" snorted Andrew, striding back down the aisle. The congregation looked on, aghast, too shocked to say anything, spellbound and hanging on every word of this new, and fascinating, development. The priest hopped uneasily from one foot to another. He was in a tight spot.

"You do?" he said into the microphone.

"Yes! They don't love each other!" shot back Christopher, his voice echoing back to him like a disembodied voice from heaven. A ripple went through the press corps. This was better copy than any had dared hope for.

"And you are?" squeaked the priest through some heavy electronic crackle.

"I'm Roderick Fraser," lied Christopher. "Heir to the throne of this country, the former Kingdom of Elphberg."

Someone screamed. A high pitched, reedy whinny that was soon lost in the rafters above. One or two giggled. The deathly silence that ensued was only marred by the sound of the bride sliding slowly to the floor, her fall cushioned by swathes of soft taffeta. She was lifted up bodily and seated in a pew, and water was fetched.

"Well, I don't know about that," stammered the priest, climbing down from his podium. He looked around desperately for a cue, but no one seemed to know what to do. No one was in charge. Or rather, the horrifying truth of it was, he was.

"But I'm afraid the church says you have to have a better reason to prevent two people getting married," he said, squinting into the gloom.

∼

The Spare and The Heir

A CAR CAME TO AN ABRUPT HALT AT THE BOTTOM OF THE STEPS just as the jabbering guard raced out of the Cathedral.

"There's someone in there with a gun," he shouted. The others turned to him. Who had a gun? The man who'd burst in? While they were arguing about what to do, Rupert Hentzau leapt out of the car and bounded up the steps. Too late they realised, and by the time they caught up with him he was already through the door. They came tumbling in behind him.

"Freeze!"

"Hold it!"

"Nobody move!"

"Get your hands off me, you idiot!" cried Hentzau as one of them tried to pull him back. He shook himself down angrily and looked around him. "Good God, what the hell's going on here?"

For a moment the security men were unsure of what to do. A bewildering array of targets presented themselves. The earlier intruder, Christopher, now appeared to be tending to Rosie at the far end of the aisle while TV people milled around, filming freely and blocking their line of sight:

"*An amazing drama has been unfolding here in Strelsau, Ruritania whilst we've been on the air,*" began a CNN reporter, crouching behind a pillar, jigging the camera up and down to make it look as though the action had already started.

On the other hand their primary client - an important distinction in the security manual, where you are taught to protect in order of importance - was now getting up and exposing himself. They kept Christopher covered as best they could, just in case he made a false move. But he didn't. He held her tight. They'd been beaten. It was phase two. Somewhere at which they should never ever allow themselves to arrive. It was over to Psych-Ops and an internal inquiry. They backed away reluctantly, misty eyed and frustrated.

"As I stand here, surrounded by all the panoply of a royal wedding," intoned the Al Jazeera anchorman, panning wildly round a sea of jostling hats.

Hentzau beat a path down the aisle. His son, Andrew, was standing next to the priest, and Rosie was nowhere to be seen. Had they started already? All around was pandemonium. What was going on?

"Ah, Mr Hentzau, you've arrived at last," said the priest, scurrying up. "We're a little short of instructions, you see that man over there…" He beckoned in the direction of Christopher, who had just let Rosie go and was trying to make himself heard amid a forest of thrusting microphones, "has raised an objection, and I'm afraid the bride took quite a turn.."

Hentzau marched towards him, manhandling guests out of the way. Rosie struggled to her feet. "I'll be alright in a minute," she stammered. But when she saw Hentzau approach her expression changed.

"And who's this?" growled Hentzau, gesturing at Christopher.

Christopher began to speak but Rosie cut him short. "Please Mr Hentzau, be lenient, he's made a terrible mistake, he was only trying to…"

"Roderick Fraser," said Christopher. They eyed each other.

"Ah yes," said Hentzau wearily. Behind them, people were starting to file out. "We were expecting you."

"What do you mean you were expecting him?" Rosie looked up, goggle eyed. "I don't understand. Who's Roderick Fraser?"

He turned to his erstwhile future daughter-in-law. His face spelt defeat.

"The wedding's postponed, Miss Elphberg. I know you'll be disappointed."

She leapt up. "Really?"

He studied her for a second with a pained expression. Then he turned abruptly to his son. "Come on, we're going. Where's your sister?"

∽

BUT TILLY WAS NOWHERE TO BE SEEN. WHILE FRANTIC EFFORTS were made to revive Rosie, she was inching her way towards the back of the church. Something had to be done. Fraser had obviously waylaid her father, and was now intent on wrecking everything. The only thing she was sure of was that he had to be stopped. By all and any means.

Why wouldn't the guards shoot at him? She kept her eyes on the two that surrounded Fraser as she hurried down the side aisle, and could see they were doing nothing to get him out. All they'd managed to do was restrain him. It was pathetically obvious. They were terrified of the press coverage.

She felt a burning sensation in the pit of her stomach. This was her moment. The time had come to act. If she didn't save the situation, no one would. She got to the last row, moseyed innocently towards a side door, and jabbed her Swiss Army knife into the ribs of the bewildered looking guard who was standing just inside it, watching the unfolding drama with ill-concealed and inexcusable inaction.

He froze, startled.

"Do exactly as I say," she hissed up at him. "Pull your hands away from your gun." Terrified, he did as he was told. She slid her hand around his body until she found his holster, yanked off the leather safety strap and slid the gun gently out. It was heavier than she'd expected.

"Now scram," she said, and he edged quickly out of the door.

Chapter 62

Nobody's Perfect

Some time later, a long cavalcade of cars made its way slowly through the pressing throng towards the gates of the Palace. In the lead vehicle were Rosie and Christopher, the string of cans rattling noisily behind them. Next came Andrew, followed by his father and his Chief of Staff. Then came a car full of officials, including Horst who, against official government policy, had sneaked off to the wedding at the last moment and, wedged in beside him, Michael, whom Christopher had insisted got a ride. Last came a fleet of hooting taxis – several for the Press, several more for Jackson and the Angels, and, bringing up the rear, one for Yuri Lougouev, fulminating vocally to his driver.

Flags waved, people cheered. No one knew what on earth was going on. Least of all Rosie. Christopher knew he owed her an explanation. But it wasn't as easy as all that. He was only part of the way through outlining to her the royal lineage of Roderick Fraser, as relayed to him by Sophie, when she interrupted him.

"But I don't understand it!" she cried, perplexed. "Why didn't you tell me? Why pretend to be Christopher..."

"The thing is Rosie, I'm not actually…I mean he…"

Rosie lunged at him, her hand clamped to his lips. "Ssh, don't say a thing, I really don't want to hear it!" She sniffed. "And that girl?" she added sullenly.

"What girl?"

"I can't believe it, you were in bed with her, how could you?"

Her eyes flashed with anger.

"Well, you see, it was all a terrible mistake," he said, blushing. "What happened is, she came in, and…"

She clamped her hands over her ears. "No!" she screamed. "No more! Don't go on, I've heard enough!" She shook her head and rolled her eyes. "You're just like all the rest."

She tossed her head away from him. He tried to touch her, but she shook him off with a little scornful flick of her hand.

"You will abdicate, of course," she said coldly.

"Abdicate?"

"Don't tell me you don't have a brother, a cousin or something?"

He hesitated. Perhaps he could play this role just a little bit longer.

"Well…yes, but…abdicate?" he teased. "I mean…d'you think that's really necessary?"

He shifted his gaze to the window. To the crowds of waving people, the babies held aloft on father's shoulders, the beaming, eager faces, the awe-struck children. He gave a tentative wave in reply.

"Because…I could really get into this… *King thing*."

He cast her a sidelong glance.

She looked shocked. "You can't be serious? You'd hate it! Shaking hands with thousands of people, small talk with endless foreign dignitaries…"

"I like meeting new people actually," he sniffed, smiling

enthusiastically at a particularly attractive teenage girl who'd climbed halfway up a lamp-post.

"And just think of all those banquets. *Ugh!*"

"Caviar, lobster, T-bone steak..." he murmured absent-mindedly, leaning forward to pour himself a glass of Bollinger from a bottle in the cooler. "Champagne?" he added, as he nodded his head regally at an old gentleman who was doffing his cap at a street corner.

"And what about parades?" she continued, her voice rising, cross now. "Taking the salute, sitting rigid for hours on a horse! Have you thought about that?" She shook him. "Look at me, Christopher, be serious. You'd never be able to ride a double decker bus again."

"Touché!" He laughed, turning to her. "But I don't understand you, Rosie, I really don't. Last time we spoke about this, you told me it was your duty, that the monarchy was some kind of sacred magic, that if the people want it, then..."

"Yes, but not me!" she cried. "It doesn't mean *I* actually want it! Now they've worked out your lineage back to Queen Flavia, there are bound to be loads of eligible people. I'm off the hook!" She snorted. "Besides, I could say the same about you!"

"Meaning?"

"Yes, what about *your* ideals?" Her eyes narrowed dangerously. "Or was that all just talk? The Boston Tea Party? The Mayflower? The Statue of Liberty? I thought you said your mother was a daughter of the French Revolution?"

"You mean the American Revolution."

"Ha!" she cried, tossing her head back. "Well there you are then! You're half American! How can you be King?"

"Nobody's perfect," he muttered.

She hit him. "Oh! You're impossible!"

He sighed. The game was up. There was no moving her.

She really had no interest in this monarchy business. It was time to come clean.

"Listen. Rosie. I've been trying to tell you. My name really is Christopher, and moreover, I've got an older brother."

She turned. "So you mean you *will* abdicate?" Her eyes were suddenly bright with hope and expectation. But slowly their expression changed. "*Say that again?*"

"I said I have an older brother."

She regarded him with heavy suspicion. "But that's impossible! Then you can't be the heir."

Christopher flung his hands in the air in exasperation. "That's exactly what I've been trying to tell you! They've all got it wrong! I'm not Roderick Fraser at all. In fact he doesn't even exist!" It took a few moments for this to sink in.

"So you're not the heir?"

"Christ no! And neither is my brother! I'm Christopher Wainwright, for God's sake, a telesales executive from Stoke Newington, London. How could I be the heir?"

"So there is no other heir?" she said heavily, deflated.

Silence. Suddenly Rosie burst into tears. It was so unexpected it took Christopher a few moments to react, but when he did she proved inconsolable.

"Oh! That means I'm the Queen after all! How could you and Sophie be so cruel, raising my hopes like that!"

"Hold on, it's not Sophie's fault. And anyway, we got you out of that marriage, didn't we?" He looked hurt.

"Yes, but see out there?" she said, grabbing for a tissue and gesturing wildly at the crowds pressing up against the crush barriers. "They'll be satisfied with nothing less than royalty now!"

"Well you bloody well abdicate then!"

"How can I? I'm the only one!" she wailed. "If it's not this Fraser person then it's me, can't you see that?"

He put his arm around her. Took a deep breath, tried one final time.

"But if we stick together, I mean, just the two of us, perhaps we can make it work."

"What, you mean get married?"

"Well…"

"A salesman from London?" she cried, almost hysterical. "Ha! Hardly fit material for a Queen's consort, I think? And besides, you forget…you've made an enemy of Hentzau now. He'd make our lives hell."

She'd got a point there. They'd need twenty-four hour security, and that was just against the homicidal daughter.

"So you won't marry me?"

She laughed bitterly. "What sort of proposal is that?" She wrung her hands. "Christopher, how can I, if I'm to be Queen? You don't seem to understand. You might have got me out of marrying that loser, for the time being, and please," she put her hand on his in a sudden display of emotion, "don't think I'm not grateful for that! But can you see you and me as the royal couple?"

"I can actually," he sniffed.

A new tear formed, swelled, and ran slowly down her cheek. He kissed it gently, tasting the salt. Despite her distress, or maybe because of it, she looked more beautiful than he'd ever seen her. Wisps of hair hung down her slender neck. His lips hovered above it, softly brushing her with his nose. Her smell was expensive. And intoxicating.

"So if you weren't the heir, you would? Marry me I mean?"

She arched her head away from him. "Don't play with me, Christopher."

"No, I'm serious, I need to know."

They looked at each other in silence for a moment, then she turned away. They were approaching the Palace.

The Spare and The Heir 391

"Well...maybe, if...but.."

"Because I love you," he said, reaching across and gently kissing her on the lips. She sank into him, exhausted. He nuzzled her ear. "And I'm going to let you into a secret."

He paused. She looked up at him with misty eyes.

"It's not entirely true that you're the only heir. I might not be the mystery heir, but it doesn't mean that there isn't one."

He reached for his mobile.

"What d'you mean?" she said, tensing as he tapped in a set of numbers. "What are you doing?"

He stroked her neck and listened for the ringing tone. Somebody answered.

"Hello? Cynthia?" He laughed. "Yes, how did you guess? Glad I found you in."

Rosie narrowed her eyes and mouthed something at him, but he was concentrating on the woman at the other end of the line.

"What? Yes, thanks, the tour has gone very well." He winked at Rosie. "Or perhaps 'well' is a bit of an exaggeration. Let's say it's been ... an experience. Yes, definitely an experience. Now," he squeezed Rosie's hand. "Which do you want first? The good news, or the bad news?"

"Who are you talking to?" hissed the woman he loved.

He put a finger to her lips, a smirk spreading across his face.

"Yes, yes, I know you've got a dinner to go to, this won't take a minute. The bad news? No, Michael was OK in the end, thanks. Nice chap actually. And yes, everybody was very happy. No probs with the air-conditioning in the hotel and the continental with juice went down a treat. What? So why am I ringing you?" He paused, looking at Rosie significantly. She stared back as if he were mad.

"It's about something else actually. You see, the bad news is that you'll never be able to ride a double-decker bus again. The good news is, you won't have to use the tube either."

He glanced idly in the rear view mirror, wondering how Cynthia was going to take it. And froze. Two eyes glittered back at him menacingly from under a peaked hat. They were large, round and little girl-ish.

No! It couldn't be true! After all he'd been through. He shivered with dread, casting about wildly. Surreptitiously he tried the door. Locked.

"What's the matter?" said Rosie, suddenly alarmed.

"Hello?" came a far away voice down the phone line. "Hello?"

She looked far too young to be driving a car. A sudden spurt on the accelerator, the screams of well-wishers crushed underfoot, the split-second oblivion of a brick wall. From what Sophie had told him, the girl was capable of anything. To come this far...

"Christopher!" Rosie dug her nails into his arm. "What is it?"

In a flash, it came to him. It wasn't just a throne he had to sell to her. It was a tough one. But not impossible. *Pitch, objection, counter, re-pitch.* He pressed the speaker button on his mobile so the rest of the car could hear this most important telesales call of his life.

"Cynthia, you still there?"

"Yes of course I'm bloody well here, what the hell's going on?"

"I'm not going to beat about the bush. He's a count, he's rich, and there's a throne waiting." He smiled at Rosie. "His...ah...his engagement's just fallen through, so if you hurry you might just be able to snap him up."

There was a deathly silence. For one awful moment Christopher thought he'd blown it, that she'd hung up.

"Cynthia? You still there? Listen, he's called Andrew. His

father the Duke has done extensive research, and you're the one he wants his son to marry."

It was a lie - it so often was when you had something to sell - but Sophie had told him how Hentzau had reacted when presented with the evidence. He would be more than satisfied. Not to mention the underage chauffeur watching him like a hawk. He wished to God she'd keep her eyes on the road.

When Cynthia finally spoke she sounded wary.

"*Rare-ly?*" she said.

But definitely interested. Fish. Hooked.

The eyes in the rear view mirror flickered away. Satisfied. For the time being.

The End.

About the Author

James D. Wood worked as a tour manager for a number of tour companies including American Express, Trafalgar Tours, and Jules Verne. He went on to build a career in the film industry, in travel technology, and as a publisher, travel writer and author. James lives in West London.

For advance news of James's new books, invitations to be a beta reader and pre-release offers, sign up at www.jdwoodbooks.com

Other Books by James

The Big Little War

The incredible true story of how a handful of RAF trainee pilots and their instructors, in antiquated biplanes, defeated the Iraqi army and the Luftwaffe in Iraq in May 1941, and changed the course of World War 2.

Printed in Great Britain
by Amazon